THE LONGMAN COMPANION TO
THE CONSERVATIVE PARTY SINCE 1830

LONGMAN COMPANIONS TO HISTORY

General Editors: Chris Cook and John Stevenson

The following Companions to History *are now available*:

Renaissance Europe, 1390–1530
Stella Fletcher

The European Reformation
Mark Greengrass

The Tudor Age
Rosemary O'Day

The Stuart Age, 1603–1714
John Wroughton

Britain in the Eighteenth Century, 1688–1820
Jeremy Gregory and John Stevenson

European Nationalism, 1789–1920
Raymond Pearson

European Decolonisation
Muriel E. Chamberlain

The Middle East since 1914
(Second Edition)
Ritchie Ovendale

America, 1910–1945
Patrick Renshaw

Nazi Germany
Tim Kirk

Britain since 1945
Chris Cook and John Stevenson

Germany since 1945
Adrian Webb

The European Union since 1945
Alasdair Blair

Imperial Russia, 1695–1917
David Longley

Napoleonic Europe
Clive Emsley

Britain in the Nineteenth Century, 1815–1914
Chris Cook

The Labour Party, 1900–1998
Harry Harmer

Russia since 1914
Martin McCauley

Britain, 1914–45
Andrew Thorpe

America, Russia and the Cold War, 1914–1998 (Second Edition)
John W. Young

Formation of the European Empires, 1488–1920
Muriel E. Chamberlain

THE LONGMAN COMPANION TO

THE CONSERVATIVE PARTY SINCE 1830

N. J. Crowson

An imprint of Pearson Education

Harlow, England · London · New York · Reading, Massachusetts · San Francisco · Toronto · Don Mills, Ontario · Sydney
Tokyo · Singapore · Hong Kong · Seoul · Taipei · Cape Town · Madrid · Mexico City · Amsterdam · Munich · Paris · Milan

Pearson Education Limited

Head Office:
Edinburgh Gate
Harlow CM20 2JE
Tel: +44 (0)1279 623623
Fax: +44 (0)1279 431059

London Office:
128 Long Acre
London WC2E 9AN
Tel: +44 (0)20 7447 2000
Fax: +44 (0)20 7240 5771
Website: www.history-minds.com

First published in Great Britain in 2001

ISBN 0 582 31292 2 PPR
ISBN 0 582 31291 4 CSD

British Library Cataloguing in Publication Data
A CIP catalogue record for this book can be obtained from the British Library

10 9 8 7 6 5 4 3 2 1

Typeset in 10/12 ITC New Baskerville by Graphicraft Limited, Hong Kong
Produced through Longman Malaysia, VVP

The Publishers' policy is to use paper manufactured from sustainable forests.

For Clementine Emily Crowson
Born 13 November 1999

Acknowledgements

I must thank Stuart Ball for reading the chapter on organisation. This form of compendium could not have been written without the efforts of countless historians in the archives over the decades. Therefore I graciously acknowledge their labours.

The publishers are grateful to the following for permission to reproduce copyright material:

Table 'Scottish Parliament' and Table 'Welsh Assembly' from *20th Century British Political Facts, 1900–2000,* reprinted by permission of Macmillan Ltd (Butler, D. and Butler, G. 2000).

CONTENTS

LIST OF TABLES

Part 1

1.1 ORIGINS AND DEVELOPMENT

1. ORIGINS AND ANTECEDENTS

Historians are unable to agree the point in history that should be the beginning of the Conservative party. Unlike the Labour and Liberal parties there is no convenient starting point: no great (or small) meeting, or document outlining its principles and criteria. If by party the historian means an organised, integrated electoral and propaganda machine no such thing existed before the 1867 Reform Act. However, the label 'Conservative' came into everyday usage during the 1830s and it was during this period under the leadership of Robert Peel, and his *Tamworth Manifesto*, that the party of today began its evolution.

The origins of its 'birth' can be traced through three different strands:

1. a tradition of opposition to change
2. the return to favour in the 1760s of the Pittites who evolved into the Tories
3. a direct response to the constitutional crises of 1827–32 that culminated in the 1832 Reform Act

The label Tory was first applied, in a political sense, in reference to a group of politicians during the reign of Charles II who could trace their political heritage back to a faction of moderate Cavaliers under Charles I. During the eighteenth century the two main political groups were the Tories (who were a party of landed gentry and opposed to change) and the Whigs (who were more disposed to change and were associated with the interests of trade). Both groups were amorphous and lacked structure and cohesion, but despite this a trend emerged for the creation of 'party' ministries that saw one particular group win the King's favour and use the position to deny patronage to the other group. The Whigs enjoyed long periods of hegemony, although from the 1760s the Tories underwent a revival displaying a willingness to create alliances and benefiting from the political advancement of the Pittites. With the Napoleonic wars, and the ministries of Lord Liverpool, the Tories enjoyed long-term political office. The constitutional crises over Catholic emancipation and franchise reform challenged the cohesion of the Tories and suggested to some the possibility, and need, to evolve with the changed political landscape. The deferment of the Duke of Wellington to Robert Peel in 1834 saw the transfer from Tory to Conservative. Yet the label 'Tory' continues to be applied to the 'Conservative' party even to this day.

2. BRIEF CHRONOLOGY

1834	Robert Peel launches his *Tamworth Manifesto.*
1846	Party splits over Corn Law repeal between Peelites who favour free trade and the Protectionists led by Bentinck and Disraeli.
1870	Disraeli forms the first majority Conservative administration since the 1846 split.
1886	Liberal Unionists begin co-ordinating their activities with the Conservatives.
1906	Conservatives suffer their worst election defeat.
1911	Liberal Unionists formally merge with Conservative party.
1915	Conservatives join the wartime coalition government.
1922	Revolt of Conservative MPs at Carlton Club ends the coalition with Lloyd George's Liberals and sees the emergence of a new leading figure, Stanley Baldwin.
1931	Baldwin and senior Conservatives agree to join a National Government to resolve the economic crisis.
1940	Winston Churchill becomes wartime prime minister.
1945	The electorate rejects Churchill and plumps for the 'New Jerusalem' offered by Attlee's Labour Party.
1951–64	Conservative electoral hegemony under Churchill, Eden, Macmillan and Home.
1965	Party adopts a ballot system for selecting future leaders.
1975	Margaret Thatcher becomes the Conservative Party's first female leader.
1990	Thatcher resigns as Prime Minister, after a leadership challenge, ending an 11-year reign: she had become the longest serving PM.
1997	Conservatives suffer their worst electoral defeat since 1906. It ends 18 years of continuous Conservative government.
2001	Second successive heavy electoral defeat.

1.2 LEADERS

1. LEADER OF THE PARTY (OR OF THE HOUSE OF COMMONS)

	Date elected or appointed as leader	Dates served as Prime Minister	Age on becoming leader (years and months)
Duke of Wellington	22 January 1828	22 January 1828–21 November 1830 17 November–9 December 1834 (Acting PM)	57 y 8 m
Robert Peel	10 December 1834	10 December 1834–8 April 1835 30 August 1841–27 June 1846	45 y 8 m
Lord Stanley (14th Earl of Derby, 1851)	July 1846	23 February–17 December 1852 21 February 1858–11 June 1859 28 June 1866–25 February 1868	47 y 3 m
Benjamin Disraeli (Earl of Beaconsfield, 1876)	27 February 1868	27 February–1 December 1868 20 February 1874–21 April 1880	63 y 2 m
H. Stafford Northcote	22 April 1881 (in House of Commons)	—	63 y 6 m
3rd Marquess of Salisbury (PM in House of Lords)	22 April 1881 (in House of Lords); 23 June 1885 (as sole party leader)	23 June 1885–28 January 1886 25 July 1886–11 August 1892 25 June 1895–11 July 1902	55 y 4 m
Arthur Balfour	14 July 1902	12 July 1902–4 December 1905	53 y 11 m
Andrew Bonar Law	13 November 1911	—	53 y 1 m
Austen Chamberlain	21 March 1921	—	57 y 5 m
Andrew Bonar Law	23 October 1922	23 October 1922–22 May 1923	64 y 1 m

	Date elected or appointed as leader	Dates served as Prime Minister	Age on becoming leader (years and months)
Stanley Baldwin	28 May 1923	23 May 1923– 22 January 1924 4 November 1924– 4 June 1929 7 June 1935– 31 May 1937	55 y 9 m
Neville Chamberlain	31 May 1937	31 May 1937– 10 May 1940	68 y 2 m
Winston Churchill	9 October 1940	10 May 1940– 26 July 1945 26 October 1951– 6 April 1955	65 y 11 m
Anthony Eden	21 April 1955	6 April 1955– 22 January 1957	57 y 10 m
Harold Macmillan	22 January 1957	22 January 1957– 11 November 1963	62 y 11 m
Alec Douglas-Home	11 November 1963	11 November 1963– 16 October 1964	60 y 4 m
Edward Heath	2 August 1965	19 June 1970– 4 March 1974	49 y 1 m
Margaret Thatcher	11 February 1975	4 May 1979– 28 November 1990	49 y 3 m
John Major	27 November 1990	27 November 1990– 1 May 1997	47 y 7 m
William Hague	19 June 1997	—	36 y 2 m

Adapted from: J. Ramsden, *An Appetite for Power* (London, 1998), pp. 511–12; A. Seldon and S. Ball, *Conservative Century* (Oxford, 1994), pp. 773–4, 781–5.

2. APPOINTMENT OF THE LEADER

Until 1965 there did not exist any formal mechanism for deciding who was Conservative party leader. Leaders 'emerged' either by securing the apparent support of a significant proportion of the senior figures in the party or because they were invited by the monarch of the day to create a ministry. At least until the Parliament Act of 1911 the leaders in the Lords and the Commons shared the responsibilities of leadership unless one of them was Prime Minister or had been a Prime Minister in the preceding Conservative government. Without a formal mechanism of leadership selection it was very difficult for the party to rid itself of a leader, as Stanley Baldwin demonstrated 1929–31. In theory a leader could be removed from office if one, or a combination of the following, occurred:

1. The leader 'lost' the confidence of a significant proportion of his front bench and was requested to resign.
2. Vote of no confidence passed at a mass party meeting of Conservative peers, MPs and prospective candidates.

The manner in which Alec Douglas-Home succeeded Harold Macmillan in 1963, however, prompted renewed criticisms of the way in which party leaders evolved. Allegations of a 'magic circle', or the 'grey men', engineering the candidate of their preferred choice to the top position, were widely criticised both from within the party and the wider media. One backbencher, Humphry Berkeley, wrote to Home proposing the institution of an electoral school. After further internal party discussion it was agreed that Home's successor would be elected by ballot. Edward Heath was the first 'elected' leader of the Conservative party in 1965. Since that date the election rules have been revised to account for both unforeseen circumstances and for political benefit. The rules and the electoral colleges are summarised in the following table.

3. THE ELECTORAL RULES AND COLLEGES

	Summary of main rules and revisions	Electoral College(s)
1965	1. Multiple ballot, to be initiated only in the event that a vacancy in the leadership arose through death or resignation: **1st Ballot**: Victory requires majority plus 15 per cent more votes than the 2nd placed candidate. If this is not achieved nominations for the first ballot would be void and a 2nd ballot required. **2nd Ballot**: To win, an overall majority was required. If no winner then a third ballot required. **3rd Ballot** to be held between the three leading candidates in 2nd ballot. The ballot would be preferential, using the alternative vote procedure. If no candidate won an overall majority, the second preferences of the candidate with the smallest number of votes would be redistributed, so giving one of the two remaining candidates a majority. 2. All candidates had to be nominated and seconded by an MP. These individuals' names to remain secret. 3. In theory, the party meeting (comprising MPs, peers, parliamentary candidates and National Union executive) has the 'right' to reject/endorse the chosen candidate.	**Members of Parliament**, all other sections of the party to convey preferences to and through them.

	Summary of main rules and revisions	Electoral College(s)
1974–75	1. Provision for annual leadership contest, within first 3 to 6 months of a new parliament or during the first 28 days of a new session. 2. The majority plus 15 per cent more votes than next candidate threshold retained – but this is now measured out of the total number of votes *eligible to be cast*, not just the number actually cast. 3. Makes formal provision for consultation with extra-parliamentary party and specified who was eligible to attend the confirmatory party meeting.	**Members of Parliament**
1989	Names of MPs nominating a candidate to be made public.	
July 1991	1. Annual re-election no longer automatic. To initiate a contest at least 10 per cent of the parliamentary party must write to the chairman of the 1922 Committee within 14 days of the opening of a new session of parliament, or within three months of the start of a new parliament. These MPs are not required to propose alternative candidates. 2. 3rd ballot is confined to top *two* candidates from 2nd ballot, but that any candidate can withdraw within 24 hours of the conclusion of the 2nd ballot.	**Members of Parliament**
February 1998	1. Contest to be triggered by a vote of confidence. This can be called either by the incumbent leader, or if 15 per cent of the parliamentary party inform the chairman of the 1922 committee in writing of the need for a confidence vote. The vote is to involve only members of the parliamentary party. 2. The next round will only occur if the existing leader fails to achieve a simple majority of all those voting. The defeated leader cannot contest the next round. If the leader wins the vote this confers immunity from further challenge for 12 months. 3. Candidates for the second ballot require only a proposer and seconder, whose names will be published. This is the only opportunity for candidates to enter the overall election contest. The election will take the form of a series of elimination ballots within the parliamentary party until the number of candidates has been reduced to two. 4. The remaining two candidates will be subjected to a final postal ballot of the whole party membership (OMOV).	***Confidence vote*: Members of Parliament** ***Elimination ballot(s)*: Members of Parliament** after consultation between individual MPs and constituency associations. ***Final Ballot*: All party members (OMOV)**

Summary of main rules and revisions	Electoral College(s)
5. The procedures stipulate a shorter time interval between the parliamentary party votes than previous rules and also restrict the period between the last parliamentary vote and the close date of the OMOV ballot to a maximum of 14 days. 6. The chairman of the 1922 Committee will be responsible for stipulating the regulations governing methods of communication, advertising and canvassing. In addition a maximum level will be decreed for campaign expenditure.	

Table compiled from: Ball and Seldon (eds), *Conservative Century* pp. 69–96; Stark, *Choosing a Leader*, pp. 20–35.

4. LEADERSHIP ELECTIONS 1965–97

Year	Ballot	Outcome
1965	First Ballot (28 July) Edward Heath 150 Reginald Maudling 133 Enoch Powell 15 Abstentions 6	Heath becomes leader. Despite securing an overall majority he had not reached the 15 per cent winning margin. However, other candidates withdrew and there was no second ballot.
1975	First Ballot (4 February) Margaret Thatcher 130 Edward Heath 119 Hugh Fraser 16 Abstentions 11	Heath and Fraser withdrew. Rule changes means new candidates can enter contest for second ballot.
	Second Ballot (11 February) Margaret Thatcher 146 William Whitelaw 79 James Prior 19 Geoffrey Howe 19 John Peyton 11 Abstentions 2	Thatcher elected as leader
1989	First Ballot (5 December) Margaret Thatcher 314 Anthony Meyer 33 Abstentions 27	Thatcher re-elected, no further ballot required
1990	First Ballot (20 November) Margaret Thatcher 204 Michael Heseltine 152 Abstentions 16	Thatcher had majority but was four votes short of securing 15 per cent margin over next candidate. A second ballot required. After deliberation Thatcher withdrew.

Year	Ballot	Outcome
1990	Second Ballot (27 November) John Major 185 Michael Heseltine 131 Douglas Hurd 56 Abstentions 0	Major 2 votes short of overall majority, the other candidates withdrew and there was no third ballot
1995	First Ballot (4 July) John Major 218 John Redwood 89 Spoilt papers 12 Abstentions 8	Major secures the necessary margin of victory.
1997	First Ballot (10 June) Kenneth Clarke 49 William Hague 41 John Redwood 27 Peter Lilley 24 Michael Howard 23 Abstentions 0	No outright victor. Lilley and Howard withdrew, and endorsed the candidature of Hague for second ballot.
	Second Ballot (17 June) Kenneth Clarke 64 William Hague 62 John Redwood 38 Abstentions 0	No outright victor. Third ballot required. Redwood was eliminated under the rules, and the next day endorsed Clarke.
	Third Ballot (19 June) William Hague 92 Kenneth Clarke 70 Abstentions 2	Hague elected leader.

Source: Stuart Ball, *The Conservative Party since 1945* (1998), pp. 185–7.

1.3 CONSERVATIVE CABINETS AND ADMINISTRATIONS

WELLINGTON'S PROVISIONAL GOVERNMENT: NOVEMBER–DECEMBER 1834

Prime Minister	Duke of Wellington
Lord Chancellor	Lord Lyndhurst
Secretary of State	Duke of Wellington
Lords Commissioners for Executing the Office of Lord High Treasurer	Duke of Wellington, Earl of Rosslyn, Lord Ellenborough, Lord Maryborough, Sir J. Beckett, J. Planta.

PEEL'S MINORITY ADMINISTRATION: DECEMBER 1834–JUNE 1835

Prime Minister and Chancellor of Exchequer	Sir Robert Peel
Lord Chancellor	Lord Lyndhurst
Foreign Secretary	Duke of Wellington
Lord President of the Council	Earl of Rosslyn
Lord Privy Seal	Lord Wharncliffe
Home Secretary	Henry Goulburn
Secretary for War and Colonies	Earl of Aberdeen
First Lord of the Admiralty	Earl de Grey
Master-General of the Ordnance	Sir George Murray
President of the Board of Trade and Master of the Mint	A. Baring
President of the Board of Control	Lord Ellenborough
Secretary at War	J.C. Herries
Paymaster-General	Sir Edward Knatchbull

PEEL'S 2ND ADMINISTRATION: AUGUST 1841–JUNE 1846

Prime Minister and First Lord of the Treasury	Sir Robert Peel
Minister without Portfolio	Duke of Wellington
Home Secretary	James Graham

President of Board of Trade	Earl of Ripon William Ewart Gladstone (May 1843) Not a cabinet post, February–December 1845 Earl of Dalhousie (December 1845)
Lord Chancellor	Lord Lyndhurst
Lord President of the Council	Lord Wharncliffe Duke of Buccleuch (January 1846)
Lord Privy Seal	Duke of Buckingham Duke of Buccleuch (January 1842) Earl of Haddington (January 1846)
Chancellor of Exchequer	Henry Goulburn
Foreign Secretary	Earl of Aberdeen
Secretary for War and Colonies	Viscount Stanley William Ewart Gladstone (December 1845)
First Lord of the Admiralty	Earl of Haddington Earl of Ellenborough (January 1846)
President of the Board of Trade	Earl of Ripon
President of the Board of Control	Lord Ellenborough (cr. Earl 1844) Lord Fitzgerald (October 1841) Earl of Ripon (May 1843)
Secretary at War	Sir Henry Hardinge Not a cabinet post, May 1844–May 1845 Sidney Herbert (May 1845)
Paymaster-General	Sir Edward Knatchbull (not a cabinet post after February 1845)
Chancellor of the Duchy of Lancaster	Lord Granville Somerset (May 1844)
First Commissioner of Woods and Forests	Earl of Lincoln (January 1845) Not a cabinet post after February 1846

DERBY'S 1ST MINORITY ADMINISTRATION: FEBRUARY–DECEMBER 1852

Prime Minister	Earl of Derby
Chancellor of Exchequer and Leader of Commons	Benjamin Disraeli
Foreign Secretary	Lord Malmesbury
Home Secretary	Spencer Walpole

Lord Chancellor	Lord St Leonards
Lord Privy Seal	Marquess of Salisbury
Secretary of State for War and Colonies	Sir John Pakington
First Lord of the Admiralty	Duke of Northumberland
President of Board of Trade	J.W. Henley
President of the Board of Control	J.C. Herries
First Commissioner of Works	Lord John Manners
Postmaster-General	Earl of Hardwicke

DERBY'S 2ND WHO'S WHO ADMINISTRATION: FEBRUARY 1858–MAY 1859

Prime Minister	Earl of Derby
Chancellor of Exchequer	Benjamin Disraeli
Foreign Secretary	Earl of Malmesbury
Home Secretary	Spencer Walpole T.H. Sotheron-Estcourt (February 1859)
Lord Chancellor	Lord Chelmsford
Lord President of the Council	Marquess of Salisbury
Lord Privy Seal	Earl of Hardwicke
Secretary for War	General Peel
Secretary for Colonies	Lord Stanley Sir E. Bulwer-Lytton (May 1858)
First Lord of the Admiralty	Sir John Pakington
President of the Board of Trade	J.W. Henley Earl of Donoughmore (February 1859)
President of the Board of Control	Earl of Ellenborough Lord Stanley (May 1858) Post abolished August 1858
First Commissioner of Works	Lord John Manners
Secretary of State for India	Lord Stanley (August 1858)

DERBY'S 3RD ADMINISTRATION: JUNE 1866–FEBRUARY 1868

Prime Minister	Earl of Derby
Foreign Secretary	Lord Stanley

Home Secretary	Spencer Walpole G. Gathorne Hardy (May 1867)
Chancellor of Exchequer	Benjamin Disraeli
Lord Chancellor	Lord Chelmsford
Lord President of the Council	Duke of Buckingham Duke of Malborough (March 1867)
Lord Privy Seal	Earl of Malmesbury
Secretary for War	General Peel Sir John Pakington (March 1867)
Secretary for the Colonies	Earl of Carnarvon Duke of Buckingham (March 1867)
First Lord of the Admiralty	Sir John Pakington H. Lowry-Corry (March 1867)
President of the Board of Trade	Sir Stafford Northcote Duke of Richmond (March 1867)
Secretary for India	Viscount Cranborne Sir Stafford Northcote (March 1867)
First Commissioner of Works	Lord John Manners
Chief Secretary for Ireland	Lord Naas (cr. Earl of Mayo 1867)
President of the Poor Law Board	G. Gathorne Hardy
Minister without Office	Spencer Walpole (from May 1867)

DISRAELI'S 1ST ADMINISTRATION: FEBRUARY–DECEMBER 1868

Prime Minister	Benjamin Disraeli
Foreign Secretary	Lord Stanley
Home Secretary	Spencer Walpole
Chancellor of Exchequer	G. Ward Hunt
Lord Chancellor	Lord Chelmsford
Lord President of the Council	Duke of Buckingham
Lord Privy Seal	Earl of Malmesbury
Secretary for War	General Peel
Secretary for Colonies	Earl of Carnarvon
First Lord of the Admiralty	Sir John Pilkington
President of the Board of Trade	Sir Stafford Northcote
Secretary for India	Viscount Cranborne
First Commissioner of Works	Lord John Manners
President of the Poor Law Board	G. Gathorne Hardy

DISRAELI'S 2ND ADMINISTRATION: FEBRUARY 1874–APRIL 1880

Prime Minister and First Lord of Treasury	Benjamin Disraeli (cr. Earl of Beaconsfield 1876)
Chancellor of Exchequer	Sir Stafford Northcote
Foreign Secretary	Earl of Derby Marquess of Salisbury (April 1878)
Home Secretary	Richard Cross
Lord Chancellor	Lord Cairns (cr. Earl 1878)
Lord President of the Council	Duke of Richmond
Lord Privy Seal	Earl of Malmesbury Benjamin Disraeli (August 1876) Duke of Northumberland (February 1878)
Secretary for the Colonies	Earl of Carnarvon Sir Michael Hicks Beach (February 1878)
Secretary for War	G. Gathorne Hardy F.A. Stanley (April 1878)
Secretary for India	Marquess of Salisbury G. Gathorne Hardy (April 1878)
First Lord of the Admiralty	G. Ward Hunt W.H. Smith (August 1877)
Postmaster-General	Lord John Manners
Chief Secretary for Ireland	Sir Michael Hicks Beach (February 1877) Not a cabinet post from February 1878
President of the Board of Trade	Viscount Sandon (April 1878)

SALISBURY'S MINORITY ADMINISTRATION: JUNE 1885–JANUARY 1886

Prime Minister	Marquess of Salisbury
Foreign Secretary	Marquess of Salisbury
Home Secretary	Richard A. Cross
Chancellor of Exchequer	Michael Hicks Beach
First Lord of the Treasury	Earl of Iddesleigh (Sir Stafford Northcote)
Lord Chancellor	Lord Halsbury (Sir Hardinge Giffard)
Lord President of the Council	Viscount Cranbrook
Lord Privy Seal	Earl of Harrowby
Secretary for the Colonies	Sir F.A. Stanley
Secretary for War	W.H. Smith (plus *Chief Secretary for Ireland* from January 1886)

Secretary for India	Lord Randolph Churchill
First Lord of the Admiralty	Lord George Hamilton
President of the Board of Trade	Duke of Richmond E. Stanhope (August 1885)
Irish Viceroy	Earl of Carnarvon
Postmaster-General	Lord John Manners
Vice-President (Education)	Hon. E. Stanley
Lord Chancellor of Ireland	Lord Ashbourne
Secretary for Scotland	Duke of Richmond (August 1885)

SALISBURY'S 2ND ADMINISTRATION: AUGUST 1886–AUGUST 1892

Prime Minister	Marquess of Salisbury
Foreign Secretary	Earl of Iddesleigh Marquess of Salisbury (January 1887)
Home Secretary	Henry Matthews
Chancellor of Exchequer	Lord Randolph Churchill George Goschen (January 1887)
Lord Chancellor	Lord Halsbury
Lord President of the Council	Viscount Cranbrook
Secretary for the Colonies	Hon. Edward Stanhope Lord Knutsford (January 1887)
Secretary for War	W.H. Smith
Secretary for India	Viscount Cross
Chief Secretary for Ireland	Sir Michael Hicks-Beach A.J. Balfour (April 1887) W.L. Jackson (October 1891)
First Lord of the Admiralty	Lord George Hamilton
President of the Board of Trade	Lord Stanley Sir Michael Hicks-Beach (February 1888)
Chancellor of the Duchy of Lancaster	Lord John Manners
Lord Chancellor of Ireland	Lord Ashbourne
Secretary for Scotland	A.J. Balfour (November 1886) Marquess of Lothian (November 1887)
First Lord of the Treasury	W.H. Smith (January 1887) A.J. Balfour (October 1991)
Minister without Office	Sir Michael Hicks Beach (March 1887–February 1888)

Lord Privy Seal	Earl of Cadogan (May 1887)
President of the Local Government Board	Charles T. Ritchie (May 1887)

SALISBURY'S 3RD ADMINISTRATION: JUNE 1895–JULY 1902

Prime Minister	Marquess of Salisbury
Foreign Secretary	Marquess of Salisbury Marquess of Lansdowne (November 1900, Liberal Unionist)
Chancellor of Exchequer	Sir Michael Hicks-Beach
Home Secretary	Sir Matthew White-Ridley Charles T. Ritchie (November 1900)
First Lord of the Treasury	A.J. Balfour
Lord Chancellor	Earl of Halsbury
Lord President of the Council	Duke of Devonshire
Lord Privy Seal	Viscount Cross Marquess of Salisbury (October 1900)
Secretary for Colonies	Joseph Chamberlain
Secretary for War	Marquess of Lansdowne (Liberal Unionist) Hon. St John Brodrick (October 1900)
Secretary for Scotland	Lord Balfour of Burleigh
Secretary for India	Lord George Hamilton
Irish Viceroy	Earl Cadogan
First Lord of the Admiralty	George Goschen Earl of Selborne (October 1900)
President of Board of Trade	G.W. Balfour (October 1900)
President of Local Government Board	Walter Long (October 1900)
President of Board of Agriculture	R.W. Hanbury (October 1900)
Postmaster-General	Marquess of Londonderry (October 1900)

BALFOUR'S ADMINISTRATION: JULY 1902–NOVEMBER 1905

Prime Minister and First Lord of Treasury	A.J. Balfour (July 1902)
Chancellor of Exchequer	Sir Michael Hicks-Beach Charles Ritchie (August 1902) Austen Chamberlain (October 1903, Liberal Unionist)
Foreign Secretary	Marquess of Lansdowne (Liberal Unionist)

Home Secretary	Charles Ritchie Aretas Akers-Douglas (August 1902)
Lord Chancellor	Earl of Halsbury
Lord President of the Council	Duke of Devonshire
Lord Privy Seal and President of the Board of Education	Marquess of Londonderry
Secretary for the Colonies	Joseph Chamberlain Alfred Lyttelton (October 1903)
Secretary for War	Hon. St John Broderick H. Arnold-Forster (October 1903)
Secretary for India	Lord George Hamilton Hon. St John Broderick (October 1903)
Secretary for Scotland	Lord Balfour of Burleigh A. Murray (October 1903) Marquess of Linlithgow (February 1905)
Chief Secretary for Ireland	Lord Wyndham Walter Long (March 1905)
First Lord of the Admiralty	Earl of Selborne Earl of Cawdor (March 1905)
Chancellor of the Duchy of Lancaster	Lord James of Hereford Sir William Walrond (August 1902)
President of the Board of Trade	George Balfour 4th Marquess of Salisbury (March 1905)
President of the Local Government Board	Walter Long G.W. Balfour (March 1905)
President of the Board of Agriculture	R.W. Hanbury Earl of Onslow (May 1903) Ailwyn Fellowes (March 1905)
Lord Chancellor of Ireland	Lord Ashbourne
First Commissioner of Works	Lord Windsor (Earl of Plymouth)
Postmaster-General	Austen Chamberlain (Liberal Unionist) Lord Stanley (October 1903)

ASQUITH'S COALITION GOVERNMENT: MAY 1915–DECEMBER 1916

Colonial Secretary	Andrew Bonar Law
Lord Privy Seal	Earl Curzon
First Lord of the Admiralty	A.J. Balfour
India Secretary	Austen Chamberlain

The key posts were held by Liberals

LLOYD GEORGE COALITION: DECEMBER 1916–OCTOBER 1922

Prime Minister	David Lloyd George (Coalition Liberal)
Chancellor of Exchequer	Andrew Bonar Law Austen Chamberlain (January 1919) Robert Horne (April 1921)
Foreign Secretary	A.J. Balfour Earl Curzon (October 1919)
Home Secretary	George Cave Edward Shortt (January 1919, Coalition Liberal)
Lord President	Lord Curzon A.J. Balfour (October 1919)
Lord Chancellor	Lord Finlay Lord Birkenhead (January 1919)
Lord Privy Seal	Earl of Crawford Andrew Bonar Law (January 1919) Austen Chamberlain (March 1921)
First Lord of the Admiralty	Sir Edward Carson Sir Eric Geddes (July 1917) Walter Long (January 1919) Lord Lee (February 1921)
Board of Agriculture and Fisheries	Rowland Prothero (cr. Lord Ernle 1919) Lord Lee (August 1919) Sir A. Griffith-Boscawen (February 1921)
Secretary for Colonies	Walter Long Viscount Milner (January 1919) Winston Churchill (February 1921, Coalition Liberal)

BONAR LAW ADMINISTRATION: OCTOBER 1922–MAY 1923

Prime Minister	Andrew Bonar Law
Chancellor of Exchequer	Stanley Baldwin Neville Chamberlain (August 1923)
Foreign Secretary	Marquess Curzon
Home Secretary	William Bridgeman
Lord President	Marquess of Salisbury
Lord Chancellor	Viscount Cave
First Lord of the Admiralty	Leo Amery

Minister for Agriculture and Fisheries	Sir Robert Sanders
Secretary for Colonies	Duke of Devonshire
President of Board of Education	Edward Wood
Minister for Health	Sir A. Griffith-Boscawen Neville Chamberlain (March 1923)
Secretary for India	Viscount Peel
Minister for Labour	Sir A. Montague-Barlow
Chancellor of the Duchy of Lancaster	Marquess of Salisbury
Postmaster-General	Sir L. Worthington-Evans
Secretary for Scotland	Viscount Novar
President of Board of Trade	Sir P. Lloyd-Greame
Minister for War	Earl of Derby

BALDWIN'S 1ST ADMINISTRATION: MAY 1923–JANUARY 1924

Prime Minister	Stanley Baldwin
Chancellor of Exchequer	Stanley Baldwin Neville Chamberlain (from August 1923)
Foreign Secretary	Marquess Curzon
Home Secretary	William Bridgeman
Lord President	Marquess of Salisbury
Lord Chancellor	Viscount Cave
Lord Privy Seal	Lord Robert Cecil
Financial Secretary to the Treasury	Sir W. Joynson-Hicks (until August 1923)
First Lord of the Admiralty	Leo Amery
Minister for Agriculture and Fisheries	Sir Robert Sanders
Minister for Air	Sir Samuel Hoare
Secretary for Colonies	Duke of Devonshire
President of Board of Education	Edward Wood
Minister for Health	Neville Chamberlain (March 1923) Sir W. Joynson-Hicks (August 1923)
Secretary for India	Viscount Peel
Minister for Labour	Sir A. Montague-Barlow
Postmaster-General	Sir L. Worthington-Evans
Secretary for Scotland	Viscount Novar
President of Board of Trade	Sir P. Lloyd-Greame
Minister for War	Earl of Derby

BALDWIN'S 2ND ADMINISTRATION: NOVEMBER 1924–JUNE 1929

Prime Minister	Stanley Baldwin
Chancellor of Exchequer	Winston Churchill
Foreign Secretary	Sir Austen Chamberlain
Home Secretary	Sir William Joynson-Hicks
Lord President	Marquess Curzon Earl of Balfour (April 1925)
Lord Chancellor	Viscount Cave Lord Hailsham (March 1928)
First Lord of the Admiralty	William Bridgeman
Minister for Agriculture and Fisheries	Edward Wood W. Guinness (November 1925)
Minister for Air	Sir Samuel Hoare
Secretary for Colonies and Dominions	Leo Amery
President of Board of Education	Lord Eustace Percy
Minister for Health	Neville Chamberlain
Secretary for India	Earl of Birkenhead Viscount Peel (October 1928)
Minister for Labour	Sir A. Steel-Maitland
Chancellor of the Duchy of Lancaster	Viscount Cecil of Chelwood Lord Cushendun
Secretary for Scotland	Sir John Gilmour
President of Board of Trade	Sir P. Lloyd-Greame (Cunliffe-Lister from Nov. 1924)
Minister for War	Sir L. Worthington-Evans
Minister for Works	Viscount Peel Marquess of Londonderry (October 1928)
Attorney-General	Sir Douglas Hogg

NATIONAL GOVERNMENT: AUGUST 1931–JUNE 1935

Prime Minister	Ramsay MacDonald (National Labour)
Chancellor of Exchequer	Philip Snowden (National Labour) Neville Chamberlain (November 1931)
Foreign Secretary	Marquess of Reading (Liberal) John Simon (November 1931, Liberal National)
Home Secretary	Herbert Samuel (Liberal) John Gilmour (September 1932)

Lord President	Stanley Baldwin
Lord Chancellor	Lord Sankey (National Labour)
Lord Privy Seal	Viscount Snowden (November 1931, National Labour)
First Lord of the Admiralty	Sir B. Eyres-Monsell (November 1931)
Minister for Agriculture and Fisheries	Sir John Gilmour (cabinet position from November 1931) Walter Elliot (September 1932)
Minister for Air	Marquess of Londonderry (November 1931)
Secretary for Colonies	J.H. Thomas (National Labour) Sir P. Cunliffe-Lister (November 1931)
Secretary for Dominions	J.H. Thomas (National Labour)
President of Board of Education	Sir D. Maclean (elevated to cabinet November 1931, Liberal) Lord Irwin (cr. Viscount Halifax 1934) (June 1932)
Minister for Health	Neville Chamberlain Sir E. Young (November 1931)
Secretary for India	Sir Samuel Hoare
Minister for Labour	Sir H. Betterton (November 1931) Oliver Stanley (June 1934)
Postmaster-General	Sir Kingsley Wood (elevated to cabinet December 1933)
Secretary for Scotland	Sir Archibald Sinclair (elevated to cabinet November 1931, Liberal) Sir Godfrey Collins (September 1932, Liberal National)
President of Board of Trade	Sir P. Cunliffe-Lister Walter Runicman (November 1931, Liberal National)
Secretary for War	Viscount Hailsham (November 1931)
Minister for Works	William Ormsby-Gore (November 1931)

BALDWIN'S NATIONAL GOVERNMENT: JUNE 1935–MAY 1937

Prime Minister	Stanley Baldwin
Chancellor of Exchequer	Neville Chamberlain
Foreign Secretary	Sir Samuel Hoare Anthony Eden (December 1935)

Home Secretary	John Simon (National Liberal)
Lord President	Ramsay MacDonald (National Labour)
Lord Chancellor	Viscount Hailsham
Lord Privy Seal	Marquess of Londonderry Viscount Halifax (November 1935)
First Lord of the Admiralty	Sir B. Eyres-Monsell (cr. Viscount Monsell 1935) Sir Samuel Hoare (June 1936)
Minister for Agriculture and Fisheries	Walter Elliot William Morrison (October 1936)
Secretary for Air	Sir Philip Cunliffe-Lister (cr. Viscount Swinton 1935)
Secretary for Colonies	Malcolm MacDonald (National Labour) J.H. Thomas (November 1935, National Labour) William Ormsby-Gore (May 1936)
Minister for Co-ordination of Defence	Sir Thomas Inskip (March 1936)
Secretary for the Dominions	J.H. Thomas (National Labour) Malcolm MacDonald (November 1935, National Labour)
President of Board of Education	Oliver Stanley
Minister for Health	Sir Kingsley Wood
Secretary for India	Marquess of Zetland
Minister for Labour	Ernest Brown (Liberal National)
Minister without Portfolio	Anthony Eden (June 1935–December 1935) Lord Eustace Percy (June 1935–March 1936)
Secretary for Scotland	Sir Godfrey Collins Walter Elliot (October 1936)
President of Board of Trade	Walter Runciman
Minister for Transport	Leslie Hore-Belisha (elevated to cabinet October 1936, Liberal National)
Secretary for War	Viscount Halifax Alfred Duff Cooper (November 1935)
Minister for Works	William Ormsby-Gore Earl Stanhope (June 1936)

CHAMBERLAIN'S NATIONAL GOVERNMENT: MAY 1937–SEPTEMBER 1939

Prime Minister	Neville Chamberlain
Chancellor of Exchequer	Sir John Simon

Foreign Secretary	Anthony Eden Viscount Halifax (February 1938)
Home Secretary	Sir Samuel Hoare
Lord President	Viscount Halifax Viscount Runciman (March 1938)
Lord Chancellor	Viscount Hailsham Lord Maugham (March 1938)
Lord Privy Seal	Earl de la Warr Sir John Anderson (October 1938, National)
First Lord of the Admiralty	Alfred Duff Cooper Earl Stanhope (October 1938)
Minister for Agriculture and Fisheries	William Morrison Sir Reginald Dorman-Smith (January 1939)
Secretary for Air	Viscount Swinton Sir Kingsley Wood (May 1938)
Secretary for Colonies	William Ormsby-Gore Malcolm MacDonald (May 1938)
Secretary for Dominions	Malcolm MacDonald Lord Stanley (May 1938) Malcolm MacDonald (October 1938) Sir Thomas Inskip (January 1939)
Minister for Co-Ordination of Defence	Sir Thomas Inskip Lord Chatfield (January 1939)
President of Board of Education	Earl Stanhope Earl de la Warr (October 1938)
Minister for Health	Sir Kingsley Wood Walter Elliot (May 1938)
Secretary for India and Burma	Marquess of Zetland
Minister for Labour	Ernest Brown
Chancellor of the Duchy of Lancaster	Earl Winterton (elevated to cabinet March 1938) William Morrison (January 1939)
Minister without Portfolio (and *Supply Minister* from July 1939)	Leslie Burgin (April 1939)
Secretary for Scotland	Walter Elliot John Colville (May 1938)
President of Board of Trade	Oliver Stanley
Minister for Transport	Leslie Burgin Euan Wallace (April 1939)
Secretary for War	Leslie Hore-Belisha

CHAMBERLAIN'S WARTIME ADMINISTRATION: SEPTEMBER 1939–MAY 1940

(N.B. * Indicates membership of war cabinet.)

Prime Minister	Neville Chamberlain*
Chancellor of Exchequer	Sir John Simon*
Foreign Secretary	Viscount Halifax*
Home Secretary	Sir John Anderson* (National)
Lord President	Earl Stanhope
Lord Chancellor	Viscount Caldecote
Lord Privy Seal	Sir Samuel Hoare* Sir Kingsley Wood
First Lord of the Admiralty	Winston Churchill*
Minister for Agriculture and Fisheries	Sir Reginald Dorman-Smith
Secretary for Air	Sir Kingsley Wood Sir Samuel Hoare (April 1940)
Secretary for Colonies	Malcolm MacDonald
Secretary for Dominions	Anthony Eden
Minister for Co-ordination of Defence	Lord Chatfield* (post abolished April 1940)
President of Board of Education	Earl de la Warr H. Ramsbottom (April 1940)
Minister for Food	William Morrison Lord Woolton (April 1940)
Minister for Health	Walter Elliot
Secretary for India and Burma	Marquess of Zetland
Minister for Information	Lord Macmillan Sir John Reith (January 1940)
Minister for Labour and National Service	Ernest Brown
Chancellor of the Duchy of Lancaster	William Morrison
Minister without Portfolio	Lord Hankey*
Secretary for Scotland	John Colville
Minister for Shipping	Sir John Gilmour Robert Hudson (April 1940)
Minister for Supply	Leslie Burgin
President of Board of Trade	Oliver Stanley Sir Alan Duncan (January 1940)
Minister for Transport	Euan Wallace
Secretary for War	Leslie Hore-Belisha* Oliver Stanley* (January 1940)

CHURCHILL'S COALITION GOVERNMENT MAY 1940–MAY 1945

(N.B. * Indicates membership of war cabinet.)

Prime Minister	Winston Churchill*
Chancellor of Exchequer	Sir Kingsley Wood (* member October 1940–February 1942) Sir John Anderson* (September 1943, National)
Foreign Secretary	Viscount Halifax* Anthony Eden* (December 1940)
Home Secretary	Sir John Anderson (National) Herbert Morrison* (October 1940, Labour)
Lord President	Neville Chamberlain* (until October 1940) Clement Attlee* (September 1943, Labour)
Lord Privy Seal	Clement Attlee* (Labour) Sir Stafford Cripps* (February–November 1942, Labour) Lord Beaverbrook* (September 1943)
Minister for Aircraft Production	Lord Beaverbrook (* from August 1940) John Moore-Brabazon (May 1941) John Llewellyn (February 1942) Sir Stafford Cripps (November 1942, Labour)
Dominions Secretary	Viscount Caldecote Viscount Cranborne Clement Attlee* (February 1942, Labour)
Minister for Labour and National Service	Ernest Bevin (* from October 1940, Labour)
Minister Resident Middle East	Oliver Lyttelton* (February 1942) Richard Casey* (March 1942–December 1943, Independent)
Minister without Portfolio	Arthur Greenwood* (Labour) Sir William Jowitt (December 1942, Labour)
Minister of State	Lord Beaverbrook* (May 1941) Oliver Lyttelton* (June 1941 until March 1942)
Minister for Reconstruction	Lord Woolton* (November 1943)
Minister for Supply	Herbert Morrison (Labour) Sir Alan Duncan (October 1940) Lord Beaverbrook* (June 1941–February 1942)
Minister for War Production	Lord Beaverbrook* (February 1942) Oliver Lyttelton* (March 1942)

CHURCHILL'S 'CARETAKER' ADMINISTRATION MAY–JULY 1945

Prime Minister and Minister of Defence	Winston Churchill
Lord President	Lord Woolton
Lord Chancellor	Viscount Simon
Lord Privy Seal	Lord Beaverbrook
Foreign Secretary	Anthony Eden
Home Secretary	Donald Somervell
First Lord of the Admiralty	Brendan Bracken
Minister for Agriculture and Fisheries	Robert Hudson
Minister for Air	Harold Macmillan
Colonial Secretary	Oliver Stanley
Dominions Secretary	Viscount Cranborne
Minister for Education	Richard Law
Secretary for India and Burma	Leo Amery
Minister for Labour and National Service	R.A. Butler
President of the Board of Trade	Oliver Lyttelton
Secretary for War	Sir John Grigg

CHURCHILL'S 1ST PEACETIME ADMINISTRATION: OCTOBER 1951–APRIL 1955

Prime Minister	Winston Churchill
Chancellor of Exchequer	R.A. Butler
Foreign Secretary	Anthony Eden
Home Secretary	Sir David Maxwell Fyfe (October 1951) Gwilym Lloyd-George (October 1954)
Defence Minister	Winston Churchill Earl Alexander (March 1952) Harold Macmillan (Oct. 1954)
Lord President	Lord Woolton 5th Marquess of Salisbury (November 1952)
Lord Chancellor	Viscount Simon Viscount Kilmuir (October 1954)
Lord Privy Seal	5th Marquess of Salisbury Harry Crookshank (May 1952)
Minister for Agriculture, Fisheries and Food	Sir Thomas Dugdale (cabinet post from September 1953) Derick Heathcoat Amory (July 1954)

Colonial Secretary	Oliver Lyttelton Alan Lennox Boyd (July 1954)
Commonwealth Relations Office	Lord Ismay 5th Marquess of Salisbury (March 1952) Viscount Swinton (November 1952)
Minister for Transport Fuel and Power Defence	Lord Leathers (position abolished September 1953)
Minister for Education	Florence Horsbrugh (elevated to cabinet September 1953) Sir David Eccles (October 1954)
Minister for Food	Gwilym Lloyd-George (elevated to cabinet September 1953) Derick Heathcoat Amory (October 1954)
Minister for Health	Harry Crookshank (until May 1952 when post no longer cabinet rank)
Minister for Housing and Local Government	Harold Macmillan Duncan Sandys (October 1954)
Minister for Labour and National Service	Sir Walter Monckton
Chancellor of the Duchy of Lancaster	Lord Woolton (November 1952)
Paymaster-General	Lord Cherwell (until November 1953)
Minister for Pensions	Osbert Peake (October 1954)
Secretary for Scotland	James Stuart
President of the Board of Trade	Peter Thorneycroft

EDEN'S ADMINISTRATION: APRIL 1955–JANUARY 1957

Prime Minister	Sir Anthony Eden
Chancellor of Exchequer	R.A. Butler Harold Macmillan (December 1955)
Foreign Secretary	Harold Macmillan Selwyn Lloyd (December 1955)
Home Secretary	Gwilym Lloyd-George
Defence Minister	Selwyn Lloyd (April 1955) Sir Walter Monckton (December 1955) Anthony Head (October 1956)
Lord President	Marquess of Salisbury
Lord Chancellor	Viscount Kilmuir
Lord Privy Seal	Harry Crookshank R.A. Butler (December 1955)

Minister for Agriculture, Food and Fisheries	Derick Heathcoat Amory
Colonial Secretary	Alan Lennox Boyd
Commonwealth Relations Office	Earl of Home
Minister for Education	Sir David Eccles
Minister for Housing and Local Government	Duncan Sandys
Minister for Labour and National Service	Sir Walter Monckton Iain Macleod (December 1955)
Chancellor of the Duchy of Lancaster	Lord Woolton Earl of Selkirk (December 1955)
Paymaster-General	Sir Walter Monckton (October 1956)
Minister for Pensions	Osbert Peake (until December 1955)
Secretary for Scotland	James Stuart
President of the Board of Trade	Peter Thorneycroft
Minister for Works	Patrick Buchan-Hepburn (December 1955)

MACMILLAN'S ADMINISTRATION: JANUARY 1957–OCTOBER 1963

Prime Minister	Harold Macmillan
Chancellor of Exchequer	Peter Thorneycroft Derick Heathcoat Amory (January 1958) Selwyn Lloyd (July 1960) Reginald Maudling (July 1962)
Foreign Secretary	Selwyn Lloyd Earl of Home (renounced 1963) (July 1960) R.A. Butler (October 1963)
Home Secretary	R.A. Butler (January 1957) Henry Brooke (July 1962)
Defence Minister	Duncan Sandys (January 1957) Harold Watkinson (October 1959) Peter Thorneycroft (July 1962)
First Secretary of State	R.A. Butler
Lord President	Marquess of Salisbury Earl of Home (March 1957) Viscount Hailsham (September 1957) Earl of Home (October 1959) Viscount Hailsham (July 1960)
Lord Chancellor	Viscount Kilmuir Lord Dilhorne (July 1962)

Lord Privy Seal	R.A. Butler Viscount Hailsham (October 1959) Edward Heath (July 1960)
Colonial Secretary	Alan Lennox-Boyd Iain Macleod (October 1959) Reginald Maudling (October 1961) Duncan Sandys (July 1962)
Commonwealth Relations Office	Earl of Home Duncan Sandys (July 1960)
Education Minister	Viscount Hailsham Geoffrey Lloyd (September 1957) Sir David Eccles (October 1959) Sir Edward Boyle (July 1962)
Health Minister	Enoch Powell (July 1962)
Minister for Housing, Local Government and Welsh Affairs	Henry Brooke Charles Hill (October 1961) Sir Keith Joseph (July 1962)
Minister for Labour and National Service	Iain Macleod Edward Heath (October 1959) John Hare (July 1960)
Chancellor of the Duchy of Lancaster	Charles Hill Iain Macleod (October 1961)
Paymaster-General	Reginald Maudling (elevated to cabinet September 1957) Lord Mills (October 1959 until October 1961)
Minister for Power	Lord Mills (until October 1959)
Minister for Science	Viscount Hailsham (October 1959)
President of the Board of Trade	Sir David Eccles Reginald Maudling (October 1959) Frederick Erroll (October 1961)
Minister for Transport and Civil Aviation	Harold Watkinson Ernest Marples (October 1959)

HOME'S ADMINISTRATION: OCTOBER 1963–OCTOBER 1964

Prime Minister	Sir Alec Douglas-Home
Chancellor of Exchequer	Reginald Maudling
Foreign Secretary	R.A. Butler
Home Secretary	Henry Brooke
Defence Minister	Peter Thorneycroft
Lord President	Viscount Hailsham

Lord Chancellor	Lord Dilhorne
Lord Privy Seal	Selwyn Lloyd
Colonial Secretary and Commonwealth Relations Office	Duncan Sandys
Minister for Education and Science	Viscount Hailsham
Minister of State for Education	Sir Edward Boyle (April 1964)
Health Minister	Anthony Barber
Minister for Housing, Local Government and Welsh Affairs	Sir Keith Joseph
Chancellor of the Duchy of Lancaster	Lord Blakenham (John Hare)
Minister for Power	Frederick Erroll
President of the Board of Trade	Edward Heath
Minister for Transport	Ernest Marples
Minister for Works	Geoffrey Rippon

HEATH'S ADMINISTRATION JUNE 1970–MARCH 1974

Prime Minister	Edward Heath
Chancellor of Exchequer	Iain Macleod Anthony Barber (July 1970)
Foreign Secretary	Sir Alec Douglas-Home
Home Secretary	Reginald Maudling Robert Carr (July 1972)
Defence Secretary	Lord Carrington Ian Gilmour (January 1974)
Lord President	William Whitelaw Robert Carr (April 1972) James Prior (November 1972)
Lord Chancellor	Quintin Hogg (cr. Lord Hailsham 1970)
Lord Privy Seal	Earl Jellicoe Lord Windlesham (June 1973)
Chief Secretary to the Treasury	Maurice Macmillan Patrick Jenkin (April 1972) Thomas Boardman (January 1974)
Minister for Agriculture, Fisheries and Food	James Prior Joseph Godber (November 1972)

Minister for Education and Science	Margaret Thatcher
Minister for Employment and Productivity	Robert Carr Maurice Macmillan (April 1972) William Whitelaw (December 1973)
Secretary of Sate for Energy	Lord Carrington (January 1974)
Minister for Energy	Patrick Jenkin (January 1974)
Minister for the Environment	Peter Walker (October 1970) Geoffrey Rippon (November 1972)
Minister for Health and Social Security	Sir Keith Joseph
Minister for Housing and Local Government	Peter Walker (until October 1970)
Chancellor of the Duchy of Lancaster (responsibility for Europe)	Anthony Barber Geoffrey Rippon (July 1970) John Davies (November 1972)
Secretary for Northern Ireland	William Whitelaw (March 1972) Francis Pym (December 1973)
Minister for Transport	John Peyton (June–October 1970 only)
Secretary for Wales	Peter Thomas

THATCHER'S GOVERNMENT: MAY 1979–NOVEMBER 1990

Prime Minister	Margaret Thatcher
Chancellor of Exchequer	Sir Geoffrey Howe (May 1979) Nigel Lawson (June 1983) John Major (October 1989)
Foreign Secretary	Lord Carrington (May 1979) Francis Pym (April 1982) Sir Geoffrey Howe (June 1983) John Major (July 1989) Douglas Hurd (October 1989)
Home Secretary	William Whitelaw (May 1979) Leon Brittan (June 1983) Douglas Hurd (September 1985) David Waddington (October 1989)
Defence Secretary	Francis Pym (May 1979) John Nott (January 1981) Michael Heseltine (January 1983) George Younger (January 1986) Tom King (July 1989)

Lord President	Lord Soames Francis Pym (September 1981) John Biffen (April 1982) Viscount Whitelaw (June 1983) John Wakeham (January 1988) Sir Geoffrey Howe (July 1989) John MacGregor (November 1990)
Lord Chancellor	Lord Hailsham Lord Havers (June 1987) Lord Mackay (October 1987)
Lord Privy Seal	Sir Ian Gilmour Humphrey Atkins (September 1981) Lady Young (April 1982) John Biffen (June 1983) John Wakeham (June 1987) Lord Belstead (January 1988)
Chief Secretary to the Treasury	John Biffen (May 1979) Leon Brittan (January 1981) Peter Rees (June 1983) John MacGregor (September 1985) John Major (June 1987) Norman Lamont (July 1989)
Minister for Agriculture, Fisheries and Food	Peter Walker Michael Jopling (June 1983) John MacGregor (June 1987) (Not a cabinet seat from July 1989)
Minister for Arts	Norman St John Stevas (until January 1981 when no longer cabinet position)
Secretary for Education and Science	Michael Carlisle Sir Keith Joseph (September 1981) Kenneth Baker (May 1986) John MacGregor (July 1989) Kenneth Clarke (November 1990)
Employment Secretary	James Prior Norman Tebbit (September 1981) Tom King (October 1983) Lord Young (September 1985) Norman Fowler (June 1987) Michael Howard (January 1990)
Energy Secretary	David Howell Nigel Lawson (September 1981) Peter Walker (June 1983) Cecil Parkinson (June 1987) John Wakeham (July 1989)

Secretary for the Environment	Michael Heseltine Tom King (January 1983) Peter Jenkin (June 1983) Kenneth Baker (September 1985) Nicholas Ridley (May 1986) Chris Patten (July 1989)
Secretary for Health and Social Security	Patrick Jenkin Norman Fowler (September 1981) John Moore (June 1987)
Secretary for Health	Kenneth Clarke (July 1988) William Waldegrave (November 1990)
Secretary for Industry	Sir Keith Joseph Patrick Jenkin (September 1981) (June 1983 reorganised as *Dept. of Trade and Industry*)
Secretary for Trade	John Nott John Biffen (January 1981) Lord Cockfield (April 1986) (June 1983 reorganised as *Dept. of Trade and Industry*) Cecil Parkinson (June 1983) Norman Tebbit (October 1983) Leon Brittan (September 1985) Paul Channon (January 1986) Lord Young (June 1987) Nicholas Ridley (July 1989) Peter Lilley (July 1990)
Chancellor of the Duchy of Lancaster	Norman St John Stevas Francis Pym (January 1981) Lady Young (October 1981) Cecil Parkinson (April 1982) Lord Cockfield (June 1983) Earl of Gowrie (September 1984) Norman Tebbit (September 1985) Kenneth Clark (also *Minister of Trade* June 1987) Anthony Newton (July 1988) Kenneth Baker (July 1989)
Secretary for Northern Ireland	Humphrey Atkins James Prior (September 1981) Douglas Hurd (September 1984) Tom King (September 1985) Peter Brooke (July 1989)
Paymaster-General	Angus Maude Francis Pym (January 1981)

	Cecil Parkinson (September 1981) (Not a cabinet post June 1983–September 1984) Kenneth Clarke (September 1985) (Position not cabinet status from June 1987)
Secretary for Scotland	George Younger Malcolm Rifkind (January 1986)
Secretary for Wales	Nicholas Edwards Peter Walker (June 1987) David Hunt (May 1990)
Social Security Minister	John Moore (July 1988) Anthony Newton (July 1989)
Secretary for Transport	Norman Fowler (elevated to cabinet January 1981) David Howell (September 1981) Tom King (June 1983) Nicholas Ridley (October 1983) John Moore (May 1986) Paul Channon (June 1987) Cecil Parkinson (July 1989)

MAJOR'S ADMINISTRATION: NOVEMBER 1990–MAY 1997

Prime Minister	John Major
Deputy Prime Minister	Michael Heseltine (July 1995)
Chancellor of Exchequer	Norman Lamont (November 1990) Kenneth Clarke (May 1993)
Foreign Secretary	Douglas Hurd
Home Secretary	Kenneth Baker (November 1990) Kenneth Clarke (April 1992) Michael Howard (May 1993)
Defence Secretary	Tom King Malcolm Rifkind (April 1992) Michael Portillo (July 1995)
Lord Chancellor	Lord Mackay
Lord President	John MacGregor Anthony Newton (April 1992)
Chief Secretary to Treasury	David Mellor Michael Portillo (April 1992) Jonathan Aitken (July 1994) William Waldegrave (July 1995)
Minister for Agriculture, Fisheries and Food	John Selwyn Gummer Gillian Shephard (May 1993) William Waldegrave (July 1994) Douglas Hogg (July 1995)

Minister for Education and Science	Kenneth Clarke John Patten (April 1992) Gillian Shephard (July 1994)
Minister for Employment	Michael Howard Gillian Shephard (April 1992) (No longer cabinet position from May 1993)
Secretary for Energy	John Wakeham (Office abolished April 1992)
Secretary for the Environment	Michael Heseltine Michael Howard (April 1992) John Selwyn Gummer (May 1993)
Minister for Health	William Waldegrave Virginia Bottomley (April 1992) (From July 1995 not a cabinet ranking post)
Chancellor of the Duchy of Lancaster	Chris Patten William Waldegrave (April 1992) David Hunt (July 1994) Roger Freeman (July 1995)
Minister without Portfolio	Jeremy Hanley (July 1994) Brian Mawhinney (July 1995)
Minister for National Heritage	David Mellor (April 1992) Peter Brooke (September 1992) Stephen Dorrell (July 1994) Virginia Bottomley (July 1995)
Secretary for Northern Ireland	Peter Brooke Sir Patrick Mayhew (April 1992)
Secretary for Scotland	Iain Lang Michael Forsyth (July 1995)
Secretary for Wales	David Hunt John Redwood (July 1994) William Hague (July 1995)
Minister for Social Security	Anthony Newton Peter Lilley (April 1992)
Secretary for Trade	Peter Lilley Michael Heseltine (April 1992) Iain Lang (July 1995)
Secretary for Transport	Michael Rifkind John MacGregor (April 1992) Brian Mawhinney (July 1994) Sir George Young (July 1995)

1.4 THE CONSERVATIVES AND THE ELECTORATE

1. GENERAL ELECTION RESULTS*

1832
Date: 10 December 1832–8 January 1833
Total electorate: 812,938
Votes cast: 827,776 (70.4%)

	Votes	% share of vote	No. of candidates	No. of unopposed seats won	Total no. of seats won
Conservative (Tories)	241,284	29.4	350	66	175
Liberal (Whigs)	554,719	66.7	636	109	441
Others	31,773	3.9	51	14	42

1835
Date: 6 January–6 February
Total electorate: 845,776
Votes cast: 611,137 (65.0%)

	Votes	% share of vote	No. of candidates	No. of uncontested seats won	Total no. of seats won
Conservative	261,269	42.6	407	121	273
Liberal	349,868	57.4	538	154	385

* From 1832–1945 inclusive the % share figures and % of electorate voting have been adjusted to take account of multi-member constituencies.

1837
Date: 24 July–18 August
Total electorate: 1,004,664
Votes cast: 798,025 (63.6%)

	Votes	% share of vote	No. of candidates	No. of uncontested seats won	Total no. of seats won
Conservative	379,694	48.3	484	121	314
Liberal	418,331	51.7	510	115	344

1841
Date: 29 June–22 July
Total electorate: 1,017,379
Votes cast: 593,445 (63.4%)

	Votes	% share of vote	No. of candidates	No. of uncontested seats won	Total no. of seats won
Conservative	306,314	50.9	498	212	367
Liberal	273,902	46.9	388	113	271
Others	13,229	2.2	30	12	20

1847
Date: 29 July–26 August
Total electorate: 1,106,514
Votes cast: 482,429 (53.4%)

	Votes	% share of vote	No. of candidates	No. of uncontested seats won	Total no. of seats won
Conservative[1]	205,481	42.2	422	213	325
Liberal	259,311	53.9	393	136	292
Others	17,637	3.9	64	18	39

1. Including Peelites thereafter

* From 1832–1945 inclusive the % share figures and % of electorate voting have been adjusted to take account of multi-member constituencies.

1852
Date: 7–31 July
Total electorate: 1,184,689
Votes cast: 743,904 (57.9%)

	Votes	% share of vote	No. of candidates	No. of uncontested seats won	Total no. of seats won
Conservative	311,481	41.4	461	160	330
Liberal	430,882	58.4	488	95	324
Others	1,541	0.2	4	0	0

1857
Date: 27 March–24 April
Total electorate: 1,235,530
Votes cast: 716,552 (58.9%)

	Votes	% share of vote	No. of candidates	No. of uncontested seats won	Total no. of seats won
Conservative	239,712	33.1	351	148	264
Liberal	464,127	65.1	507	176	377
Others	12,713	1.8	20	4	13

1859
Date: 28 April–18 May
Total electorate: 1,271,900
Votes cast: 565,500 (63.7%)

	Votes	% share of vote	No. of candidates	No. of uncontested seats won	Total no. of seats won
Conservative	193,232	34.3	394	196	298
Liberal	372,117	65.7	465	183	356
Others	151	0.0	1	0	0

* From 1832–1945 inclusive the % share figures and % of electorate voting have been adjusted to take account of multi-member constituencies.

1865
Date: 11–24 July
Total electorate: 1,350,404
Votes cast: 854,856 (62.5%)

	Votes	% share of vote	No. of candidates	No. of uncontested seats won	Total no. of seats won
Conservative	346,035	39.8	406	142	289
Liberal	508,821	60.2	516	161	369

1868
Date: 17 November–7 December
Total electorate: 2,484,713
Votes cast: 2,333,251 (68.5%)

	Votes	% share of vote	No. of candidates	No. of uncontested seats won	Total no. of seats won
Conservative	903,318	38.4	436	91	271
Liberal	1,428,776	61.5	600	121	387
Others	1,157	0.1	3	0	0

1874
Date: 31 January–17 February
Total electorate: 2,753,142
Votes cast: 2,466,037 (66.4%)

	Votes	% share of vote	No. of candidates	No. of uncontested seats won	Total no. of seats won
Conservative	1,091,708	43.9	507	125	350
Liberal	1,281,159	52.7	489	52	242
Others	93,170	3.4	84	10	60

* From 1832–1945 inclusive the % share figures and % of electorate voting have been adjusted to take account of multi-member constituencies.

1880
Date: 31 March–27 April
Total electorate: 3,040,050
Votes cast: 3,359,416 (72.2%)

	Votes	% share of vote	No. of candidates	No. of uncontested seats won	Total no. of seats won
Conservative	1,426,351	42.0	521	58	237
Liberal	1,836,423	55.4	499	41	352
Others	96,642	2.6	83	10	63

1885
Date: 24 November–18 December
Total electorate: 5,708,030
Votes cast: 4,638,235 (81.2%)

	Votes	% share of vote	No. of candidates	No. of uncontested seats won	Total no. of seats won
Conservative	2,020,927	43.5	602	10	249
Liberal	2,199,998	47.4	572	14	319
Others	417,310	9.1	164	19	102

1886
Date: 1–27 July
Total electorate: 5,708,030
Votes cast: 2,974,163 (74.2%)

	Votes	% share of vote	No. of candidates	No. of uncontested seats won	Total no. of seats won
Conservative[1]	1,520,886	51.4	563	118	393
Liberal	1,353,581	45.0	449	40	191
Others	99,696	3.6	103	66	86

1. Including Liberal Unionists thereafter

* From 1832–1945 inclusive the % share figures and % of electorate voting have been adjusted to take account of multi-member constituencies.

1892
Date: 4–26 July
Total electorate: 6,160,541
Votes cast: 4,598,319 (77.4%)

	Votes	% share of vote	No. of candidates	No. of uncontested seats won	Total no. of seats won
Conservative	2,159,150	47.0	606	40	314
Liberal	2,088,019	45.1	532	13	271
Others	351,150	7.9	165	10	85

1895
Date: 13 July–7 August
Total electorate: 6,330,519
Votes cast: 3,866,282 (78.4%)

	Votes	% share of vote	No. of candidates	No. of uncontested seats won	Total no. of seats won
Conservative	1,894,772	49.1	588	132	411
Liberal	1,765,266	45.7	447	11	177
Others	206,244	5.2	145	46	82

1900
Date: 1–24 October
Total electorate: 6,730,935
Votes cast: 3,523,482 (75.1%)

	Votes	% share of vote	No. of candidates	No. of uncontested seats won	Total no. of seats won
Conservative	1,767,958	50.3	579	163	402
Liberal	1,572,323	45.0	402	22	184
Labour	62,698	1.3	15	0	2
Others	120,503	3.4	116	58	83

* From 1832–1945 inclusive the % share figures and % of electorate voting have been adjusted to take account of multi-member constituencies.

1906
Date: 12 January–8 February
Total electorate: 7,694,741
Votes cast: 5,626,091 (83.2%)

	Votes	% share of vote	No. of candidates	No. of uncontested seats won	Total no. of seats won
Conservative	2,422,071	43.4	574	13	156
Liberal	2,751,057	49.4	539	27	399
Labour	329,748	5.9	51	0	30
Others	131,300	2.4	132	74	87

1910
Date: 15 January–10 February
Total electorate: 7,694,741
Votes cast: 6,667,400 (86.8%)

	Votes	% share of vote	No. of candidates	No. of uncontested seats won	Total no. of seats won
Conservative	3,104,407	46.8	516	19	272
Liberal	2,866,157	43.5	600	1	274
Labour	505,657	7.6	78	0	40
Others	120,503	3.4	119	55	83

1910
Date: 3–19 December
Total electorate: 7,709,981
Votes cast: 5,235,238 (81.6%)

	Votes	% share of vote	No. of candidates	No. of uncontested seats won	Total no. of seats won
Conservative	2,420,169	46.6	548	72	272
Liberal	2,293,869	44.2	467	35	272
Labour	371,802	6.4	56	3	42
Others	149,398	2.8	120	53	85

* From 1832–1945 inclusive the % share figures and % of electorate voting have been adjusted to take account of multi-member constituencies.

1918
Date: 14 December
Total electorate: 21,392,322
Votes cast: 10,786,818 (57.2%)

	Votes	% share of vote	No. of candidates	No. of uncontested seats won	Total no. of seats won
Conservative[1]	4,144,192	38.4	445	41	382
Liberal (Coalition)	1,396,590	13.0	145	23	127
Liberals (Non-Coalition)	1,388,784	12.9	276	4	36
Labour (Coalition)	53,962	0.5	5	1	4
Labour (Non-Coalition)	2,245,777	20.8	361	4	57
Others (Coalition)	166,108	1.5	19	0	10
Others (Non-Coalition)	1,391,405	12.9	372	27	91

1. Includes both Coalition and Non-Coalition Conservatives

1922
Date: 15 November
Total electorate: 20,874,456
Votes cast: 14,392,330 (73.0%)

	Votes	% share of vote	No. of candidates	No. of uncontested seats won	Total no. of seats won
Conservative	5,502,298	38.5	482	42	344
Labour	4,237,349	29.7	414	4	142
National Liberal	1,471,317	9.9	151	5	53
Liberal	2,668,143	18.9	334	5	62
Others	513,223	3.0	60	1	14

* From 1832–1945 inclusive the % share figures and % of electorate voting have been adjusted to take account of multi-member constituencies.

1923
Date: 6 December
Total electorate: 21,283,061
Votes cast: 14,547,695 (71.1%)

	Votes	% share of vote	No. of candidates	No. of uncontested seats won	Total no. of seats won
Conservative	5,514,541	38.0	536	35	258
Labour	4,439,780	30.7	427	3	191
Liberal	4,301,481	29.7	457	11	158
Others	291,893	1.6	26	1	8

1924
Date: 29 October
Total electorate: 21,730,988
Votes cast: 16,640,279 (77.0%)

	Votes	% share of vote	No. of candidates	No. of uncontested seats won	Total no. of seats won
Conservative	7,854,523	46.8	534	16	412
Labour	5,489,087	33.3	514	9	151
Liberal	2,928,737	17.8	339	6	50
Others	367,932	2.1	40	1	12

1929
Date: 30 May
Total electorate: 28,854,748
Votes cast: 22,648,375 (76.3%)

	Votes	% share of vote	No. of candidates	No. of uncontested seats won	Total no. of seats won
Conservative	8,656,225	38.1	590	4	260
Labour	8,370,417	37.1	569	0	287
Liberal	5,308,738	23.5	513	0	59
Others	312,995	1.3	58	3	9

* From 1832–1945 inclusive the % share figures and % of electorate voting have been adjusted to take account of multi-member constituencies.

1931
Date: 27 October
Total electorate: 29,952,361
Votes cast: 21,656,373 (76.4%)

	Votes	% share of vote	No. of candidates	No. of uncontested seats won	Total no. of seats won
National Government					
Conservative	11,905,925	55.0	518	49	470
Liberal	1,372,595	6.5	111	5	32
National Liberal	807,302	3.7	41	7	35
National Labour	341,370	1.5	20	0	13
National	100,193	0.5	4	0	4
Non-National Government					
Labour	6,649,630	30.9	516	6	52
Others	476,998	1.9	82	0	9

1935
Date: 14 November
Total electorate: 31,374,449
Votes cast: 21,997,054 (71.1%)

	Votes	% share of vote	No. of candidates	No. of uncontested seats won	Total no. of seats won
National Government					
Conservative and National Liberal[1]	11,362,654	51.7	559	26	420
National Labour	339,811	1.5	20	0	8
National	53,189	0.3	4	0	1
Non-National Government					
Labour	8,325,491	37.8	552	13	154
Liberal	1,443,093	6.6	161	0	21
Others	472,816	2.1	52	1	11

1. Includes National Liberals thereafter

* From 1832–1945 inclusive the % share figures and % of electorate voting have been adjusted to take account of multi-member constituencies.

1945
Date: 5 July
Total electorate: 33,240,391
Votes cast: 25,095,195 (72.8%)

	Votes	% share of vote	No. of candidates	No. of uncontested seats won	Total no. of seats won
Conservative	9,972,010	39.6	618	1	210
Labour	11,967,746	48.0	603	2	393
Liberal	2,252,430	9.0	306	0	12
Others	903,009	3.4	156	0	25

1950
Date: 23 February
Total electorate: 34,412,255
Votes cast: 28,771,124 (83.9%)

	Votes	% share of vote	No. of candidates	No. of uncontested seats won	Total no. of seats won
Conservative	12,492,404	43.5	619	2	298
Labour	13,266,176	46.1	617	0	315
Liberal	2,621,487	9.1	475	0	9
Others	391,055	1.5	157	0	3

1951
Date: 25 October
Total electorate: 34,919,331
Votes cast: 28,596,594 (82.6%)

	Votes	% share of vote	No. of candidates	No. of uncontested seats won	Total no. of seats won
Conservative	13,718,199	48.0	617	4	321
Labour	13,948,883	48.8	617	0	295
Liberal	730,546	2.6	109	0	6
Others	198,966	0.6	33	0	3

* From 1832–1945 inclusive the % share figures and % of electorate voting have been adjusted to take account of multi-member constituencies.

1955
Date: 26 May
Total electorate: 34,852,179
Votes cast: 26,759,729 (76.8%)

	Votes	% share of vote	No. of candidates	No. of uncontested seats won	Total no. of seats won
Conservative	13,310,891	49.7	624	0	345
Labour	12,405,254	46.4	620	0	277
Liberal	722,402	2.7	110	0	6
Others	321,182	1.2	55	0	2

1959
Date: 8 October
Total electorate: 35,397,304
Votes cast: 27,862,652 (78.7%)

	Votes	% share of vote	No. of candidates	No. of uncontested seats won	Total no. of seats won
Conservative	13,750,875	49.3	625	0	365
Labour	12,216,172	43.8	621	0	258
Liberals	1,640,760	5.9	216	0	6
Others	254,845	0.9	74	0	1

1964
Date: 15 October
Total electorate: 35,894,054
Votes cast: 27,657,148 (77.1%)

	Votes	% share of vote	No. of candidates	No. of uncontested seats won	Total no. of seats won
Conservative[1]	12,002,642	43.4	630	0	304
Labour	12,205,808	44.1	628	0	317
Liberal	3,099,283	11.2	365	0	9
Others	354,415	1.3	134	0	0

1. Includes Ulster Unionists

* From 1832–1945 inclusive the % share figures and % of electorate voting have been adjusted to take account of multi-member constituencies.

1966
Date: 31 March
Total electorate: 35,957,245
Votes cast: 27,264,747 (75.8%)

	Votes	% share of vote	No. of candidates	No. of uncontested seats won	Total no. of seats won
Conservative	11,418,455	41.9	629	0	253
Labour	13,096,629	48.0	622	0	364
Liberals	2,327,457	8.6	311	0	12
Others	422,206	1.5	145	0	1

1970
Date: 18 June
Total electorate: 39,342,013
Votes cast: 28,344,798 (72.0%)

	Votes	% share of vote	No. of candidates	No. of uncontested seats won	Total no. of seats won
Conservative	13,145,123	46.4	628	0	330
Labour	12,208,758	43.1	625	0	288
Liberal	2,117,035	7.5	332	0	6
Others	873,882	3.1	252	0	6

1974
Date: 28 February
Total electorate: 39,753,863
Votes cast: 31,340,162 (78.8%)

	Votes	% share of vote	No. of candidates[1]	No. of uncontested seats won	Total no. of seats won
Conservative	11,872,180	37.9	623	0	297
Labour	11,645,616	37.2	623	0	301
Liberal	6,059,519	19.3	517	0	14
Scottish National	633,180	2.0	70	0	7
Plaid Cymru	171,374	0.6	36	0	2
Others	958,293	3.0	266	0	14

1. Hereafter until 1997 no major political parties contested the 12 Northern Irish seats.

* From 1832–1945 inclusive the % share figures and % of electorate voting have been adjusted to take account of multi-member constituencies.

1974

Date: 10 October
Total electorate: 40,072,970
Votes cast: 29,189,104 (72.8%)

	Votes	% share of vote	No. of candidates	No. of uncontested seats won	Total no. of seats won
Conservative	10,462,565	35.8	622	0	277
Labour	11,457,079	39.2	623	0	319
Liberal	5,346,704	18.3	619	0	13
Scottish National	839,617	2.9	71	0	11
Plaid Cymru	166,321	0.6	36	0	3
Others	916,818	3.2	281	0	12

1979

Date: 3 May
Total electorate: 41,095,649
Votes cast: 31,221,362 (76.0%)

	Votes	% share of vote	No. of candidates	No. of uncontested seats won	Total no. of seats won
Conservative	13,697,923	43.9	622	0	339
Labour	11,532,218	36.9	623	0	269
Liberal	4,313,804	13.8	577	0	11
Scottish National	504,259	1.6	71	0	2
Plaid Cymru	132,544	0.4	36	0	2
Others	1,040,614	3.4	647	0	12

1983

Date: 9 June
Total electorate: 42,192,999
Votes cast: 30,671,137 (72.7%)

	Votes	% share of vote	No. of candidates	No. of uncontested seats won	Total no. of seats won
Conservative	13,012,316	42.4	633	0	397
Labour	8,456,934	27.6	633	0	209
Liberal	4,210,115	13.7	322	0	17
Social Democrat	3,570,834	11.7	311	0	6
Scottish National	331,975	1.1	72	0	2
Plaid Cymru	125,309	0.4	38	0	2
Others	963,654	3.1	569	0	17

* From 1832–1945 inclusive the % share figures and % of electorate voting have been adjusted to take account of multi-member constituencies.

1987
Date: 11 June
Total electorate: 43,180,753
Votes cast: 32,529,578 (75.3%)

	Votes	% share of vote	No. of candidates	No. of uncontested seats won	Total no. of seats won
Conservative	13,760,583	42.3	633	0	376
Labour	10,029,807	30.8	633	0	229
Liberal	4,173,450	12.8	327	0	17
Social Democrat	3,168,183	9.7	306	0	5
Scottish National	416,473	1.3	71	0	3
Plaid Cymru	123,599	0.4	38	0	3
Others	857,433	2.7	317	0	17

1992
Date: 9 April
Total electorate: 43,240,084
Votes cast: 33,610,162 (77.7%)

	Votes	% share of vote	No. of candidates	No. of uncontested seats won	Total no. of seats won
Conservative[1]	14,093,890	41.9	645	0	336
Labour	11,559,857	34.4	634	0	271
Liberal	5,995,712	17.8	632	0	20
Scottish National	629,552	1.8	35	0	3
Plaid Cymru	154,439	0.5	72	0	4
Others	1,176,692	3.5	366	0	17

1. Includes 11 conservative candidates fielded in Northern Ireland.

* From 1832–1945 inclusive the % share figures and % of electorate voting have been adjusted to take account of multi-member constituencies.

1997

Date: 1 May
Total electorate: 43,240,084
Votes cast: 33,610,162 (77.7%)

	Votes	% share of vote	No. of candidates	No. of uncontested seats won	Total no. of seats won
Conservative[1]	9,600,940	30.7	648	0	165
Labour	13,517,911	43.2	638	0	418
Liberal Democrat	5,243,440	16.8	639	0	46
Scottish National	622,260	22.1	72	0	6
Plaid Cymru	161,030	9.9	40	0	4
Others	2,142,621	6.8	1,686	0	20

1. Includes 9 Conservative candidates fielded in Northern Ireland

2001

Date: 7 June
Total electorate: 44,391,464
Votes cast: 26,368,530 (59.4%)

	Votes	% share of vote	No. of candidates	No. of uncontested seats won	Total no. of seats won
Conservative[1]	8,357,292	31.8	643	0	166
Labour	10,740,168	40.8	640	0	413
Liberal Democrat	4,815,249	18.3	639	0	52
Scottish National	464,314	1.8	72	0	5
Plaid Cymru	195,892	0.8	40	0	4
Others	1,800,032	6.5	1,273	0	19

1. Includes 3 conservative candidates fielded in Northern Ireland.

* From 1832–1945 inclusive the % share figures and % of electorate voting have been adjusted to take account of multi-member constituencies.

2. BY-ELECTIONS

2a. Significant By-elections for the Conservatives since 1918

Constituency	Date	Outcome for Conservatives	Significance
Bothwell	16 July 1919	Loss	Labour gain from Coalition Conservatives.
Dover	12 January 1921	Loss	Anti-Waste League capture seat illustrating threat Independents could pose on the anti-spending ticket. Further gains at Hereford and St George's Westminster encourage Conservatives to take up anti-spending message and weaken coalition.
Camberwell North	20 February 1922	Loss	Labour gain indicative of improving stature of the party and consolidation of its gains made in local elections. One of eight net gains by summer 1922.
Newport	18 October 1922	Gain	Conservative gain from Coalition Liberals; prompted by local Conservative hostility to Licensing Act (1921). It crystallises anti-coalitionist support on the eve of the Carlton Club meeting which heralded the downfall of Lloyd George.
Mitcham	3 March 1923	Loss	Labour gain. Conservative candidate, a minister, also challenged by an Independent Conservative, supported by Lord Rothermere. Signified dissatisfaction with government inaction and the decontrol of rents.
East Toxteth, Liverpool	5 February 1931	Gain	Conservative gain in straight contest with Labour. Indicative of growing dissatisfaction with MacDonald's Labour government.

Constituency	Date	Outcome for Conservatives	Significance
St George's, Westminster	19 March 1931	Hold	Duff Cooper, the Conservative candidate, fights off the challenge laid down by Beaverbrook's Empire Crusade campaign. Helps secure Baldwin's leadership.
East Fulham	25 October 1933	Loss	With a swing of 30% Labour snatch the seat from the Conservatives. Campaign fought over 'pacifist' question.
Wavertree, Liverpool	6 February 1935	Loss	Intervention of Randolph Churchill, as an independent Conservative, against the official Conservative, splits the right's vote and enables Labour to win seat.
Oxford	27 October 1938	Hold	Quintin Hogg holds the seat for the Conservatives from an Independent. Seen as a referendum on Chamberlain's appeasement policy.
Bridgwater	17 November 1938	Loss	Vernon Bartlett, an Independent, defeats the Conservatives. An 'appeasement' by-election.
Kinross and West Perth	21 December 1938	Hold	The Duchess of Atholl, having resigned her seat in protest at the Munich agreement and her treatment by her local Association, stands as an Independent, but is defeated by the official Conservative candidate.
Kennington Lambeth	24 May 1939	Loss	Labour gain with 11.2% swing. The highest achieved by Labour since the 1935 general election. This would also prove to be Labour's last by-election gain from the Conservatives for over 17 years.
Grantham	25 March 1942	Loss	An Independent narrowly defeats Conservatives; first of series of wartime defeats of government candidates.

Constituency	Date	Outcome for Conservatives	Significance
Skipton	7 January 1944	Loss	Conservatives lose seat to Common Wealth; similar result follows at Chelmsford 26 April 1945
Sunderland South	13 May 1953	Gain	First occasion since 1924 that a government candidate won a by-election seat from the Opposition and only third time since 1918.
Lewisham North	14 February 1957	Loss	Labour's first gain from Conservatives for 17 years.
Torrington	27 March 1958	Loss	In a three-way contest the Liberals snatch the seat from the Conservatives. This is the first Liberal by-election victory since 1929.
Orpington	14 March 1962	Loss	Liberals overturn a safe Conservative seat with a 6% swing. The loss of the seat added to Harold Macmillan's problems.
South Dorset	22 November 1962	Loss	Labour gain after Conservative candidate finds himself challenged by an anti-Common Market candidate.
Leyton	21 January 1965	Gain	Conservative victory inflicts maximum embarrassment upon Labour. It had been hoped by the Wilson government to find a seat for Patrick Gordon Walker (Foreign Secretary) who had lost at Smethwick the previous October.
Dudley	28 March 1968	Gain	Is the largest swing, 21%, achieved during the 1966–70 Wilson government. Turned a Labour majority of 10,022 in 1966 general election into an 11,656 Conservative majority.

Constituency	Date	Outcome for Conservatives	Significance
Meriden	28 March 1968	Gain	Conservatives overturn a Labour 1966 majority of 4,581 into a 15,263 Conservative majority. This is despite internal divisions within the local party. Evidence of Conservative resurgence since Heath's election as leader.
Swindon	30 October 1969	Gain	Majority of 478. Indicative of the unpopularity of the Wilson government's trade union policy.
Sutton and Cheam	7 December 1972	Loss	Liberals snatch one of the safest suburban Conservative seats. Indicated electorate's dissatisfaction with prices and mortgage rates and concern over U-turns.
Isle of Ely	26 July 1973	Loss	Loss to the Liberals. The Conservative 1970 majority of 9,606 is overturned into a Liberal majority of 1,470. Another example of vulnerability of normally 'safe' Conservative seats and highlights the electorate's continued dissatisfaction with Heath's policies.
Ripon, Yorkshire	26 July 1973	Loss	Conservative loss to Liberals, who gained a narrow majority of 946.
Berwick-upon-Tweed	8 November 1973	Loss	Another Conservative defeat at the hands of the Liberals, again by a very narrow Liberal majority of 57. Commentators remained unconvinced of Liberal's ability to translate by-election successes into a credible general election result.
Walsall North	4 November 1976	Gain	Recording a swing of 22.6% the Conservatives convincingly capture the normally safe Labour stronghold. The largest swing of the 1974–79 Parliament to a Conservative.

Constituency	Date	Outcome for Conservatives	Significance
Ashfield	28 April 1977	Gain	Conservatives gain this normally safe Labour mining constituency with the narrowest of margins, 264. Result indicated union dissatisfaction with the Callaghan government's 'social contract'.
Crosby	26 November 1981	Loss	Shirley Williams victorious for the newly formed SDP, capturing a safe Conservative seat.
Glasgow Hillhead	25 March 1981	Loss	Roy Jenkins secures the marginal seat for the SDP from the Conservatives, pushing them into third place.
Northfield, Birmingham	28 October 1982	Loss	Labour victory in aftermath of Falklands. First gain from Conservatives since 1971.
Ryedale	8 May 1986	Loss	One of the Alliance's most convincing victories during the Thatcher second ministry.
Vale of Glamorgan	4 May 1989	Loss	Labour gain on a swing of 12.4%. Their largest gain since 1935 begins to suggest the electoral liability that Thatcher may present the Conservatives.
Mid-Staffordshire	23 March 1990	Loss	Labour exploits the unpopularity of Thatcher's community charge (poll tax), securing the largest swing from Conservative to Labour in 50 years. Result encouraged some to doubt Thatcher's continued suitability to lead the Conservatives.
Ribble Valley	7 March 1991	Loss	Liberal Democrat gain clearly signalling end of the honeymoon period for the Conservatives' new leader, John Major.
Monmouth	16 May 1991	Loss	Labour gain, exploiting the electorate's fear of the Conservatives' plans for the privatisation of the NHS.

Constituency	Date	Outcome for Conservatives	Significance
Newbury	6 May 1993	Loss	Liberal Democrat gain in a Conservative stronghold. The Lib Dems would still have won without the extensive Labour tactical voting.
Christchurch	29 July 1993	Loss	Liberal Democrat gain in what was previously a safe Conservative seat with 38.7% swing. Reduced Conservative majority in House of Commons to 17. The result heightens Conservative concerns about Liberal Democrat potential advances in the south of England.
Dudley West	15 December 1994	Loss	Labour gain overturning Conservative 1992 majority of 5,789 into 20,694. Increases expectations of Labour victory at next general election.
Staffordshire South East	11 April 1996	Loss	Labour wins the seat from the Conservatives, inflicting a 22.2% swing against them.
Wirral South	27 February 1997	Loss	Foretaste of 1997 general election as Labour win the safe Conservative seat.
Romsey	4 May 2000	Loss	Liberal Democrat gain from Conservatives. This was the Conservatives' 51st safest seat. It took the gloss off Conservative gains in the local elections and raised fresh questions about Hague's electability.

2b. By-elections 1832–2001[1]

	Total seats*	Total changes	Conservative gains	Conservative losses
1832–35	58	15	11	2
1835–37	89	27	17	10
1837–41	105	19	15	4
1841–47	231	38	15	13
1847–52	172	36	14	13
1852–57	218	32	10	22

	Total seats*	Total changes	Conservative gains	Conservative losses
1857–59	90	8	6	1
1859–65	221	40	26	14
1865–68	141	15	6	9
1868–74	176	49	32	7
1874–80	193	31	13	17
1880–85	193	29	20	6
1885–86	38	3	2	0
1886–92	179	24	2	22
1892–95	103	14	9	5
1895–1900	113	18	3	14
1900–5	114	31	2	27
1906–10	100	16	12	—
1910 Jan. to Dec.	21	—	—	—
1910–18[2]	247	30	16	4
1918–22	108	26	4	13
1922–23	16	6	1	4
1923–24	10	3	2	1
1924–29	63	20	1	16
1929–31	36	7	4	1
1931–35	62	10	—	9
1935–45	219	30	—	29
1945–50	52	4	3	—
1950–51	16	—	—	—
1951–55	48	1	1	—
1955–59	52	6	1	4
1959–64	62	9	2	7
1964–66	13	2	1	1
1966–70	38	16	12	1
1970–74	30	9	—	5
1974	1	—	—	—
1974–79	30	7	6	—
1979–83	20	7	1	4
1983–87	31	5	—	4
1987–92	23	8	—	7
1992–97	18	10	—	9
1997–2001	16	2	—	1

Source: F.W.S. Craig, *Chronology of British Parliamentary By-Elections 1832–1987* (1987), pp. 313, 324; C. Cook and J. Ramsden (eds), *By-Elections in British Politics* (1997), p. 4.

Notes:

* The number of by-elections up to 1918, and to a lesser extent to 1926, is artificially increased by the practice that Ministers stand for re-election on appointment. In 53 such cases the returns were unopposed.

1. Includes Irish by-elections up until 1922 and Northern Irish seats thereafter.
2. With the outbreak of the First World War on 4 August 1914 the Conservative, Labour and Liberal parties observed an electoral truce during the war by nominating only for seats which they had previously held.

3. Local Elections

	Number of seats available	Conservatives elected	Conservative % share of seats	Conservative % share of the vote
LONDON				
GLC[1]				
1964	100	36	36.0	39.8
1967	100	82	82.0	51.9
1970	100	65	65.0	50.8
1973	92	32	33.7	37.9
1977	92	64	69.6	52.5
1981	91	41	44.6	39.7
Boroughs				
1964	1,859	668	35.9	38.8
1968	1,858	1,441	77.6	58.5
1971	1,863	601	32.3	38.5
1974	1,867	713	38.2	40.7
1978	1,908	960	50.3	48.9
1982	1,914	984	51.4	41.5
1986	1,914	685	35.8	35.2
1990	1,914	731	38.2	37.2
1994	1,917	518	27.0	31.3
1998	1,917	538	28.1	32.0
METROPOLITAN				
Counties 1973–81				
1973	601	141	23.5	36.2
1977	601	360	59.9	52.8
1981	601	122	20.3	30.7
Boroughs				
1973	2,518	697	27.7	35.4
1975	838	446	53.2	45.8
1976	854	410	48.0	45.2
1978	875	354	40.5	45.0
1979	980	320	32.6	39.7
1980	1,364	340	24.9	35.4
1982	1,339	418	31.2	32.5
1983	845	239	28.3	33.6
1984	853	195	22.9	31.0
1986	862	143	16.6	26.5
1987	873	234	26.8	31.6
1988	857	179	20.9	31.6
1990	860	114	13.3	26.4
1991	840	186	22.1	31.7
1992	843	273	32.4	39.5
1994	850	76	8.9	22.7
1996	836	72	8.6	22.7
1998	849	107	12.6	26.0
2000	884	203	23.0	31.4

	Number of seats available	% which were contested by Conservative candidates	Conservative % share of seats	Conservative % share of the vote
ENGLISH SHIRES				
Counties				
1973	3,129	80.1	45.2	42.1
1977	3,127	90.0	75.3	58.1
1981	3,096	90.9	48.2	40.7
1985	3,005	92.8	43.6	38.4
1989	3,005	95.0	47.3	42.2
1993	2,998	94.6	31.2	35.6
1997	2,203	93.1	39.6	36.9
Districts				
1973	13,535	59.3	32.5	32.1
1976	13,589	70.3	50.8	42.1
1978	677	94.4	59.5	52.5
1979	12,184	76.6	48.8	41.9
1980	1,607	89.6	42.8	40.6
1982	1,579	87.7	49.3	39.5
1983	10,405	73.1	49.2	40.0
1984	1,899	91.4	42.9	39.3
1986	1,951	90.2	33.3	34.6
1987	10,021	75.0	47.9	39.5
1988	1,799	95.3	43.8	41.2
1990	1,855	90.7	24.6	30.7
1991	10,121	75.9	38.4	35.9
1992	1,783	94.5	50.8	45.2
1996	1,528	91.2	22.7	29.7
1998	1,372	93.5	30.8	34.8
2000	1,608	96.1	47.8	43.0
WALES				
Counties				
1973	574	24.0	12.0	12.5
1977	577	43.7	24.4	22.0
1981	600	36.8	12.8	17.1
1985	552	34.4	9.1	15.2
1989	505	32.3	7.3	16.5
1993	502	33.5	6.4	12.5
Districts				
1973	1,476	18.5	9.1	11.0
1976	1,523	22.7	14.6	15.0
1979	1,519	28.5	12.8	18.6
1983	1,479	24.0	13.0	16.3
1987	1,360	21.2	10.1	14.1
1991	1,367	18.9	7.6	13.3

	Number of seats available	% which were contested by Conservative candidates	Conservative % share of seats	Conservative % share of the vote
SCOTLAND				
Districts				
1974	2,560	21.1	9.4	26.8
1977	2,571	21.1	10.8	27.2
1980	2,452	22.3	9.3	24.1
1984	2,835	20.1	6.7	21.4
1988	3,130	20.0	5.2	19.4
1992	3,180	19.3	6.4	23.2
Regions				
1974	1,148	22.1	9.8	28.6
1978	1,047	27.9	13.0	30.3
1982	1,294	21.9	9.2	25.1
1986	1,390	18.6	4.7	16.9
1990	1,515	21.3	3.4	19.6
Unitary				
1995	1,159		7.1	
1999	1,222		8.8	
ENGLISH/WELSH				
Unitary				
1996	658	91.2	14.6	29.7
1997	1,044	78.7	22.3	31.3
1998	206	94.2	18.0	26.7
2000	882	94.3	40.4	39.3

Sources: C. Rallings and M. Thrasher (eds), *Local Elections in Britain: A Statistical Digest*, pp. vii–xxvii; C. Rallings and M. Thrasher (eds), *Local Elections Handbook 1993, 1994, 1997*; *http://www.lgcnet.com/pages/products/elections* Local Government Network

Note:

1. The GLC was abolished 8 May 1986

Part 2

CHRONOLOGIES

2.1 GOVERNMENT AND OPPOSITION 1832–46

OPPOSITION 1832–DECEMBER 1834

Chronology of main events

1832

June	Royal assent for Reform Act: disenfranchises 56 boroughs, creates new seats in the more populous areas and widens franchise to 813,000.

1834

November	The King, having dismissed Lord Melbourne's ministry, invites Wellington to accept office. He declines in favour of Peel. This is the last time a British monarch uses their legal entitlement to dismiss a government.
December	Peel forms minority administration.

PEEL'S MINORITY ADMINISTRATION DECEMBER 1834–JUNE 1835

Chronology of events

1834

December	Peel's *Tamworth Manifesto* claims him as leader of 'the Great Conservative Party'. While addressed to his constituents it is in fact an appeal to the whole electorate intended to distinguish himself from his predecessor, the Duke of Wellington, and demonstrate his own brand of political beliefs to both the electorate and his party.

1835

February	New parliament meets. Although Conservatives have improved total number of MPs in election, still a minority administration.
March	Ecclesiastical Commission established. This is one of the few achievements of Peel's hundred-day administration.
April	Peel resigns after administration loses a vote on the appropriations. The Whigs and Irish combine in the 'Lichfield House Pact'.

OPPOSITION APRIL 1835–AUGUST 1841

Chronology of events

1835

September	Peel co-operates with the Whigs in passing English Municipal Corporations Act.

1837

June	Death of King requires a general election in which Conservatives improve numerical standing in House of Commons.
August	Stanley and Graham (who had been key figures in Grey's 1834 ministry) cross the floor to join Peel's party.

1839

May	'Bedchamber crisis'. After the resignation of Whig ministry Peel makes the appointment of some Conservative ladies to act as Ladies of the Bedchamber to the Queen conditional upon him accepting office. When the young Queen Victoria refuses, Peel declines to form a ministry.
Autumn	Peel resists the secularisation of national education.

1841

August	Following the defeat of the Whig ministry on a vote of confidence an election is called which results in a 70-seat Conservative majority. The party polled particularly strong support in the English and Welsh counties.

PEEL'S SECOND ADMINISTRATION AUGUST 1841–JUNE 1846

Chronology of events

1842

April	85 Conservatives rebel against an attempt to remove the ban on the import of cattle.
June	Budget repeals duties on 750 items, but also introduced the measure of income tax in peacetime and lowered the rate of protection offered by the Corn Law.

1843

May	70 rural Conservative MPs meet at Carlton Club and resolve to vote against the bill to lower duty on Canadian corn, even if it risks the fall of the administration. In the event government secures a majority of 83.
July	'Young England' quartet of Disraeli, George Smyth, Lord John Manners and Henry Baille-Cochrane gain national prominence when they oppose the Irish Arms bill.

1844

March	Government defeated on new Factory bill after group of rebel Conservatives combined with official opposition. This is indicative of the MPs' independence despite the growth of party feeling since the 1830s. Decision reversed after threat of resignation from Peel.
June	Defeated over the sugar tariff by combination of protectionist Conservative and Liberal free traders. Peel again threatens resignation to force the House of Commons to rescind. Party meeting fails to reach agreement on sugar tariff. Peel speaking in Parliament upsets many of his supporters with the tone of his speech, however secures a majority. This event and March's Factory bill had the consequence of weakening the party's personal loyalty to its leader and also of encouraging a belief that it is faced with executive despotism.

1845

April	Budget repeals duties on further 450 items; Disraeli begins his attacks on Peel.
February–May	Maynooth grant only carried with support of Liberals. Opposed by 150 Conservatives.
November–December	Cabinet are reluctant to accept Peel's proposals for Corn Law repeal. Early November Stanley presented a memorandum arguing repeal irrelevant to Irish famine thereby fatally weakening the 'necessity' argument for repeal.
December	Peel resigns but resumes office two weeks later.

1846

January	Lord George Bentinck emerges as the leader of Tory malcontents opposed to repeal. Quickly claims support of 180 anti-Peel Conservatives. Repeal of Corn Laws presented to Parliament. Protectionists determined to prolong the passage of the legislation, and have support of two-thirds of Conservative parliamentary party.
March	Lord Stanley decides to speak and vote against repeal.
April	Bentinck formally accepts leadership of anti-Peelite protectionist party in Commons, Lord Stanley leads from Lords, although does not formally acknowledge role until after 1846 parliamentary session. Disraeli still needs to prove his credentials to fellow Conservatives.
May	Lord Ellenborough suggests that Peel should stand down as Conservative leader to enable a unity candidate to heal divisions. Peel rejects the proposal as impossible and constitutionally unacceptable.

June	As Corn Law repeal receives third reading in House of Lords, the Protectionist leaders decide to support a whig amendment to the Coercion bills for Ireland. 69 Protectionists join with Whigs 25 June and defeat the government. Peel resigns.

Resignations

1842

January	Duke of Buckingham (Lord Privy Seal) resigns after cabinet debates about duty on corn and the possibility of re-introducing income tax.

1845

January	Gladstone (President of Board of Trade) resigns over Maynooth grant.
February	Sir E. Knatchbull (Paymaster General).
November	Lord Stanley (Secretary for War) and Duke of Buccleuch (Lord Privy Seal) over Corn Laws.
December	Peel resigns at loss of two ministers, but Whigs unable to form a ministry so Peel returns to office at end of month.

1846

June	Peel resigns from premiership.

2.2 OPPOSITION AND MINORITY GOVERNMENT 1846–68

OPPOSITION JUNE 1846–FEBRUARY 1852

Chronology of events

1846

July — Duke of Richmond hosts a dinner for the Protectionist Party at which Lord George Bentinck proclaims Lord Stanley as leader in both houses of parliament.
Attempts to re-unite Peelites and Protectionists in opposition to Whig government's sugar bill fail.

December — Bentinck defies Stanley and seeks to revive the opposition to the malt tax. Henry Goulburn tells Peel that the Peelites are a party of observation.

1847

January — Bentinck and Beresford, against Stanley's express wishes, lend support to radical John Bright in the Manchester by-election. His principal rival is Lord Lincoln, Peelite and a politician considered as a possible future Conservative leader.

July — As Parliament re-assembles party circulars are only sent to Protectionist Conservatives. Exclusion of the Peelites from distribution lists is due to fear of irrevocable damage and of driving them into the arms of the Whigs.

September — John Croker writing in *Quarterly Review* declares the split in the Conservatives is irreversible. Stanley does not share this view.

December — Bentinck speech in favour of religious toleration during Jewish emancipation debate offends the majority of his Protestant supporters. Beresford informed him that he no longer commanded his party's support. Bentinck resigns as party's leader of the Commons.

1848

March — Stanley intervenes to prevent the defeat of the Russell government on its bill to reduce sugar duties. Motivated by a realisation that the Protectionists would be unable to form a government.

July — Public Health Bill secured support of 88 per cent of free-trade Peelites and was voted against by 56 per cent of Protectionists opposed to its centralising features.

August	Disraeli sums up session for Protectionist Conservatives.
September	Bentinck dies.
1849	
March	Leadership of Protectionist party in Commons to be shared between J.C. Herries, Marquess of Granby and Disraeli. Arrangement exists only in name. Disraeli rapidly acknowledged as the Commons leader.
1850	
February	Gladstone and 34 Peelites support Disraeli's motion seeking to relieve agricultural poverty by reducing poor law levies. Russell's government survives with a majority of 21.
June	Peelites join forces with Protectionists and vote against Palmerston during Don Pacifico debate. This action blocks all likelihood of Peelites joining a Whig administration while Palmerston in office.
July	Death of Peel. Aberdeen now leads the Peelites.
August	*The Conservative Magazine* complains that the Protectionist Party is not a working party let alone an official opposition.
1851	
January/ February	Peelites further distanced from Whigs by opposing the Ecclesiastical Titles bill. This sought to appease Protestant sensitivities after the Catholic Cardinal Wiseman adopted the title 'Archbishop of Westminster' the previous October.
February	Russell resigns and advises Queen to send for Stanley. After a week of negotiations, in which the Peelites refused to serve under Stanley, he declines offer to form a ministry because the Queen refuses to grant him a dissolution of parliament. In a statement to the House of Lords, Stanley takes the line agreed at an earlier party meeting that his party is still committed to a fixed duty on wheat.
June	Lord Stanley succeeds to title of Earl of Derby upon death of father.
1852	
February	Lord Derby asked to form a ministry after Palmerston engineers the fall of Russell's administration.

DERBY'S FIRST MINORITY GOVERNMENT: FEBRUARY–DECEMBER 1852

Chronology of events

1852	
February	Leading Peelites Gladstone, Herbert and Newcastle consider whether to join Derby administration. Decline opportunity.

April	Disraeli postpones the budget until after the general election.
June	Government appeals to English Protestantism by reminding Catholics that the law forbids religious Catholic parades.
July	Parliament dissolved. Protectionists gain seats in the general election, but not enough to give them a majority. Beresford embroiled in a bribery scandal. Threat of prosecution eventually dropped in 1854 due to lack of evidence.
September	Death of Duke of Wellington.
November	New Parliament recalled for Disraeli's budget. Aims to relieve financial burdens on landed classes and apply direct taxation as universally as indirect taxes. Acknowledgement of permanency of free trade signalled by Derby administration's acceptance of a Commons resolution on the issue. Some view Disraeli's budget as essentially being free trade.
December	Government defeated 305 to 286 on budget with every Peelite voting against. Their objection was upon the grounds that it committed financial heresy by breaking the golden rule that chancellors aim to secure surpluses, as well as contempt for Disraeli. Derby resigns.

OPPOSITION DECEMBER 1852–FEBRUARY 1858

Chronology of events

1852

December	15 Peelites join the Aberdeen government, including 6 at cabinet status, finalising the split in the Conservative party.

1853

September	Malmesbury estimates that 'dependable' Conservative MPs can only be numbered at 150.
December	'Cabinet Council' held including Disraeli, Malmesbury and Hardwicke to evaluate the state of the party.

1854

April	Disraeli offends many of his own supporters when he combines with the Manchester Radicals to vote for the abolition of advertisement duty in newspapers.
June	Party splits in division over the Aberdeen government's India Administration bill.

1855

January–February	Derby refuses to form a purely Conservative ministry when Aberdeen's government falls over Crimean War. This

	was after he had invited Palmerston, Gladstone and Sidney Herbert to form a coalition but they declined.
February	Derby defends his decision to a party meeting of 170 MPs and 50 Peers.
May	Disraeli moves a motion of censure on Palmerston government's conduct of Crimean war. Conservative vote holds but still unable to defeat government.
1856	
September	Gladstone writing in *Quarterly Review* complains that the Protectionist Party under Bentinck and Disraeli is failing to provide opposition to Russell's government.
1857	
March	202 Conservatives combine with mixture of Liberals and Peelites to defeat Palmerston over bombardment of Canton. Palmerston still collected votes of 39 Conservatives. Dissolution.
May	At least seven Conservatives elected to new parliament inform Chief Whip that they can no longer support a party in opposition to Palmerston.
1858	
February	Conspiracy bill votes indicate continued Conservative flirtations with Palmerston as 112 vote with the government while Disraeli, and 145 other Conservatives, successfully oppose the bill. Government resigns. Derby forms the 'Who's Who' administration.

DERBY'S SECOND ADMINISTRATION FEBRUARY 1858–MAY 1859

Chronology of events

1858	
June	Property qualification for members of parliament abolished.
July	Jews admitted to Parliament.
1859	
March	Defeat of government on reform bill introduced by Disraeli by 39 votes.
April	Parliament dissolved. Conservatives increase numerical representation, but still ten short of absolute majority. Overtures to Palmerston rebuffed.
June	Willis's tearoom meeting formally merges Peelites with Liberals, ending a seven-year period in which Peelite supporters

of the coalition called themselves Liberal Conservatives. Government defeated in vote of confidence by 13 votes.

Resignations

1858

May — Earl of Ellenborough (President of Board of Control) resigns after nearly bringing the government down by publishing a dispatch disapproving of the Governor-General Lord Canning's conduct.

1859

February — Spencer Walpole (Home Secretary) and J.W. Henley (President of Board of Trade) object to a provision of the reform bill for a uniform £10 franchise in counties as well as boroughs.

OPPOSITION JUNE 1859–JUNE 1866

Chronology of events

1860

January — Derby informs Palmerston that in the event of his administration falling he will not seek to form an alternative administration.

1861

January — Malmesbury renews official pledge to Palmerston provided his administration does not attempt parliamentary reform or become embroiled in war with Austria.

1866

June — Alliance of Whigs and Conservatives defeats the Liberal Reform Bill; Derby forms government.

DERBY'S THIRD ADMINISTRATION JUNE 1866–FEBRUARY 1868

Chronology of events

1867

February — Parliament meets, but government still undecided on details for a reform bill. Senior figures threaten resignation in opposition to household suffrage after party meeting at Carlton Club.

March — Disraeli addresses meeting of party's MPs to outline the nature of the reform bill.

August — 2nd Reform Act receives royal assent: increases electorate to 1,057,000 in England and Wales and in the towns working-class voters are in a majority.

Resignations

1867

March — Cranborne (Colonial Secretary), Carnarvon (India Secretary) and General Peel (Secretary for War) resign from cabinet over reform bill.

1868

February — Lord Derby resigns due to ill health and Disraeli becomes Prime Minister.

DISRAELI'S FIRST ADMINISTRATION FEBRUARY–DECEMBER 1868

Chronology of events

1868

December — Disraeli administration resigns following general election, the first held under the new franchise.

2.3 GOVERNMENT AND OPPOSITION 1868–85

OPPOSITION DECEMBER 1868–FEBRUARY 1874

Chronology of events

1869

October	Salisbury attacks Disraeli's leadership in *Quarterly Review* article 'The past and the future of Conservative policy'. The death of Lord Derby consolidates Disraeli's position since the new Earl undecided about his political future, but also weakens it because Disraeli loses an important ally.

1870

February	Carnarvon tries to engineer Salisbury's elevation to the leadership of the party in the House of Lords, but is thwarted when Salisbury rules himself out. Position is assumed by the compromise figure of Duke of Richmond.

1871

October	Number of leading Conservatives, including Carnarvon, Salisbury and Northcote, after discussions with trade unionists, make call for the party to promote a more advanced seven-point social programme, the 'New Social Alliance'. In part this is due to growing awareness of urban conditions, but also events in continental Europe, especially the bloodshed associated with the Paris Commune.

1872

January	Meeting of senior party figures at Burghley decides to urge Disraeli to stand down in favour of Derby in light of continued party discontent.
February	Attending the thanksgiving service for the recovery of the Prince of Wales from typhoid fever, Disraeli finds himself cheered while the crowds greet Gladstone with hostility.
April	Disraeli addresses mass rally of 6,000 supporters at Manchester Free Trade Hall rounding off a week of campaigning in the North West. Links the party's traditional values of monarchy and empire with the newer strain of social reform. This is the first occasion that Disraeli has used the forum of a mass audience, unlike his rival Gladstone.

June — Disraeli addresses National Union rally at Crystal Palace and claims that the Conservatives are the party of empire and speaks of 'the elevation of the condition of the people.'

October — Salisbury in *Quarterly Review* makes argument against the Conservatives' forming a minority administration should the opportunity arise. Disraeli employed the same arguments six months later.

1873

March — Gladstone resigns after unexpected defeat for his Irish University Scheme because of an alliance between Conservatives and Catholics. Disraeli refuses to take office, persuading his colleagues that it would be inopportune to form a minority Conservative administration. Thus Gladstone obliged to return to office for a further ten months. In the House of Commons Disraeli likens the government to a 'range of exhausted volcanoes'.

May — Disraeli's Bath by-election letter provides an innovation in terms of a party leader endorsing a candidate. The exuberance of the letter backfires when the seat was lost against the prevailing trend in by-elections.

1874

January — Gladstone dissolves parliament and goes to the country pledging to abolish income tax.

DISRAELI'S SECOND ADMINISTRATION FEBRUARY 1874–APRIL 1880

Chronology of events

1874

July — Public Worship Regulation bill passes House of Commons without a vote after the intervention of Disraeli anxious to reinforce Protestantism. In the Lords Salisbury and the Conservatives resist the bill.

November — Disraeli seriously ill. Salisbury and Derby contemplate a possible successor.

1875

July — Cabinet decide to abandon merchant shipping legislation only to resuscitate a temporary version after Plimsoll's outburst and the ensuing controversy.

1876

June — Government aware from this point onwards of growing unease about Bulgarian atrocities.

July	Failing health obliges Disraeli to offer to move to the Lords and although retaining the premiership passes the leadership of the party in the House of Commons to Stafford Northcote.
September	Gladstone publishes *Bulgarian Horrors and the Question of the East.*
1878	
January	Dyke (Chief Whip) reports to cabinet that a 'united party' is prepared to back British military intervention in the Russian-Turkish war.
July	Disraeli and Salisbury return from Berlin Congress claiming 'peace with honour'. Congratulatory banquet held in the men's honour by Conservative members of both Houses of Parliament.
August	Disraeli advised not to dissolve parliament. However, loss of Newcastle-under-Lyme by-election suggests that the post-Berlin congress honeymoon is over. Disraeli and Salisbury receive 1,000 delegates from Conservative Associations at Foreign Office.
1879	
July	Zulu resistance in South Africa finally crushed.
September	British Afghan mission is slaughtered.
November	Gladstone begins his Midlothian campaign.

Resignations

1875	
July	Clare Read resigns minor office after Disraeli tries to abandon Agricultural Holdings bill.
1876	
August	Malmesbury (Lord Privy Seal) retires.
1878	
January	Carnarvon (Colonial Secretary) resigns over the moving of the British fleet through the Dardannelles.
March	Derby (Foreign Secretary) resigns. The public justification is his opposition to the sending of British reserve troops to the Mediterranean to deter the Russians. The real reason was his opposition to secret plans to occupy Cyprus.

OPPOSITION APRIL 1880–JUNE 1885

Chronology of events

1880	
May	Bridgwater House venue for the first rally of Conservative MPs and peers since election.

August — Leadership of Northcote openly attacked during Carlton Club meeting.

1881

February — Northcote leads Conservative supporters out of House of Commons chamber in protest at Gladstone's attempts to push through the Speaker's reforms of the Commons' procedures.

March — Disraeli makes his last appearance in the House of Lords.

April — Death of Disraeli.

May — Salisbury elected Conservative leader of House of Lords.

1882

March–October — Churchill sidelined from politics by illness.

1883

April — Northcote presented with an address of confidence signed by all Conservative MPs who had not held office in the previous administration, except for Churchill and Newdegate.

July — Churchill elected to National Union Central Council on casting vote of its chairman. Two members resign in protest.

1884

February — Churchill defeats Chaplin to secure chair of National Union Council.

July — Carlton Club party meeting takes stock of reform bill and prepares for recess.

July — At the Sheffield Conference Salisbury and Churchill make a public display of rapprochement.

November — Party chiefs divided over whether to force dissolution over opposition to franchise reform without redistribution; Northcote and Salisbury meet Liberal leadership to agree redistribution details.

December — Gladstone announces the redistribution of seats. Denounced by Lord Claud Hamilton as 'political suicide'.

1885

February — Northcote and Salisbury move motions of censure (in their respective Houses) over fall of Khartoum. Highlights difference in approach between two men. Northcote's motion is designed to prevent the ousting of the government while Salisbury is willing to push to the limit. Salisbury's is carried, and Northcote's fails. This guarantees Salisbury's primacy.

2.4 GOVERNMENT AND OPPOSITION 1885–1906

SALISBURY'S MINORITY ADMINISTRATION JUNE 1885–JANUARY 1886

Chronology of events

1885

June	Salisbury summoned to Balmoral after Gladstone resigns following defeat on an amendment to the Crime Act. Salisbury finds forming his cabinet difficult with Churchill unprepared to serve alongside Northcote and Cross. Compromise reached with Northcote's elevation to Lords and the sidelining of Raikes.
October	With a general election imminent Salisbury's Newport speech to conference sees Conservatives vying for votes of newly enfranchised county occupiers. Salisbury's first appearance before the party as leader.
November	Parnell and O'Connor urge Irish voters in Britain to vote against Liberals. Contemporaries debated whether it gained the Conservatives 20 extra seats.
December	Gladstone's 'Hawarden Kite'. It enables the Conservatives to shed their Irish 'allies' and gives them a cause around which to re-unite.

1886

January	Government defeated on Jesse Colling's 'three acres and a cow' amendment to the Address. Salisbury resigns.

OPPOSITION JANUARY–AUGUST 1886

Chronology of events

1886

March	Salisbury meets Hartington, leader of the Liberal Unionists.
April–June	Conservative parliamentary resistance to Gladstone's Irish Home Rule bill culminates in its defeat.
June	General election co-operation in the constituencies between Conservatives and Liberal Unionists ensures survival of 78

Liberal Unionists, the election of 316 Conservatives and the reduction of the Liberals to 191.

SALISBURY'S SECOND ADMINISTRATION AUGUST 1886–AUGUST 1892

Chronology of events

1886

December — Resignation of Churchill (Chancellor of Exchequer) obliges cabinet reshuffle.

1887

January — Iddesleigh (formerly Northcote) having been reshuffled in the cabinet drops dead on farewell visit to Salisbury at Downing Street. Goschen become the first Whig to join a Conservative cabinet.

1888

February — Joseph Chamberlain sends Salisbury a summary of his position.

1889

November — Attending the Nottingham party conference Salisbury makes the case for 'assisted' (i.e. free) elementary education.

1890

March — At a party meeting at the Carlton Club Salisbury seeks to rally party behind government legislation and urges party not to prejudge elementary education issue until the government has published its proposals.

June — After a series of minimal majorities in House of Commons votes Salisbury warns the Queen that the position is critical and important legislation will have to be postponed until the next session.

1891

November — Chamberlain dismisses likelihood of Liberal Unionists rejoining Liberal Party.

December — Hartington succeeds as 8th Duke of Devonshire leaving Liberal Unionist leadership of Commons vacant; falls to Chamberlain.

1892

May — Joint meeting of Unionist leaders to debate timing for next election and tactics.

July — *Campaign Guide* condemns the eight-hour day for rising prices and lowering efficiency.

August — Government defeated on vote of confidence.

Resignations

1886

December	Randolph Churchill (Chancellor) after disagreements over his budget proposals. Followed only by Dunraven, the fair trade colonial under-secretary.

1887

February	Resignation of Michael Hicks Beach (Chief Secretary for Ireland) due to failing eyesight. Replaced by A.J. Balfour.

OPPOSITION AUGUST 1892–JUNE 1895

Chronology of events

1892

September	Chamberlain speaks in Birmingham of need for legislation to restrict hours and labour of shop workers.

1894

November	Chamberlain memorandum on imperial and social policies proposes among many things compensation for industrial injuries, old age pensions and restrictions on alien immigration.

1895

January	Randolph Churchill dies aged 44.
June	National Union holds banquet in honour of Liberal Unionists, Hartington and Chamberlain.
July	*Campaign Guide* proposes pensions, although only for a contributions scheme which would have excluded the most vulnerable.

SALISBURY'S THIRD ADMINISTRATION JUNE 1895–JULY 1902

Chronology of events

1897

August	Workmen's Compensation Act offends many natural Conservative supporters and in September fails to reap rewards when miners of East Denbighshire reject the Conservatives in a by-election.

1898

November	Bankruptcy of financier Ernest Hooley causes considerable embarrassment. Carlton Club obliged to return donations totalling £10,000 and Central Office £50,000 to help pay Hooley's creditors.
November	Joseph Chamberlain makes speech on nature of Unionism.

1899

October — South African war begins.

1900

January — Middleton begins to press for changes to Electoral Disabilities Removal Act (1891) to ensure volunteers serving in South African War are not disqualified from voting in next election.

October — 'Khaki' election returns Conservatives but with reduced majority.

1902

March — At insistence of Balfour and Devonshire, Cabinet agrees to implement an Education bill, including rate support. This reverses the cabinet's rejection of rate support the previous December. The bill proposes the abolition of School Boards and transfers power to local authorities.

April — Michael Hicks-Beach (Chancellor) obliged to increase income tax and impose duties on imported corn to pay for cost of the South African war.

May — South African war ends.

Resignations

1900

November — Salisbury hands over running of Foreign Office to Lansdowne.

BALFOUR'S ADMINISTRATION JULY 1902–NOVEMBER 1905

Chronology of events

1902

July — Balfour elected leader at a meeting of MPs and peers at the Foreign Office. However, before he had accepted the King's commission he had consulted with Joseph Chamberlain.

October — Critical meeting of Birmingham Liberal Unionist Association debates the Education bill. Chamberlain speaks.

November — Cabinet overrules the chancellor and decides to include imperial preference on corn duties in next budget.

December — Joseph Chamberlain departs for a ministerial tour of South Africa. He returns in the New Year.

1903

April — Ritchie (Chancellor) demands the lifting of duties on corn, threatening resignation if his ultimatum is rejected.

May — Joseph Chamberlain launches tariff reform campaign with speech in Birmingham urging imperial preference.

	Henry Chaplin leads a party deputation to Balfour to press for protection.
July	Unionist Free Food League formed by 60 MPs. A week later the opposition respond by forming the Tariff Reform League.
August	'Chamberlain policy' attacked by Sir W. Harcourt; Balfour anxious to preserve unity tries to offer compromise. Decision postponed.
October	Balfour's address to the annual conference provides Devonshire with pretext to resign. The Sheffield conference affirms Balfour's 'middle course'.
November	Chamberlain makes his 'two loaves' speech in Birmingham.
1904	
February	112 tariff reform MPs threaten to defeat government unless it withdraws a compromise to the free-fooders. Liberals seek to exploit Conservative divisions with a free-trade motion. 26 Conservative MPs support it with a further 12 abstaining.
June	Balfour decides that tariff debate will not be resumed during current parliamentary session.
July	177 MPs gather to celebrate Joseph Chamberlain's birthday. First annual meeting of Tariff Reform League presided over by Chamberlain.
August	Liberal vote of censure narrowly defeated after 52 Conservative MPs abstain.
October	Balfour makes public pledge not to introduce imperial preference until after a second general election.
1905	
February	Balfour and Chamberlain meet to discuss election, but Balfour unwilling to concede on tariff reform.
March	Balfour humiliated in House of Commons. Rather than vote on free food resolutions, Balfour leads his supporters out of the chamber.
April	Party deputation of 245 (out of 374) Conservative MPs to Balfour pushing for tariffs.
May	After initially agreeing to meet demands of Chamberlain, Balfour reverses his decision after protests from free-fooders.
November	Annual conference shows clear support for tariff reform and makes demands for a more democratic party; Chamberlain in a speech in Bristol appears to have split from Balfour.

Resignations

1903	
September	Joseph Chamberlain (Colonial Secretary) offers resignation from cabinet to devote time to tariff campaign. Balfour sacks

	three key 'free-food' cabinet ministers. Devonshire tries to resign in sympathy with 'free-fooders' but dissuaded.
1904	
March	George Wyndham (Chief Secretary for Ireland) resigns when it emerges that his civil servants were preparing a scheme for the devolution of power to Ireland.
1905	
November	Balfour (Prime Minister) resigns and seeks dissolution, hoping that the Liberals will split themselves over Irish Home Rule.

2.5 OPPOSITION 1906–15

OPPOSITION JANUARY 1906–MAY 1915

Chronology of events:

1906

February — Chaplin, Long and Austen Chamberlain try to mediate between Balfour and Joseph Chamberlain. It results in the publication of the 'Valentine Letters'. In these Balfour accepts tariff reform.

July — Joseph Chamberlain paralysed by a stroke. This effectively ends his political career.

December — Conservatives in Lords use majority to defeat Liberals' Education bill.

1907

February — Balfour reaffirms his support for tariff reform.

March — Conservatives win control of London County Council and retain control until 1933.

November — Following party meeting of Conservative peers at Lansdowne House they use their majority in Lords to defeat Liberals' flagship Licensing bill.

1908

Malmesbury publishes *The New Order*: an attempt to seize the policy-making initiative within the party given Balfour's inertia. Argues that the party should advocate both tariff reform and moderate social policies.

1909

June — Walter Long forms Budget Protest League.

September — The parliamentary party in the House of Commons resists the 'People's Budget' line-by-line.

November — 'People's Budget' passes through House of Commons but overwhelmingly rejected by the Conservative-dominated House of Lords, 350 to 75 votes.

1910

June — Constitutional inter-party conference seeking to overcome crisis between Liberal government and Conservative-dominated House of Lords.

October	Unionists reject Lloyd George's coalition offer.
November	Balfour rejects Lloyd George's offer of a Liberal–Conservative coalition. Constitutional conference fails.
1911	
July	After a close vote the shadow cabinet decides against opposing the Parliament bill; Lansdowne and Balfour appeal to their Conservative peers to abstain on the vote, but diehard opposition gathering momentum led by Halsbury.
August	Parliament bill passes through House of Lords. Majority of Conservatives grudgingly abstain, but 114 diehards vote against. Only carried when 37 Conservative peers led by Curzon vote for the bill, thereby avoiding the mass creation of Liberal peers.
October	Steel-Maitland fails to dissuade Halsbury from sanctioning formation of a permanent Halsbury Club. Leo Maxse's *National Review* attacks Balfour's leadership urging that 'Balfour Must Go'.
November	Balfour resigns as leader.
1912	
April	Shadow cabinet decide to abandon referendum pledge and return to a full tariff policy.
November	Part of the Liberal Home Rule bill defeated in House of Commons; annual conference hears Lansdowne offer a revised tariff reform position. Conservatives force a snap vote in the House of Commons and defeat government. The post-vote chaos obliges the Speaker to suspend the House for fear of fighting breaking out.
December	Party once again in crisis over tariff reform after Bonar Law endorses the new policy.
1913	
January	Tariff reform crisis continues with threats from Lancashire MPs to pass vote of no confidence in leadership while Bonar Law and Lansdowne threaten resignation.
January	Bonar Law announces new policy of limited industrial tariffs and no food taxes.
1914	
July	Buckingham Palace Speaker's conference.
1915	
January	Shadow cabinet consider opposition strategy and possibility of joining coalition.

February	National Union executive refuse to sanction the use of party agents in military recruitment.
April	National Union executive refuse to discuss resolution urging compulsory military service because of party truce.
May	Bonar Law agrees to join Asquith in coalition government; but major posts remain in Liberal hands.

2.6 COALITION, GOVERNMENT AND OPPOSITION 1915–31

ASQUITH'S COALITION GOVERNMENT MAY 1915–DECEMBER 1916

Chronology of events

1915

September	Bonar Law declines to discuss the issue of compulsion for military recruitment with the National Union executive.
November	Bonar Law elevated, along with Balfour, to Asquith's reconstituted war cabinet.

1916

February	Despite numerous Conservative Association resolutions for conscription the National Union executive refuse to debate issue.
June	National Union executive pass a resolution demanding a more active prosecution of the war.
November	Nigeria debate on disposal of enemy assets highlights divisions among parliamentary party as Bonar Law manages to persuade a narrow majority of his party (73 to 65) to support the government.
December	Conservative cabinet ministers demand a reconstruction of the government. Bonar Law declines the King's offer to form a cabinet, recommending instead that Lloyd George be given the opportunity.

Resignations

1915

November	Edward Carson (Attorney General) resigns over direction of war effort and promptly becomes chair of the newly formed Unionist War Committee.

1916

May	Augustine Birrell (Chief Secretary for Ireland) resigns following Easter Rising in Dublin.
June	Earl of Selborne (President, Board of Agriculture and Fisheries) resigns in protest over Lloyd George's Home Rule policy after the Easter Rising.

LLOYD GEORGE COALITION DECEMBER 1916–OCTOBER 1922

Chronology of events

1917

February	National Union executive discuss the proposals from the Speaker's conference for extension of franchise. React with hostility.
June	National Union executive agrees to franchise reform provided it includes a redistribution of Irish seats, reform of the House of Lords and votes for servicemen; Central Council critical of Winston Churchill's recall to office.

1918

March	Subcommittee comprising Law, Long, Younger and Clyde convened to consider the possibility of fighting a general election alongside Lloyd George.
May	Only 40 Conservative MPs vote against second reading of Representation of the Peoples bill.
July	Two sides of coalition agree that 150 coalition Liberal candidates will be given a free run at next election.
October	Bonar Law and Lloyd George confirm their intention to fight next election in coalition.
November	Decision by Bonar Law to fight next election on a coalition platform with Lloyd George is approved by meeting of party's MPs. Official candidates to receive 'coupon' letter from both party leaders.

1919

April	233 Conservative MPs sign a telegram to Lloyd George, who is attending the Paris Peace Conference, urging stronger action over reparations.

1920

March	Balfour formally proposes merger between Conservatives and Lloyd George Liberals. Birkenhead writes a series of articles in favour of fusion. Idea rejected by meeting of Coalition Liberal ministers, although 95 Conservative MPs had expressed support for proposal.
June	Conference divided over fusion proposals. The executive is opposed but over 62 per cent of delegates in favour. Compromise motion debated.
July	Amritsar debate. Parliamentary party divided with 122 to 93 Conservative MPs voting against government.

1921

March	Bonar Law resigns due to ill health.
June	4th Marquess of Salisbury attacks coalition in *Morning Post.*

December — Senior coalition figures meet to decide whether to call a snap election on the back of the Irish settlement. Decision postponed for party soundings to be taken.

1922

January — Circular to constituency associations from party chairman suggests an election before the House of Lords issue has been resolved would be ill-advised. Crystallises party hostility to a snap election obliging the shelving of the idea at the end of the month.

February — 'Geddes Axe' cuts public spending. This is an effort to appease the anti-waste lobby.

March — Open letter sent from chairman of National Union Central Council to Austen Chamberlain urging reform of House of Lords.

May — National Union executive rebuke government for its failure to reform House of Lords.

June — Honours scandal reaches climax with the appointment of a Royal Commission to investigate.

August — Junior ministers in a series of meetings press Austen Chamberlain for an assurance that a Conservative majority at an election would lead to a Conservative prime minister. Indicative of a desire to be rid of Lloyd George but not necessarily the coalition.

October — Bonar Law writes to *The Times* criticising Lloyd George's handling of Chanak crisis and the 'war party' in the coalition. Marks Bonar Law out as a credible alternative to Lloyd George. National Union executive criticise the decision to call an election and resolve to debate the matter at a special conference. Provokes Austen Chamberlain to convene meeting of MPs at Carlton Club.

The anti-coalition forces gain momentum after the success of candidate in the Newport by-election. Following day Carlton Club meeting rejects Chamberlain's advice to continue with the coalition. An additional 40 to 50 votes given to anti-coalitionists by disgruntled figures from the agricultural lobby. Chamberlain and Lloyd George resign the next day.

Resignations

1917

January — Steel-Maitland (Party Chairman) resigns in protest at not securing a cabinet post and only being offered a ministerial post under his rival Walter Long.

1921

July — Christopher Addison (Minister without Portfolio) resigns over government's abandonment of social reform.

1922

March — Edward Montagu (India Secretary) resigns in protest against government's pro-Greek and anti-Turkish policy over Turkey.

October — Griffith Boscawen (Agricultural Minister) resigns over importation of Canadian cattle.
Austen Chamberlain (Party Leader) and Lloyd George (Prime Minister) resign positions from the coalition after Carlton Club vote.

BONAR LAW'S ADMINISTRATION OCTOBER 1922–MAY 1923

Chronology of events

1922

October — Bonar Law formally re-elected leader at Hotel Cecil. He pledges that there will be no fundamental change in the party's attitude to protection.

November — 49 pro-coalition MPs attend a dinner held to honour Austen Chamberlain.

1923

January — Bonar Law threatens resignation after losing argument in cabinet over Baldwin's proposed settlement of British war debts to United States.

February — Government majority reduced to 22 on a motion calling for universal old age pensions. It is a sign of disquiet and the lack of impetus among the parliamentary party.

April — A snap vote defeats government by 5 votes on issue of unemployment among ex-servicemen.
Austen Chamberlain declines an offer from Bonar Law to return to office.

Resignations

1923

May — Bonar Law resigns as Prime Minister but unwilling to provide King with advice on a potential successor.

BALDWIN'S FIRST ADMINISTRATION MAY 1923–JANUARY 1924

Chronology of events

1923

October	Baldwin concludes the necessity of abandoning free trade to help solve unemployment. Since this is a direct contradiction to Bonar Law's 1922 pledge a general election appears the likely outcome. This catches the party machine off guard. Baldwin gives his first public indication of the policy reversal in a speech at London Guildhall. When cabinet meet to discuss policy change, the objections of free traders overlooked without causing their resignations, but majority wish to avoid early election. Party conference hears Baldwin explicitly declare for protection at Plymouth.
November	King asked to dissolve Parliament.
December	Conservatives are the largest party following the election but with no overall majority. Cabinet decide to face Parliament.

1924

January	Combined forces of Labour and Liberals defeat Baldwin's minority administration in a vote on an amendment to the address. Baldwin resigns the seals of office.

Resignations

1923

November	Albert Buckley (Secretary for Overseas Trade) in defence of his free trade beliefs.

OPPOSITION JANUARY–NOVEMBER 1924

Chronology of events

1924

February	Party meeting and shadow cabinet re-unite the pro- and anti-coalition factions for first time since Carlton Club meeting. Agree to revert to Bonar Law's 1922 tariff pledge. National Union Central Council strongly criticises the decision to call the election, but avoids a direct attack on the leadership of Baldwin; this is shortly after a meeting at Hotel Cecil has ratified Baldwin's continuation as leader and heard his exposition of 'New Conservatism'.
March	Churchill's by-election campaign in Westminster Abbey as a 'Constitutionalist' reveals the continuing divisions amongst the ex- and anti-coalitionists.

May	Splits within the Conservative leadership are allegedly revealed when the *People* published an interview with Baldwin in which he attacks Birkenhead, Beaverbrook and Rothermere. Baldwin forced to deny making the statements.
June	*Looking Ahead* published as a Conservative policy document. Drafted by Neville Chamberlain it provides the basis for much of the legislation of the 1924–29 Conservative administration. It is also the Conservatives first ever policy document.
September	Conservatives move a no-confidence motion on Labour's handling of the Campbell case.
October	Conservatives combine with Liberals to support an amendment calling for a select committee enquiry into Campbell case. Defeat the minority Labour government 364–199. Parliament dissolved. *Daily Mail* publishes the forged Zinoviev letter during the election campaign, heightening the 'red scare'. Joseph Ball, of Central Office, is thought to be behind its leaking to the press.

BALDWIN'S SECOND ADMINISTRATION NOVEMBER 1924–JUNE 1929

Chronology of events

1925

January–February	Dispute between Admiralty and Treasury over naval expenditure for cruisers escalates with Bridgeman (First Lord of the Admiralty) resisting Churchill (Chancellor of Exchequer) and threatening resignation. Crisis defused by passing matter to a cabinet committee.
March	Baldwin dramatically intervenes, in one of his finest speeches, in a parliamentary debate, to persuade MPs not to support F.A. Macquisten's bill on trade union law.
April	Churchill returns Britain to the Gold Standard.
July	'Cruiser crisis' erupts again as cabinet committee support Treasury view; Bridgeman, this time with increased party support, threatens resignation. Baldwin secures a compromise deal. Temporary subsidy granted to coal industry to stave off threatened strike.
December	Baldwin announces decision to refuse to apply protection to steel industry. Contributory pensions introduced while the minimum age to qualify for a pension is reduced from 70 to 65 years of age. Austen Chamberlain, foreign secretary, adds his signature to the Locarno Treaty which confirms Germany's Western borders and allows her entry to League of Nations.

1926

March	Samuel Royal Commission report on coal industry.
May	Talks between TUC and Cabinet over coal industry break down after trade unionists prevent printing of *Daily Mail*. General strike begins on 3 May. Abandoned nine days later.

1927

	J.C.C. Davidson (Party Chairman) pays off Donald im Thurn from party funds to buy his silence over role in Zinoviev letter.
March	A convention is broken when Sanders is elected chairman of National Union in preference to the senior vice-chairman, Colonel Gretton. He blames party chairman, Davidson. Gretton re-elected vice-chairman and subsequently secures the chairmanship the next year, but now implacably opposed to Davidson.
May	Trade Disputes Act passed. ARCOS raid. Joynson-Hicks (Home Secretary) authorises police raid on premises of the Soviet trade delegation. Leads to break in Anglo-Soviet diplomatic relations.
June	Bill to reform House of Lords opposed by over 100 Conservative MPs, effectively killing off the bill.
August	Unemployment Insurance Act reforms system and reduces benefits.

1928

May	Revised Prayer Book is rejected by Parliament.
July	Pressure for introduction of tariffs grows in the party. Evidenced by Baldwin meeting a delegation from Empire Industries Association who argue for the extension of duties for the iron and steel industries. Also public divisions within cabinet revealed in parliamentary debate.
August	Baldwin rebuffs the protectionists, and publicly reaffirms his 1924 commitment not to introduce tariffs.
December	National Union executive angry at government's failure to reform House of Lords, disclaims all responsibility for any future constitutional crisis.

1929

March	Local Government Act abolishes Poor Law guardians and reforms local authority finances.

Resignations

1927

August	Viscount Cecil (Chancellor of Duchy of Lancaster) over government's failure to disarm.

OPPOSITION JUNE 1929–AUGUST 1931

Chronology of events

1929

June	Conservative amendment calling for more protection for British industry proposed in response to the Labour government's King's speech.
July	Criticisms of Baldwin's 'safety first' general election campaign encourage National Union Central Council to begin enquiry into the causes of the defeat. This takes the form of a questionnaire distributed to the constituency associations.
October	Baldwin accepts a motion on empire trade at conference proposed by Henry Page Croft, Conservative backbencher and chairman of the protectionist Empire Industries Association (EIA). This token gesture is intended to quell pro-protection voices in the shadow cabinet and outflank Lord Beaverbrook who the previous month published his protection programme *Empire Free Trade.*
November	Baldwin commits Conservatives to the Irwin declaration on India and its policy of bi-partisanship.

1930

February	United Empire Party launched by Beaverbrook and Rothermere campaigning on single issue of protection.
March	Agreement is reached between Baldwin and Beaverbrook. It is agreed that a referendum on food taxes could be used to resolve protection issue. In return Beaverbrook suspends activities of United Empire Party.
June	Truce between Beaverbrook and Baldwin broken after the press baron objects to content of a series of Baldwin's speeches. United Empire Party campaign is re-launched. Baldwin denounces the activities of the press barons at a meeting at the Caxton Hall.
October	Meeting at Caxton Hall backs Baldwin's stance on tariffs.
December	Churchill openly sides with the diehards on India in speech to Indian Empire Society.

1931

January	Churchill resigns from shadow cabinet in protest at Baldwin's bi-partisan approach to India.
February	Neville Chamberlain (Party Chairman) is presented with a memorandum criticising Baldwin's leadership and suggesting he 'reconsider his position'. He decides to give the document to Baldwin who resolves to resign, only to change his mind.

March	Baldwin attacks again the role of the press barons, this time in regard to the United Empire Party's campaign in the St George's by-election that has been turned into a mini-referendum on Baldwin's leadership. Neville Chamberlain negotiates a truce with Beaverbrook.
August	Baldwin and Chamberlain break their holidays to return to London to meet senior Labour figures in an attempt to resolve the financial crisis precipitated by publication of the May Report. Within a matter of days, following intervention of the King, a provisional National Government has been formed with Baldwin agreeing to serve under MacDonald.

2.7 NATIONAL GOVERNMENT 1931–40

MACDONALD'S NATIONAL GOVERNMENT AUGUST 1931–JUNE 1935

Chronology of events

1931	
August	Baldwin's decision to participate in the National government receives party approval at meeting in Kingsway Hall.
September	Attempts to resolve financial crisis oblige the cabinet to agree cuts in public expenditure, then following a run on the pound the Gold Standard is abandoned.
October	In keeping with the spirit of economic retrenchment the Conservative Party conference cancels all social events connected with it. Ultimately the conference itself is cancelled because of the election campaign.
October	Cabinet agree to decision for an election seeking a 'doctor's mandate'.
December	Churchill's amendment critical of the government's India policy secures the support of 44 Conservative backbenchers.
1932	
February	Neville Chamberlain (Chancellor) introduces the Import Duties bill, the first tariff measure.
August	Baldwin leads the British delegation to the Imperial Conference at Ottawa.
September	National government is re-shuffled after departure of the Samuelite Liberals who were unable to accept the introduction of protection.
November	Baldwin warns the House of Commons that the 'bomber will always get through' and consequently adds to the growing concern that Britain has no viable defence against an aerial knockout blow.
November	Five special subcommittees of 1922 Committee publish reports (initially commissioned at suggestion of the Chancellor of Exchequer) that recommend budget cuts of nearly £1 million. Conservative and press outcry obliges 1922 Committee to disown the reports. Within one month it has elected a new chairman, for the first time since 1922.
1933	
February	National Union Central Council narrowly approves leadership's policy in India by 181 to 165 votes with 151 abstentions.

April–July	Trial of British engineers in USSR sours relations and leads to imposition of embargo on Soviet exports.
June	Special meeting of Central Council again accepts Baldwin's Indian policy by 838 to 356 votes.
July	Party chairman denies that Central Office finances the Union of Britain and India (UBI). This is only half true.
October	Conference accepts amendment approving Indian policy by 737 to 344 votes.
1934	
June	British Union of Fascists hold rally at Olympia. It ends in violence. Rothermere publicly breaks his press empire's support for BUF and Tory MPs who have previously expressed support for Mosley begin distancing themselves.
October	Leadership secures narrow victory for its Indian policy at conference. Result was 543 votes to 520 with nearly 700 abstentions.
December	Central Council at special meeting backs Baldwin's India policy by 712 majority.
1935	
January–February	Government retreats from introducing new benefit scales as proposed by the recently constituted Unemployment Assistance Board. This is after Conservative backbenchers combine with Labour and Liberals to object to the equalisation of social security payments.
February	India bill given second reading despite rebellion of 80 Conservative MPs.

Principal resignations

1932	
September	Viscount Samuel and the Liberal free traders plus Viscount Snowden resign in protest at adoption of protection.

BALDWIN'S NATIONAL ADMINISTRATION JUNE 1935–MAY 1937

Chronology of main events

1935	
August	Government of India bill finally passed. Baldwin hopes with a general election coming before end of year that this is the end of intra-party warfare.
October	Conference adopts unanimously Churchill's motion demanding the increasing financing of rearmament.

December — Terms of Hoare–Laval pact, which seeks to resolve the Abyssinian crisis, are leaked to press. Outrage amongst Conservative backbenchers and especially the backbench Foreign Affairs Committee. Cabinet obliges Hoare to resign as foreign secretary.

1936

January — George V dies and is succeeded by Edward VIII.

March — The appointment of Thomas Inskip as minister for the co-ordination of defence is badly received by many backbenchers.

June — Neville Chamberlain attacks the continuation of sanctions against Italy as the 'very midsummer of madness'. Some commentators see the speech as a leadership bid.
National Union Central Council adopts motion rejecting the restitution of ex-German colonies.

July — A deputation of senior backbenchers meets Baldwin to discuss rearmament position.

October — Conference rejects calls from leadership and adopts a motion flatly rejecting the return of former German colonies; Baldwin misses the party conference with heir apparent, Neville Chamberlain, deputising.

December — Abdication of Edward VIII after political outcry over King's intention to marry American divorcee Wallace Simpson. Hailed as one of Baldwin's greatest political achievements. Succeeded by George VI. Winston Churchill discredited for over-zealous support of the King.
Public Order Act bans the wearing of political uniforms. This is a deliberate counter-measure against BUF.

1937

May — Two weeks before Baldwin formally stands down as prime minister, his successor, Neville Chamberlain, begins appointing his cabinet. Chamberlain elected leader at the end of the month at a party meeting held in Caxton Hall. Nominated by Derby and Churchill.

Resignations

1935

December — Samuel Hoare (Foreign Secretary) resigns after cabinet and party abandon him and the Hoare–Laval pact.

1936

May — J.H. Thomas (Colonial Secretary) resigns after found to be responsible for a budget leak.

June — Harold Macmillan, backbench MP, resigns 'national' government whip in protest at abandonment of sanctions against Italy.

NEVILLE CHAMBERLAIN'S NATIONAL GOVERNMENT MAY 1937–SEPTEMBER 1939

Chronology of events

1937

June — Chamberlain's successor at Treasury, Sir John Simon, obliged after rebellion by backbenchers, to abandon Chamberlain's plans for a National Defence Contribution Tax (NDC).

November — Lord Halifax (Lord President) visits Germany to ascertain Hitler's intentions. Diplomatic incident narrowly avoided when Halifax mistakes Hitler for a footman.

1938

March — Germany annexes Austria creating Anschluss. Growing calls from within the Conservative party for a guarantee of Czechoslovakia; calls resisted by Chamberlain.

July — National Union Central Council grudging about slum-clearance plans demands a revision of the compensation rates for property owners.

September — Chamberlain signs the Munich agreement at a four-power conference seeking to resolve the Czechoslovak crisis.

October — House of Commons four-day Munich debate. Attack from Winston Churchill, but rebels small in numbers and only 22 abstain.

November — Agricultural Committee of MPs begins campaign for protection in farming.
Bill introduced to extend holiday pay to all workers.

1939

January — National Service introduced, but only a voluntary scheme. Growing pressure for compulsion has been mounting in Conservative party since mid-1938.

April — Conscription introduced both as a sop to the French and to pacify Conservative advocates of compulsion.

June — National Union Central Council calls for programme of public works to generate employment.

Resignations

1938

February — Anthony Eden (Foreign Secretary), Bobbety Cranborne (under-secretary at Foreign Office) and Mark Patrick (Eden's

	parliamentary private secretary) resign over Chamberlain's Italian policy.
May	Viscount Swinton (Air Minister) forced to resign after deputy, Earl of Winterton, made a poor performance on the air estimates in the House of Commons. Swinton had also angered Chamberlain over his support for compulsion in industry.
October	Duff Cooper (First Lord of Admiralty) resigns in protest at Munich agreement.

CHAMBERLAIN'S NATIONAL WARTIME ADMINISTRATION SEPTEMBER 1939–MAY 1940

Chronology of events

1939

September	Following the invasion of Poland by Germany, which Chamberlain had guaranteed in March, Britain declares war after the expiry of an ultimatum. Period of 'phoney war' follows.

1940

January	Hore-Belisha sacked as war minister after criticism from senior generals.
April	Lord Salisbury's Watching Committee formed. Played influential role in events of May 1940.
May	British troops forced to evacuate from Norway. Parliamentary outrage during Norway debate and although Chamberlain receives a majority he resigns when Labour refuse to join a new coalition. The next day the war in western Europe begins when Germany invades the Low Countries.

2.8 COALITION GOVERNMENT AND OPPOSITION 1940–51

CHURCHILL'S COALITION GOVERNMENT MAY 1940–MAY 1945 AND 'CARETAKER' GOVERNMENT MAY 1945–JULY 1945

Chronology of events

1940

May	Churchill becomes prime minister after Lord Halifax declines the opportunity.
July	180 Conservatives swamp meeting of Clement Davies's All-Party Committee to ensure resolution of confidence in government is passed.
December	Churchill formally elected leader of the Conservative Party after death of Chamberlain.

1941

July	The Post-War Problems Central Committee, chaired by R.A. Butler, is announced with a remit to evaluate and devise policy for post-war reconstruction.

1942

July	Churchill survives a censure motion after the fall of Tobruk. Despite being moved by senior backbencher, John Wardlaw-Milne, the margin of victory for the government is comfortable, 476 to 25 with 27 abstentions.
December	Publication of the Beveridge Report.

1943

February	Party discontent with the apparently socialist agenda of Labour coalition ministers is expressed when 116 Conservative MPs vote against the Catering Wages bill.
March	Tory Reform Committee established after a group of Conservative backbenchers favourable to the principles of the Beveridge Report decide to co-ordinate their activities. However, this goes against the grain of the official leadership whose spokesmen sound unenthusiastic during a parliamentary debate.
May	First party conference held since 1937. Eden stands in for Churchill who is visiting Washington.

1944

March — Tory Reform Group MPs force a division on the issue of equal pay for women. They succeed in defeating the government by 117 to 116; the vote is later reversed.

August — Butler Education Act passed, raising age of school leavers.

1945

May — Labour party leave the coalition. Churchill remains as prime minister of a 'caretaker' government pending a general election.

June — Churchill makes his Gestapo wireless broadcast in the finale of the general election campaign.

Resignations

1940

September — Neville Chamberlain (Lord President) resigns after spread of cancer makes him too ill to continue in office.

1941

January — Robert Boothby (under-secretary for food) over financial misconduct and blocked Czechoslovakian assets. Churchill suspended him from ministerial duties in November 1940 while the Select Committee investigated his conduct.

1945

May — Labour party leave coalition.

OPPOSITION JULY 1945–OCTOBER 1951

Chronology of main events

1945

October — Policy statement *Forward – by the Right* published by Tory Reform Committee with support of 41 Conservative MPs.

September — Creation of policy committees to assist Conservative front bench while in opposition.

December — Despite the decision of the shadow cabinet to abstain, 74 Conservative MPs vote against the terms of the USA loan negotiated by the Labour government.

1946

March — Churchill makes his Fulton 'Iron Curtain' speech.

1947

May — *Industrial Charter* published.
Merger of Liberal Nationals into Conservatives formalised by Woolton–Teviot agreement.

1948

June — *The Agricultural Charter* published.

1949

March — With the failure to win the Hammersmith South by-election the previous month questions rose once more about Churchill's suitability as leader. His meeting with the 1922 Committee is turbulent.

May — Despite strong Conservative hostility the Labour government succeeds in getting the legislation to nationalise the iron and steel industries through its third and final reading.

June — *Imperial Policy* statement published.

July — *The Right Road for Britain*, a Conservative policy statement, is published.

1950

March — The Conservatives managed to inflict a defeat upon the Labour government by forcing a snap division.

October — Annual conference forces upon the leadership the inclusion of a specific target for building 300,000 new houses when they return to power.

1951

February — The parliamentary party seeks to draw public attention to its hostility to Labour policies by tabling three censure motions in eight days: on coal, steel nationalisation and meat shortages.

March — Parliamentary party continues its guerrilla warfare against the government by using procedural devices to prolong sittings.

July — Parliamentary party manages to inflict a defeat upon a government amendment to the Forestry bill.

2.9 GOVERNMENT 1951–64

CHURCHILL'S PEACETIME ADMINISTRATION OCTOBER 1951–APRIL 1955

Chronology of events

1951

November	Government commits itself to denationalise iron and steel and road haulage. Balance of payments crisis obliges severe economies.

1952

January	Commonwealth finance ministers' conference in London to co-ordinate policy of the sterling area. Restrictions imposed on imports and hire purchase.
October	Britain's first atomic bomb exploded. Kenya is gripped by Mau Mau revolt.

1953

May	Denationalisation of iron and steel industry.
June	Churchill's stroke is kept secret.
July	Korean War armistice signed.
October	Conference carries a motion urging renegotiation of GATT to enable imperial preference.
November	National Service Act maintains conscription for another five years.
December	Eden (Foreign Secretary) suspends negotiations with Egyptian leader Nasser regarding the Suez Canal zone. It is a sop to rebellious Conservative backbenchers.

1954

July	End of food rationing. 'Suez Group' of Conservative backbenchers flex their political muscle by indicating their intention to vote against withdrawal from the Suez Canal zone.
August	End of hire-purchase controls.
October	Parts of annual conference televised for first time. Final agreement on Britain's withdrawal of troops from Suez Canal zone.

1955

February	Decision to produce hydrogen bomb announced.

Resignations

1954

July	Thomas Dugdale (Agriculture Minister) resigns over the Crichel Down affair.

EDEN'S ADMINISTRATION APRIL 1955–JANUARY 1957

Chronology of events

1955

May	The formal occupation of Germany by the Allied victors ends and Germany admitted to NATO.
October	R.A. Butler (Chancellor) increases taxation in a post-election supplementary budget in an attempt to restrain inflationary pressures in the economy.

1956

January	The *Daily Telegraph* questions Eden's authority. It accuses the prime minister of lacking the 'smack of firm government.'
April	Soviet leaders Khrushchev and Bulganin visit Britain.
October	Anglo-French forces launch an attack on the Suez Canal Zone, following Nasser's nationalisation of the canal in July. Hostilities ended after one week because of international, especially American, pressure.
November	Eden holidays in Jamaica 'on doctor's orders' to recover from exhaustion. In his absence R.A. Butler is acting PM.
December	Anglo-French forces formally end the Suez invasion by acceptance of UN resolutions for the withdrawal of their forces. Government survives a vote of confidence over the Suez invasion, although 15 Conservative MPs abstain.

Resignations

1956

October	Anthony Nutting (minister of state, Foreign Office) resigns in protest at Eden's Suez policy.
November	Edward Boyle (Economic Secretary) resigns in protest at Suez invasion.

1957

January	Eden (Prime Minister) resigns due to ill health.

MACMILLAN'S FIRST ADMINISTRATION JANUARY 1957–OCTOBER 1959

Chronology of events

1957

May	Macmillan allows British ships again to use Suez canal. This decision was a de facto admission of the complete failure of the Suez campaign. Later in the month 14 Conservative MPs abstain when Labour move a motion of censure over Suez. Sandys' Defence White Paper ends emphasis upon conventional forces and instead places the core of British defence policy around the nuclear deterrent.
June	National newspaper advertising campaign launched in Sunday papers designed to emphasise the Conservative party's association with prosperity and opportunity and with a view to re-establishing its reputation in the aftermath of Suez. Campaign is co-ordinated by Colman, Prentis and Varley.
July	Macmillan declares that 'Most of our people have never had it so good.'
September	Bank rate increased to 7 per cent.

1958

January	Macmillan at an airport news conference shortly before beginning a Commonwealth tour dismisses as 'a little local difficulty' the resignation of his entire Treasury team. The episode reinforces Macmillan's image for unflappability.
May	Macmillan conducts his first television interview with Ed Murrow.
October	Hire-purchase restrictions removed.
December	Partial convertibility between Sterling and US Dollar announced.

1959

February	Macmillan flies to Moscow to meet Soviet leader, Khrushchev. Publicises his image as an international statesman.
April	Budget cuts taxes by £350 million, including a two-penny reduction in the duty per pint of beer.
August	President Eisenhower visits Britain. He and Macmillan conduct a 'fireside chat' for the benefit of the television cameras.

Resignations

1957

March	Marquess of Salisbury (Lord President of the Council) quits in protest at the release of the Cypriot, Archbishop Makarios.

1958

January	Entire Treasury team resign led by Chancellor of Exchequer, Peter Thorneycroft. They were angered by Macmillan's reversal of support for tough anti-inflationary economic policy.
November	Ian Harvey (parliamentary secretary, Supply Ministry) quits as result of a homosexual affair.

MACMILLAN'S SECOND ADMINISTRATION OCTOBER 1959–OCTOBER 1963

Chronology of events

1960

February	Macmillan delivers his 'winds of change' decolonisation speech to an audience in Cape Town, South Africa.
April	Blue Streak rocket project abandoned as Britain's nuclear warhead delivery system. Hire-purchase restrictions re-introduced and credit squeeze begins.
July	Deflationary emergency budget; 'pay pause' for government employees.
October	Macmillan reshuffles his cabinet.

1961

January	Hire-purchase controls relaxed.
February	Increase in NHS prescription charges announced.
July	Introduction of 'pay pause'.

1962

March	Loss of Orpington by-election.
July	'Night of the long knives.' Macmillan dismisses, without warning, 7 of his 21 cabinet ministers. Observers consider his action a sign of panic.
October	Conference calls for imperial preference.
November	Vassall affair.
December	USA agrees to sell Polaris missiles to Britain.

1963

March	National Union Central Council expresses discontent with Macmillan's leadership.
June	Profumo affair leads to vote of confidence. Although 27 Conservatives abstain, Macmillan's government survives.
July	Peerage bill receives royal assent. Peers may now renounce titles.

August	Britain signs partial nuclear test ban treaty.
October	Following a health scare, Macmillan's resignation as PM and leader of the party announced at the start of the Annual Conference. The battle for succession is publicly conducted on the conference platform and at fringe meetings while behind the scenes the so-called 'magic circle' engineer the succession of 14th Earl of Home.

Resignations

1962

November	Thomas Galbraith (Under-Secretary of State, Scotland) resigns due to association with John Vassall while a junior minister in the Admiralty 1957–59. Subsequently exonerated and given new office in May 1963.

1963

June	John Profumo (Defence Minister) quits after lying to House of Commons about relationship with Christine Keeler.

DOUGLAS-HOME'S ADMINISTRATION OCTOBER 1963–OCTOBER 1964

Chronology of events

1963

October	Powell and Macleod refuse to serve in Home's cabinet.
November	Home returns to House of Commons in a by-election after renouncing his peerage.

1964

March	Controversy dogs Alec Douglas-Home over the abolition of Resale Price Maintenance. 31 Conservative MPs rebel in a vote.

2.10 OPPOSITION AND GOVERNMENT 1964–79

OPPOSITION OCTOBER 1964–JUNE 1970

Chronology of events

1964

October	The composition of the shadow cabinet (or 'Consultative Committee') is announced by Home.

1965

January	*Sunday Times* poll of Conservative MPs showed three out of four were broadly satisfied with Home's leadership.
July	Home announces to 1922 Committee his intention to stand down. The first electoral leadership contest conducted. Heath victorious.
October	*Putting Britain Right Ahead* launched at conference making pledges on taxation, trade unions, European policy and social security. Contemporaries saw it as a break from the ingrained Conservative ideology of 1950s. Heath breaks with tradition by attending the entire duration of the annual conference.
December	The implementation of sanctions against Rhodesia causes considerable controversy. Becomes apparent during a parliamentary division, 50 Conservatives defy leadership's policy of abstention and vote against, while 31 supported the Labour government in the Aye lobby. During the passage of Labour's Finance bill Conservative speakers propose 680 amendments.

1966

January	Enoch Powell launches a sustained attack on the Labour government's incomes policy; however the past Conservative administrations of the early 1960s are also criticised for their reliance on 'indicative planning'.

1967

April	Conservatives gain control of 18 county councils and in the Greater London Council elections win 82 seats to Labour's 18. This is the first time since 1934 that the Tories control London.
May	Borough elections net Conservative gain of 535.

October — Conference delegates, dissatisfied with the leadership's policies on education, force a ballot; the first ballot since the 1950 conference. The leadership manage to win by 1,302 votes to 816.

1968

April — Edward Heath dismisses Enoch Powell from the shadow cabinet.

June — Conservative peers defy their leader and succeed in defeating the Mandatory Sanctions Order against Rhodesia that was due for renewal. As a consequence the Labour government terminates its private discussions with Conservative representatives about reforming the House of Lords.

1970

January — Secret shadow cabinet policy weekend held at Selsdon Park Hotel, Croydon. Agreement is reached about creating a radical manifesto for the forthcoming election based upon the principles of the free-market.

HEATH'S ADMINISTRATION JUNE 1970–MARCH 1974

Chronology of events

1970

July — Iain Macleod (Chancellor of Exchequer) dies suddenly from a heart attack.

October — Conference calls for an end to support for 'lame duck' industries. Thatcher (Education Secretary) ends free school milk.

November — A government motion seeking to renew sanctions against Rhodesia causes 23 Conservative MPs to vote against.

December — Industrial Relations bill published. Within two weeks it has secured its second reading. Becomes law in 1971, giving registered unions legal status but insisting upon strike ballots and compulsory 'cooling off' periods.

1971

January — 'Angry Brigade' bomb attack on home of Robert Carr (Secretary for Employment).

February — Rolls Royce nationalised after bankruptcy.

March — Anthony Barber's budget revises the taxation rules creating conditions for the 'Barber boom'.

August — Sterling is allowed to float within upper and lower parameters of new currency system following ending of Bretton Woods system.

November — Keith Joseph drops plan for cost-related prescription charges.

1972

February — State of emergency declared as a result of the miners' strike.

March — The budget cuts taxation by £1.2 billion but there is also a rise in public expenditure.

May — Government U-turn indicated by publication of Industry bill.

June — Pound floats freely on currency markets against other European currencies.

November — Wage freeze and a statutory prices and incomes policy introduced.

1973

April — Phase two of the Prices and Incomes Policy.
Elections for the new Country Authorities, established under 1972 Local Government Act, held for first time.

December — Three-day working week introduced after miners' work to rule.

1974

January — Pressure within party grows for an early election. A meeting of Area Agents in London favours an early poll, although 1922 Committee less certain.

Resignations

1971

July — Teddy Taylor (Under-Secretary for Scotland) resigns in opposition to EEC entry.

October — Jasper More (Vice-Chamberlain) resigns in opposition to EEC entry.

1972

July — Reginald Maudling (Home Secretary) resigns due to 'Poulson' corruption enquiry.

1973

May — Lord Lambton (Under-Secretary for Air) and Earl Jellicoe (Lord Privy Seal) both resign because of sex scandals involving 'call girls'.

November — Norman Tebbit (parliamentary private secretary) resigns to free himself to speak against Heath's policies.

OPPOSITION YEARS, MARCH 1974–MAY 1979

Chronology of events

1974

March — Heath resigns as prime minister after negotiations with the Liberals fail to achieve a working majority.

	Maurice Macmillan and Julian Amery argue within party that the front bench should seek to defeat the minority Labour government over its Queen's speech, opening up the possibility of a national government should the Queen refuse to grant a dissolution.
May	London borough election results suggest a slight swing to the Conservatives.
September	Conservative manifesto is leaked.
October	Sir Keith Joseph causes outrage when speaking in Birmingham on birth control in poor families. It ends any ambitions he may harbour for the party leadership.
November	Lord Home charged with chairing a special party committee to review the leadership election rules.
1975	
January	Heath accepts the newly revised leadership rules and calls a contest for February.
February	Heath withdraws after Thatcher beats him in the first round. She goes on to win the second and becomes leader.
April	Keith Joseph endorses, despite his attachment to free market principles, the Labour government's decision to financially guarantee British Leyland with a £400 million advance. Many Conservative MPs and candidates, with marginal seats in the Midlands, were conscious of the necessity of being seen to support British Leyland.
1976	
October	The new attachment of the leadership to the free market enshrined in the policy manifesto *The Right Approach.*
1977	
March	A Conservative censure motion causes the Labour government to conclude a pact with the Liberals enabling it to comfortably survive the division.
October	Reginald Prentice takes the Conservative whip nine months after resigning from the Labour cabinet.
1978	
August	Saatchi and Saatchi poster campaign launched. Most famously included 'Labour still isn't working'.
September	Party report on use of referendums proposes their use for validating constitutional changes.
October	Pay policy issue highlights divisions between Thatcher and Heath at Annual Conference.
November	116 Conservative backbenchers defy leadership and vote for an end to sanctions against Rhodesia. Rebels Winston

	Churchill and John Biggs-Davidson are dismissed as front-bench spokesmen.
1979	
March	Vote of no confidence carried against the Callaghan Labour government by 311 to 310 votes. Election called for 3 May. Airey Neave murdered in House of Commons car park by INLA bomb.

Resignations

1976	
November	Reginald Maudling (shadow Foreign Secretary), with his reputation already tarnished by association with the Poulson scandal, sacked from front bench, after personality and policy clashes with Thatcher. This Poulson scandal had already obliged Conservative backbencher John Cordle (MP Bournemouth East) to resign from House of Commons in July.
December	Alick Buchanan-Smith (shadow Scottish Secretary) and Malcolm Rifkind (front-bench Scottish spokesman) resign in opposition to the three-line whip imposed against the Scottish and Welsh devolution bills. Thatcher refuses to accept the resignation of four other shadow front-benchers.
1977	
February	John Biffen (shadow Industry spokesman) resigns.

2.11 GOVERNMENT 1979–97

THATCHER'S FIRST ADMINISTRATION MAY 1979–JUNE 1983

Chronology of events

1979

June	Income tax cuts and increased public spending are the key features of Howe's first budget. VAT is increased to 15 per cent.
August	The beginning of 'privatisation' when Sir Keith Joseph announces that British Aerospace will be sold to private investors.
September	Lancaster House conference on Rhodesia convenes. Agreement reached in December.

1980

January	Decision to station Cruise missiles at American military installations, including Greenham Common, in Britain is announced.
May	Privatisation of British Aerospace.
August	The Housing bill gives council tenants the opportunity to purchase their local authority homes.
October	Annual party conference at Brighton told by Mrs Thatcher, when defending her economic policy, that 'the lady's not for turning'.

1981

January	Thatcher drops Norman St John Stevas as leader of House of Commons. Formation of new political party, the SDP, announced. Over the coming months it succeeds in winning a series of by-elections including in November the Conservative safe seat of Crosby. Only one Conservative MP defects to the fledgling party.
March	The £3.2 billion cut in public spending in the budget not welcomed by the 'wets' within Cabinet. Thoughts of resignation do not materialise. Indirect taxation increased. This budget is seen as evidence of the government's desire to break with Keynesian orthodoxy. 364 leading academics write to *The Times* urging a return to Keynesianism.
April	Unemployment passes 2.5 million.
September	Thatcher purges her government of the 'wets', either sacking or demoting, after a cabinet row over economic policy.

1982

January	Unemployment passes 3 million. Opinion polls put the Alliance two points ahead of the Conservatives.
March	Government majority reduced to 20 when 13 Conservative MPs vote to reverse the reduction in unemployment benefit.
April	Argentina invades the Falkland Islands and South Georgia provoking emergency Commons debate and the Cabinet's decision to dispatch a naval task force.
June	Port Stanley is surrendered to British forces.

Resignations

1982

April	Lord Carrington (Foreign Secretary) resigns after the Argentinean invasion of the Falkland Islands. Humphrey Atkins (Lord Privy Seal) and Richard Luce (Minister of State, Foreign Office) also accept responsibility and resign too.
May	Nicholas Budgen (whip) resigns over Northern Ireland policy.

1983

January	John Nott (Defence Secretary) had offered to resign at the time of the invasion of the Falklands.

THATCHER'S SECOND ADMINISTRATION JUNE 1983–JUNE 1987

Chronology of events

1984

January	Rate Capping bill gets second reading.
March	Miners' strike begins, although the miners of the Nottinghamshire fields remain at work.
April	39 Conservatives rebel over second reading of bill paving way for GLC abolition.
October	IRA bomb attack on party conference.
November	British Telecom privatised with shares being four times oversubscribed and raising £8 billion for the Treasury. This is the first public utility to be privatised.
December	Plans to increase parental contributions to student grants withdrawn by Keith Joseph after pressure from Conservative backbenchers. Britain and China agree the return of Hong Kong to China in 1997.

1985

January	Oxford University academics vote two to one to refuse the granting of Thatcher an honorary degree.

May	Local elections produce 24 hung councils out of 39 English counties with a 13 per cent drop in the Conservative vote.
June	Green paper on social security suggests end to income-related pensions.
July	Conservative parliamentary revolt over 'Top people' pay increases proposed for senior public servants.
October	Thatcher resists demands at Commonwealth conference for imposition of sanctions against South Africa's apartheid policies.
1986	
January	Westland helicopter crisis.
February	Official signing for the Channel Tunnel at Canterbury.
April	Rebellion by 68 Conservative MPs defeats the bill proposing to liberalise Sunday trading, 296–282. This is despite a three-line whip.
May	Local council elections show some Conservative gains.
November	Chancellor Lawson announces £5bn increase in public spending.
December	Privatisation of British Gas.
1987	
January	First formal general election campaign preparation meeting takes places between Thatcher and senior Conservatives at home of Lord McAlpine.
March	Pre-election budget takes two pence off income tax. The National Union Central Council signals its approval for the budget and urges an early election. Thatcher visits Moscow and Russian President Gorbachev.
April	Drafting of manifesto *The Next Moves Forward* for June general election completed.

Resignations

1983	
October	Cecil Parkinson (Party Chairman) resigns from Cabinet over affair with secretary Sara Keays and fathering an illegitimate child.
1985	
November	Ian Gow (Treasury minister) resigns in protest at Anglo-Irish agreement.
1986	
January	Michael Heseltine (Defence Secretary) resigns having stormed out of a cabinet meeting over the Westland affair. He felt he

	was denied the opportunity to make the case for Westland being sold to a European consortium rather than to Sikorsky. This resignation is followed shortly afterwards by that of Leon Brittan (Trade and Industry Secretary) after it emerged that information was leaked on the proposed sale.
October	Jeffrey Archer (deputy Party Chairman) resigns after allegations of liaison with prostitute.

THATCHER'S THIRD ADMINISTRATION JUNE 1987–NOVEMBER 1990

Chronology of events

1987	
October	Calls for the immediate introduction of the 'poll tax' to replace the rates system made at party conference forcing the government to abandon the earlier decision for phased stages.
1988	
February	Plans to privatise the electricity industry announced, confirming a pledge made by Lamont during an election news conference in previous June.
March	Lawson (Chancellor) introduces a budget that makes significant cuts to income tax, the consequence of this is an inflation-led consumer boom. The budget delights Conservative backbenchers.
April	Community charge (or 'poll tax') is given its third reading in the Commons, although it attracted the opposition of 17 Conservative MPs and reduces the government's majority to 25.
July	Education Act comes into force, introducing a national curriculum, regular testing and the potential for schools to 'opt out' of local education authority control.
October	Promise is made to privatise the coal industry.
November	British Steel privatised.
1989	
January	Plans to introduce market forces to NHS outlined in white paper *Working for Patients.*
November	Sir Anthony Meyer forces a leadership contest against Thatcher.
1990	
January	'Poll tax' legislation comes into force. One unforeseen consequence was people failing to add their names to the voter register to avoid detection by the authorities, and therefore liability for the tax.

March–April	Poll tax riots, and further Conservative rebellions in the House of Commons over the tax.
May	Local elections, the first since poll tax bills have been issued. Despite the net loss of Conservative seats, the leadership point to the success of Conservative flagship councils of Westminster and Wandsworth as vindication.
August	Iraq invades Kuwait. Thatcher and Bush in joint press conference demand withdrawal.
November	Howe's resignation speech mortally wounds Thatcher. Fails to win sufficient majority in first ballot and obliged to resign. Major wins leadership ballot on second round.

Resignations

1988

January	William Whitelaw (Lord President) resigns after suffering a stroke.
December	Edwina Currie (Under-Secretary, Health) resigns over salmonella in eggs health scare.

1989

October	Nigel Lawson (Chancellor of Exchequer) resigns, protesting about the role assumed in economic affairs by Sir Alan Walters, Mrs Thatcher's advisor.

1990

February	18 Conservative councillors in West Oxfordshire resign the whip in protest at the poll tax, losing the party control of the council.
July	Nicholas Ridley (Trade and Industry Secretary) resigns after expressing anti-German and anti-European views in an interview with *The Spectator.*
November	Geoffrey Howe (Foreign Secretary) resigns over Mrs Thatcher's European policy. His statement to a packed House of Commons two weeks later draws an analogy with cricket and gives direct momentum to those forces wishing to remove Thatcher.

MAJOR'S FIRST ADMINISTRATION NOVEMBER 1990–MAY 1992

Chronology of events

1990

December	Review of the 'poll tax' announced by Heseltine, newly returned to the cabinet as Environment Secretary.

1991

January	War commenced against Iraq. Land assault begins late February. Major 'the war leader' addresses British forces in the desert.
April	The widely anticipated demise of the 'poll tax' is announced and a successor banded 'council tax' unveiled.
May	Conservatives lose 900 seats in local elections.
July	Major launches *The Citizen's Charter.*
October	14 Conservative MPs rebel against cuts in defence.

1992

January	Conservatives' launch 'Labour's Tax Bombshell' campaign.
March	Labour's 'Jennifer's ear' party political broadcast attacks the Conservatives' NHS provision.
April	Major wins general election victory against most expectations. Took the campaign to the voters with his 'soap box'. The Conservative majority is 21.

Resignations

1992

January	Peter Brooke (Northern Ireland Secretary) resigns after appearing on Irish TV singing 'Oh My Darling Clementine' just hours after an IRA bomb kills seven.

MAJOR'S SECOND ADMINISTRATION APRIL 1992–MAY 1997

Chronology of events

1992

April	Major takes the opportunity for a cabinet reshuffle; Chris Patten, the party chairman and one of the 'high profile' victims of the general election when he lost his Bath seat, appointed Governor of Hong Kong. He is expected to oversee the return of the colony to China.
September	'Black Wednesday'.
October	Government announce the closure of 31 coal pits. The political furore, especially from the Conservative backbenches, leads to a temporary reprieve.
November	Following the collapse of the Matrix-Churchill legal case, at which former minister Alan Clark admitted lying, the Scott Inquiry into arms for Iraq is instigated.

1993

March — Lamont's tax increasing budget poorly received not least because of the introduction of VAT on fuel. This occurred despite a manifesto pledge to the contrary in 1992.

April — Government launch 'Care in Community' programme.

May — The Conservatives lose the Newbury by-election with a record swing and control of 15 County Councils. The Conservatives control only one shire county (Buckinghamshire).
Lamont sacked as chancellor and replaced by Kenneth Clarke.

June — Michael Heseltine suffers a heart attack while holidaying in Venice. Political pundits see this health scare as finally ending Heseltine's ambitions to become party leader.

July — After losing vote on Maastricht bill, Major wins a vote of confidence by 40 votes.

October — At party conference Major launches 'Back to Basics' crusade. Commentators assume the speech, following as it does others attacking single mothers by leading Conservatives, is the clarion call for a new moral social agenda. However conference is overshadowed by publication of extracts from Thatcher's memoirs that criticise leading Conservatives.

November — Parliament passes the railway privatisation bill.
Clarke introduces first unified budget. Despite increasing taxation the budget is well received by Conservative MPs.

1994

January — *The Spectator* publishes outspoken article attacking Major's government for abandoning Thatcherism.
Sunday Times publishes articles suggesting David Ashby (MP Leicestershire North West) shared a bed with a man. In December 1995 Ashby loses libel action against the paper.

May — The Conservative Party experiences severe losses in the local elections.

October — In response to the wave of scandals Major established the Nolan Committee into Public Standards.

November — Major survives a confidence vote on European Communities (Finance) bill 330–303. The whip is withdrawn from 8 Tory Euro-sceptics. Sir Richard Body resigns the whip in sympathy.

December — Government defeated on proposal to raise VAT on fuel from 8 to 17.5 per cent.

1995

April — Graham Riddick and David Tredinnick (both Conservative MPs) suspended from the House of Commons over cash for questions. They had been exposed by a *Sunday Times* 'insight'

	investigation in July 1994. Meanwhile a decision is taken to restore the whip to the 8 Conservative Euro-rebels.
May	Huge Conservative losses of 1,800 seats in local elections. This is the worst election performance of the century. Clarke overrules the Bank of England on interest rate rise.
June	In an attempt to re-assert his authority Major resigns as party leader and submits himself to re-election. Although challenged by John Redwood (Welsh Secretary), Major survives by 218 votes to 89 with 22 abstentions.
November	Nicholas Soames (MP for Crawley and friend of Prince Charles) launches outspoken attack on Princess Diana, after she admits adultery in a *Panorama* interview. He suggests she is in the 'advanced stages of paranoia'.
December	David Lightbown, the whip with a reputation for using his physical presence to corral wayward backbenchers, collapses at Twickenham's Varsity Match and dies, further reducing Major's working majority.
1996	
February	Lord Justice Scott produces his report on 'Arms to Iraq'. Government narrowly survive censure vote over Scott enquiry 319–318.
May	District Auditor surcharges Westminster City councillors (including Dame Shirley Porter, the Tesco heiress and former Conservative leader of Westminster council) £31m. The recipients vow to challenge the ruling via the High Court.
1997	
February	Major's government loses its overall majority in the House of Commons following defeat in the Wirral South by-election.

Resignations

1992	
September	David Mellor (Minister for National Heritage or the 'minister of fun' to his detractors) after allegations in the *News of the World* about an extramarital affair with Antonia de Sancha.
1993	
May	Michael Brown (government whip) resigns after being 'outed' by *News of the World.*
June	Michael Mates (junior Northern Ireland minister) resigns. It emerged that Asal Nadir, the disgraced tycoon, had received a watch from him with the inscription 'don't let the buggers get you down'. This was a reference to the Serious Fraud Office investigation into Nadir's business activities.

1994

January	Alan Duncan (parliamentary private secretary to Mawhinney at Health) resigns over irregularities with a council house purchase; Timothy Yeo (Environment Minister) resigns after allegations about his private life; similarly the Earl of Caithness (Minister for Aviation and Shipping).
October	Allegations of sleaze dog the Major government as Tim Smith (junior Northern Ireland minister) resigns following his failure to disclose payments from Al-Fayed, Harrod's owner, in the Parliamentary register. Neil Hamilton (Corporate Affairs Minister) resigns following allegations of undeclared payments in 'brown paper bags' to ask questions on behalf of Harrods. In seeking to clear his reputation Hamilton and his wife become minor celebrities.
November	Patrick Nicholls (Party Vice-Chairman) resigns after derogatory comments to his constituents about Germany and France.

1995

February	Allan Stewart (Scottish Office junior minister) resigns after confronting a group of anti-motorway protestors by waving an axe.
March	Bob Hughes (parliamentary secretary to Office of Public Service and Science) resigns following *News of the World* exposé of extramarital affair.
April	Richard Spring (Mayhew's PPS) resigns over *News of the World* revelation of sex scandal.
June	John Major (Leader) resigns and initiates a leadership contest challenging his party to 'put up or shut up'. John Redwood (Welsh Secretary) stands down from Cabinet to challenge Major in the leadership contest.
July	Jonathan Aitken (Chief Secretary to Treasury) resigns to fight libel action against *Guardian* relying upon the 'simple sword of truth'. Case collapses when it emerges he had persuaded his daughter to lie under oath. Aitken is jailed for perjury in June 1999 and declared a bankrupt.

1996

June	Rob Richards (Welsh junior minister) resigns over affair with a public relations officer.
July	Derek Heathcoat Amory (Paymaster-General) resigns in protest at Major's European policy.
December	David Willetts (Paymaster-General) obliged to resign after he admits that he misled a Select Committee.

1997

March	Tim Smith (MP for Beaconsfield) resigns over cash for questions.
April	Sir Michael Hirst (Scottish Conservative Chairman) obliged to resign on first day of general election campaign after admitting to 'past indiscretions'.

2.12 OPPOSITION 1997–2001

Chronology of events

1997

May	Following the party's hammering at the polls (its worst result since the Liberal landslide of 1906), Major announces he will step down as party leader. Michael Howard (a leadership candidate) attacked by Anne Widdecombe, his former deputy. She suggests 'there is something of the night in his personality'. Hague wins the subsequent contest.
August	Conservatives win Uxbridge by-election with a 5 per cent swing.
October	Shadow cabinet decides to rule out EMU for ten years, but leading pro-Europeans Curry, Dorrell and Young absent from meeting. Conservative MPs gather in Eastbourne for a 'bonding' session with instructions to dress casually. The media is scathing about the MPs' fashion sense.

1998

January	Sweeping changes of party's leadership rules announced.
October	On eve of party conference *The Sun* tabloid newspaper carries a front-page obituary for the Conservative Party. A photograph of a blue parrot hanging upside down, with William Hague's face superimposed, adorns the cover.
December	Viscount Cranborne (Conservative leader in the Lords) sacked by Hague after negotiating with the Labour government about House of Lords reform; Shaun Woodward is sacked from the front bench for opposing Section 28 that prevents councils from promoting homosexuality.

1999

February	Tom Spencer (MEP) forced to admit his bi-sexuality after customs officials seize drugs and homosexual pornography in his luggage. He resists calls to stand down.
March	Kitchen-table politics announced by Hague, apparently drawing inspiration from Texan republican governor, George W. Bush.
April	Peter Lilley (deputy leader), on the 20th anniversary of Thatcher's 1979 election victory, seeks to distance party from Thatcherism and suggests that the NHS and education

	are too important to be entrusted to the private sector and free-market economy. Provokes outrage from the right.
June	Hague 'stars' in TV documentary 'How to be Leader of the Opposition'. At same time the opportunity is taken to re-shuffle shadow cabinet and some 'key' figures in Central Office following the sacking of Peter Lilley.
	Jonathan Aitken is jailed for perjury. He had resigned as a minister in April 1995 to fight a libel action.
September	Michael Portillo admits to homosexual experiences in his youth.
October	Lord Archer chosen as Conservative candidate in London Mayor election. Hague launches 'The Common Sense Revolution' manifesto pledging the Conservatives' five guarantees: sterling, taxation, education, law and order and to cut bureaucracy. The publication of John Major's and Norman Lamont's memoirs threatens to overshadow the Blackpool conference.
November	Michael Portillo returns to Westminster in Kensington and Chelsea by-election; Archer quits as party's London mayoral candidate after it emerges that he persuaded a friend to lie in his 1987 libel case. He is subsequently committed to stand trial for perjury.
December	Search for Conservative mayoral candidate in chaos after selection panel excludes Steven Norris, but is obliged to re-instate his name after intervention from Michael Ancram (Party Chairman).
2000	
January	Steven Norris chosen at second attempt to be Conservative candidate in the London Mayor election.
February	Portillo appointed Shadow Chancellor of Exchequer, while right-winger John Redwood is demoted to the back benches. John Maples, one of the casualties of the reshuffle, writes an open letter attacking Hague's leadership and warns of the dangers of the party drifting too far rightward. Archer is expelled from the party for a five-year duration.
June	Rob Richards (former Conservative leader of the Welsh Assembly) is acquitted of assault.
July	Conservative peers led by Lady Young block repeal of Section 28 on the promotion of homosexuality.
August	Defection to Labour of gay millionaire Ivan Massow (who had challenged to become the party's London mayoral candidate) claiming Conservatives 'intolerant and just plain nasty'.
September	Hague derided after he claims in a magazine interview to have consumed 14 pints of beer a day while working as a

	deliveryman in his youth. Following problems over fuel protests and the Millennium Dome the Conservatives jump ahead of Labour in the polls for first time in eight years. Proves a temporary phenomenon.
December	Portillo gives interviews claiming he has no interest in becoming party leader. Hague and Portillo launch proposals for significant tax cuts if elected at next election.
2001	
January	A £5 million pounds donation is made to the Conservative election war-chest by betting tycoon, Stuart Wheeler. He claimed that recent multi-million pound donations to the Labour party, by Lord Hamlyn, Lord Sainsbury and Christopher Ondaatje, prompted his gesture.
April	Local elections due for 3 May are postponed, as is the general election, due to foot and mouth crisis. Renewed speculation about a leadership challenge to Hague after the general election'. Rumours suggest the possibility of a Portillo–Clarke axis.
May	Blair calls general election for 7 June. Opinion polls suggest Labour will increase its majority to as much as 250 seats.
June	Hague resigns immediately after election defeat. John Paul Getty Jur makes multi-million pound donation. Portillo, Clarke, lain Duncan Smith, Michael Ancram and David Davies enter leadership contest.

Resignations

1997	
October	Piers Merchant (MP for Beckenham) stands down after disclosures about his relationship with an 18-year old nightclub hostess. Ian Taylor (shadow Northern Ireland spokesman) resigns claiming Hague's anti-Euro policy 'marginalising' the party.
November	Resignation of David Curry from shadow cabinet over EU policy.
1999	
June	Raymond Robertson (Scottish Conservative chairman) resigns after losing a party vote. Personality clashes with David McLetchie (leader of Conservative MSPs) also played a part. He is persuaded to withdraw his resignation.
August	Rob Richards (leader of Conservative group in Welsh Assembly) resigns when colleagues refuse to back his deputy, David Davies, as stand-in leader while he withdrew temporarily to defend himself against a charge of assaulting a young woman.

Part 3

3.1 CONSERVATIVE PARTY ORGANISATION

The structure of the Conservative party comprises three principal elements: the professional, the parliamentary and the voluntary.

PROFESSIONAL

Carlton Club

From the 1832 Reform Act, the Carlton Club, located in Pall Mall, acted as the informal venue for officials to organise the activities of the party. Many of its duties were entirely ad hoc with club officials primarily concerned with the party in parliament. At elections officials did seek to scrutinise the electoral registers and between elections made some efforts to encourage Conservative Associations in the constituencies to register voters. The Carlton Club committee, chaired by Granville Somerset, was weakened by the hostility of the county squirearchy who were unwilling to donate to central funds and who resented interference in their own electoral business. When Peel split with the party in 1846 the organisational side of the Carlton Club lost direction.

Since its creation it has also acted as a gentleman's club for senior Conservatives. Its membership is limited to Conservatives and until recently contained almost all Conservative MPs as members. In recent years there have been moves to admit women as members. When damaged by German bombing in 1940 it re-located to its current premises in St James's Street. During its history the Club has hosted several 'key' party meetings, most famously the one that toppled the Lloyd George coalition government in October 1922.

Conservative Central Office

Created in 1870 as the headquarters for the Conservative party organisation, for the first four decades of its existence it was under the control of the principal agent, acting on behalf of the chief whip. Since the creation of the post of party chairman in 1911 it has been under the authority of this individual. The founding of Central Office was a direct consequence of the expansion of the franchise towards a mass electorate. Since its establishment Central Office has been housed in a number of different locations close to Westminster. From 1958 it has occupied its current premises of 32 Smith Square, although financial crisis obliged the party to mortgage the property in the 1990s.

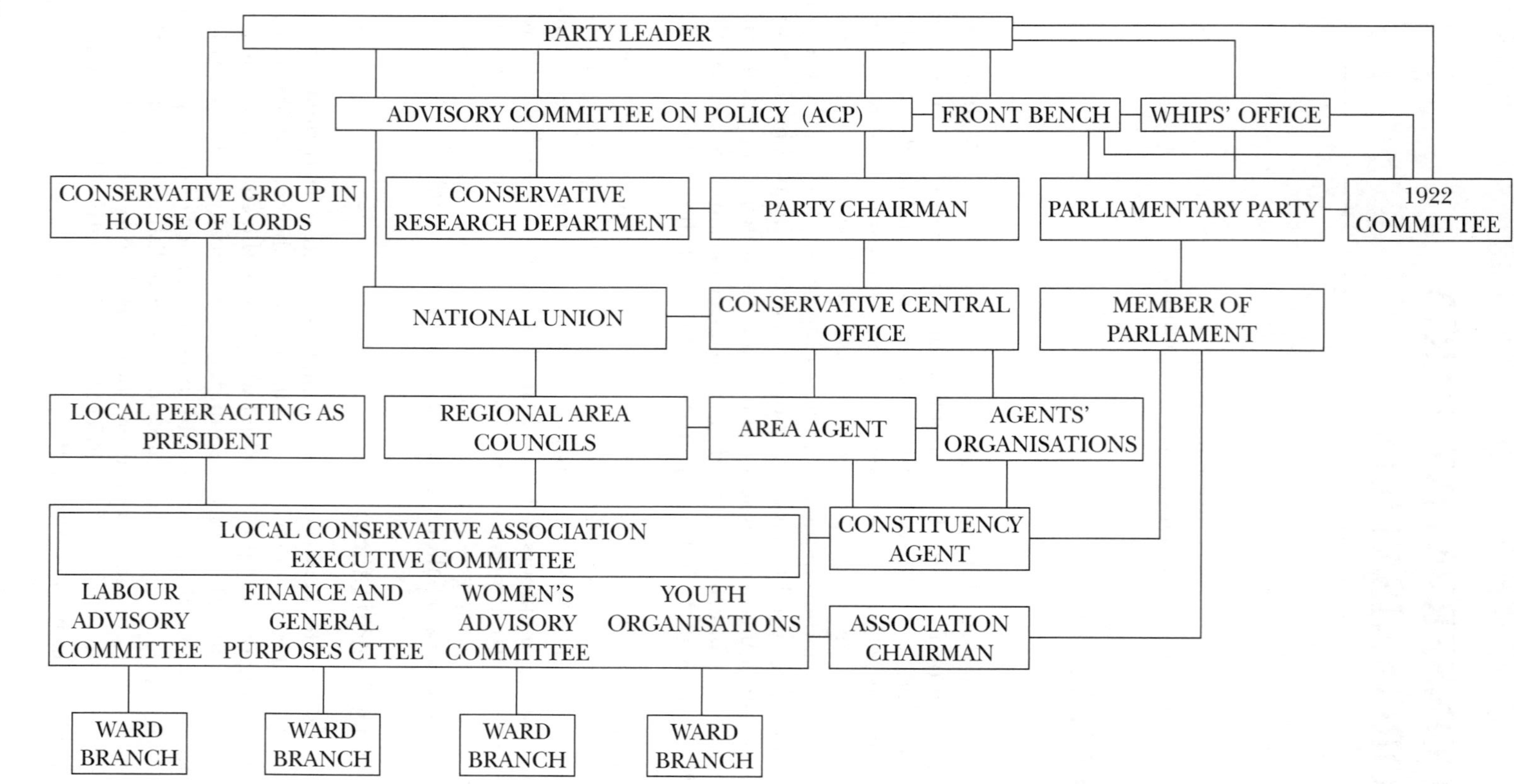

Figure 3.1 Structure of the Conservative party organisation
Adapted: N.J. Crowson, *Facing Fascism: The Conservative Party and the European Dictators* (1997)

Party Chairman

The chairman is the personal appointee of the party leader, and is responsible for overseeing the activities of the professional and voluntary wings of the party. The position was formally established in 1911.

Party Chairmen since 1911

	Date appointed
Arthur Steel-Maitland	June 1911
Sir George Younger	January 1917
Francis Stanley Jackson	March 1923
J.C.C. Davidson	November 1926
Neville Chamberlain	June 1930
1st Baron Stonehaven	April 1931
Douglas Hacking	March 1936
Thomas Dugdale	March 1942
Ralph Assheton	October 1944
1st Baron Woolton	July 1946
Oliver Poole (1st Baron Poole from 1958)	November 1955
2nd Viscount Hailsham	September 1957
R.A. Butler	October 1959
Iain Macleod	October 1961
Iain Macleod and 1st Baron Poole – Joint Chairmen	April 1963
1st Viscount Blakenham	October 1963
Edward du Cann	January 1965
Anthony Barber	September 1967
Peter Thomas	July 1970
6th Baron Carrington	April 1972
William Whitelaw	June 1974
Lord Thorneycroft	February 1975
Cecil Parkinson	September 1981
John Selwyn Gummer	September 1983
Norman Tebbit	September 1985
Peter Brooke	November 1987
Kenneth Baker	July 1989
Christopher Patten	November 1990
Sir Norman Fowler	May 1992
Jeremy Hanley	July 1994
Brian Mawhinney	July 1995
Lord Parkinson	June 1997
Michael Ancram	October 1998*

* Resigned June 2001 to contest leadership.

Principal Party Organisers

Until 1911 the role of the principal party organiser was to co-ordinate the activities of the party's organisation. Before the creation of Central Office in 1870 the key task was to encourage the registration of voters. The effectiveness of the organisation was closely linked to the personality, skill and devotion of the organiser. With the party split in 1846 the party organisation lost its direction until Central Office was created and John Gorst appointed as principal agent with the remit to administer the affairs of Central Office while linking together the leader, parliamentary party and the mass voluntary organisation. After Gorst, who had held the job in conjunction with being an MP, the appointment became a professional post. Although some of these duties were subsumed by the appointment of a party chairman from 1911, the principal agent (or namesake) effectively became a chief executive, a professional party organiser working for Central Office running the day to day organisation.

Principal Party Organisers since 1832

	Title	Tenure
Francis R. Bonham		1832–46
Philip Rose		1853–59
Markham Spofforth		1859–70
Sir John Gorst	Principal Agent	April 1870–February 1874
W.B. Skene	Principal Agent	1877–July 1880
Sir John Gorst	Principal Agent	July 1880–November 1882
G.C.T. Bartley	Principal Agent	February 1883–December 1884
Robert W.E. Middleton	Principal Agent	July 1885–July 1903
Lionel Wells	Principal Agent	July 1903–November 1905
Alexander Haig	Principal Agent	November 1905–December 1906
Percival Hughes	Principal Agent	December 1906–May 1912
John Boraston	Principal Agent	May 1912–June 1915
John Boraston and William Jenkins	Joint Principal Agents	June 1915–December 1920
Sir Malcolm Fraser	Principal Agent (Honorary)	December 1920–March 1923
Sir Reginald Hall	Principal Agent	March 1923–March 1924
Herbert Blain	Principal Agent	March 1924–January 1927
Sir T.J. Leigh Maclachlan	Principal Agent	January 1927–February 1928
H. Robert Topping	Principal Agent (General Director, February 1931)	February 1928–October 1945
Stephen Pierssene	General Director	October 1945–August 1957
William Urton	General Director	August 1957–June 1966
Richard Webster	Director of Organisation	June 1966–February 1976
Anthony Garner	Director of Organisation	February 1976–September 1988
John Lacy	Director of Organisation and Campaigning	September 1988–August 1992
Tony Garrett	Director of Campaigning (Chief Agent)	August 1992–July 1998
Archie Norman	Chief Executive	July 1998–June 1999
D. Prior	Chief Executive	June 1999–

Director-General

This occasional position was created as an overall additional co-ordinating figure. Its creation came about by the decision to lighten the administrative load of Sir Michael Fraser who had acted as both deputy chairman October 1964–October 1975 and chief executive of the professional organisation. This arrangement has been invoked on three subsequent occasions.

Director-Generals since 1974

	Tenure
Michael Wolff	April 1974–March 1975
Paul Judge	November 1992–February 1995
Martin Saunders	February 1995–June 1997

Conservative Research Department

Created on 23 October 1929, the CRD was intended to provide a forum for the initiation of policies, and to provide MPs and candidates with information about 'key' issues for use in meetings, speeches and articles. Until 1979 it operated under the auspices of its own chairman, independently of Central Office, and had the right of access to the Leader. Many of the party's brightest political stars, such as Rab Butler, Enoch Powell and Chris Patten, served their political apprenticeships in the CRD.

Chairmen of Conservative Research Department

	Tenure
Neville Chamberlain	1930–40
Sir Kingsley Wood	1940–43
Sir Joseph Ball (Acting Chairman)	1943–45
R.A. Butler	1945–64
post vacant	1964–70
Sir Michael [Lord] Fraser	1970–74
Sir Ian Gilmour	1974–75
Angus Maude	1974–79

Note: The position of the CRD chairman was abolished in 1979 and the duties absorbed by the Party Chairman.

Directors of Conservative Research Department

	Tenure
Sir Joseph Ball	1930–39
post vacant	1939–45
David Clarke and Henry Hopkinson	1948–50
David Clarke and Percy Cohen	1950–51
Michael Fraser and Percy Cohen	1951–59
Michael Fraser	1959–64
Brendon Sewill	1964–70
James Douglas	1970–74
Christopher Patten	1970–79
Alan Howarth	1979–82
Peter Cropper	1982–84
post vacant	1984–85
Robin Harris	1985–89
Andrew Lansley	1989–95
Danny Finkelstein	1995–99
R. Nye	1999–

Advisory Committee on Policy (ACP)

The ACP was reconstituted in 1945 from the Post-war Problems Central Committee and then reformed under the 1949 Maxwell Fyfe reforms. Under this latter revision it was no longer a committee of the National Union and was instead responsible to the leader, advising upon policy recommendations. It is federal in structure drawing a membership that includes the party chairman, the directors of the Conservative Research Department and the Conservative Political Centre as well as representatives from the parliamentary party and the National Union. It offers guidance on policy usually formulated by a network of specialist policy groups chaired by front-bench spokesmen. These policy groups comprise MPs, members of the National Union and sympathetic outside 'specialists'. Once in office the importance of the ACP has tended to diminish. Its future since 1997 has been unclear.

Treasurers (Joint Treasurers)

Responsible for overseeing the party's finances, the post of Treasurer has never been easy and the need to raise funds has always been a priority ever since the first Treasurer, Lord Farquhar, succeeded in raising over £600,000 in 1914.

Party (Joint) Treasurers since 1911

	Tenure
1st Earl Farquhar	1911–23
1st Viscount Younger	1923–29
Sir Samuel Hoare	1929–31
1st Baron Ebbisham	1931–33
1st Viscount Greenwood	1933–38
1st Viscount Marchwood	1938–47
Christopher Holland-Martin	1947–60
6th Baron De L'Isle	1948–52
Oliver Poole	1952–55
Sir Henry Studholme	1955–62
Robert Allan	1960–65
Richard Stanley	1962–66
Lord Chelmer	1965–77
Sir Tatton Brinton	1964–74
Sir Arnold Silverstone (Lord Ashdown, 1974)	1974–77
William Clark	1974–75
Robert Alistair (Lord) McAlpine	1975–90
Lord Boardman	1979–82
Sir Oulton Wade	1982–90
Sir Charles (Lord) Johnston	1984–88
Lord Laing	1988–93
3rd Viscount Beaverbrook	1990–92
Sir John Cope	1991–92
Tim Smith	1992–93
Charles (Lord) Hambro	1993–97
Sir Philip (Lord) Harris	1993–97
Sir Graham Kirkham	1997–98
Michael Ashcroft	1998–

Principal Publicity Officers

The holder of this post is responsible for the party's literature, publications and propaganda. The position was created in 1927.

Principal Publicity Officers since 1927

	Tenure
Sir Joseph Ball	1927–30
Sir Patrick Gower	1930–39
post vacant	1939–45
Edward O'Brien	1945–46
Mark Chapman-Walker	1946–55
Guy Schofield	1955–57
Ronald Simms	1957–61
George Hutchinson	1961–64
Roger Pemberton	1964–65
post vacant	1965
Tim Rathbone	1966–68
Geoffrey Tucker	1968–70
Russell Lewis	1970–71
Donald Harker	1971–75
Alec Todd	1975–77
Tom Hooson	1977–78
Gordon Reece	1978–80
Sir Harry Boyne	1980–82
Anthony Shrimsley	1982–85
Harvey Thomas	1985–86
Michael Dobbs	1986–89
Brendan Bruce	1989–91
Shaun Woodward	1991–92
Tim Collins	1992–94
Hugh Colver	1994–95
Tim Collins	1995
Charles Lewington	1996–97
Francis Halewood	1997
post vacant	1997
A. Cooper (Director of Political Operations and Communications)	1997–99
G. MacKay (Director of Media)	1998
Amanda Platell (Director of Media)	1999–
C. Evans (Director of Presentation)	1999–

Conservative Political Centre (CPC)

Established in December 1945 the CPC is responsible for political education, running courses and producing literature to encourage dialogue between the leadership and activists. Much of the CPC's work is conducted at a constituency level in discussion groups. Attempts to create a national network of 'political' bookshops proved unsuccessful and were abandoned in the early 1950s. The CPC at Central Office regularly dispatches literature and topics for discussion to the constituencies that in turn provide reports on the suggested topics. These are collated and then forwarded to senior party figures and the

ACP. Despite criticisms that the constituency discussion groups are cliques that fail to communicate the political message more widely the CPC remains popular with activists. Whereas for the period 1967–69 an average of 379 discussion groups responded to the circulars, in 1990 this figure was 438. The 1993 Annual Review claimed that there existed 770 CPC discussion groups.

PARLIAMENTARY

Parliamentary party

The parliamentary party comprises those Conservative MPs elected to the House of Commons and peers in the House of Lords who take the Conservative whip. Within both Houses the party can be further divided between those who serve on the front bench (as ministers in times of government or as shadow spokespersons when in opposition) and the majority who sit on the back benches.

Whips' office

The chief whip and his deputies are the personal appointees of the leader. They are the means of securing the loyalty and support of the party's MPs. They act as a channel of information, gossip and grievance while at the same time acting in concert with their opposite numbers in the Labour party to organise the work of the House of Commons. They hold the power of patronage, making recommendations on candidates suitable for posts, which can be a powerful tool for maintaining loyalty. Withdrawal of the whip from an MP is one of the ultimate means of censure whilst an individual MP resigning the whip can be a means of last resort protest. (See 4.10 conservative Factions, Rebels and Defectors.) Essentially the whips' office is a means of two-way communication between the leadership and the parliamentary party.

Chief Whips, House of Commons from 1835

	Tenure
Sir George Clerk	1835–37
Sir Thomas Fremantle	1837–44
Sir John Young	1844–46
William Beresford	1846–50
Forbes MacKenzie	1850–53
Sir William Jolliffe	1853–59
Colonel T.E. Taylor	1859–68
Gerard Noel	1868–73
Colonel T.E. Taylor	1873–74
Sir William Hart Dyke	1874–80
Rowland Wynn	1880–85
Aretas Akers-Douglas	1885–95
Sir William Walrond	1895–1902

Chief Whips, House of Commons from 1835 (cont'd)

	Tenure
Sir Alexander Acland-Hood	1902–11
Lord Balcarres	1911–12
Lord Edmund Talbot	1912–21
Leslie Wilson	1921–23
Sir Bolton Eyres-Monsell	1923–31
David Margesson	1931–41
James Stuart	1941–48
Patrick Buchan-Hepburn	1948–55
Edward Heath	1955–59
Martin Redmayne	1959–64
William Whitelaw	1964–70
Francis Pym	1970–73
Humphrey Atkins	1973–79
Michael Jopling	1979–83
John Wakeham	1983–87
David Waddington	1987–89
Timothy Renton	1989–90
Richard Ryder	1990–95
Alastair Goodlad	1995–97
James Arbuthnot	1997–

Chief Whips, House of Lords since 1870

	Date of appointment
Lord Skelmersdale (cr 1st Earl of Lothian, 1880)	1870
Earl of Kintore	1885
Earl of Limerick	1889
Earl Waldegrave	1896
Duke of Devonshire	1911
Lord Hylton	1916
Earl of Clarendon	1922
Earl of Plymouth	1925
Earl of Lucan	1929
Lord Templemore	1940
Earl Fortescue	1945
Earl St Aldwyn	1958
Lord Denham	1977
Lord Hesketh	1991
Viscount Ullswater	1993
Lord Strathclyde	1994
Lord Henley	1998

Party in House of Lords

Until 1958 the Conservative party in the House of Lords comprised hereditary peers who took the Conservative whip. The 1958 Peerage Act created an additional breed of peer – the life peer – who was granted a title and a seat in the Lords for the remainder of their lifetime. In 1999, after a protracted battle, the House of Lords Act abolished the right of hereditary peers to sit in the House of Lords, except for a small group of 92 individuals who would be elected by their fellow peers. A number of Conservative hereditary peers were granted life peerages. The hereditary peerage elections were conducted 27–28 October and 3–4 November 1999. Subsequently 51 out of the 92 elected hereditary peers were Conservative.

Conservative Party strength in House of Lords

	Conservative peers	Total number of peers
1900	354	589
1920	491	716
1938	519	775
1955	507	855
1975	292	1,139
1 November 1999	483	1,211
1 December 1999	233	656

Source: D. Butler and G. Butler, *Twentieth Century British Political Facts* (2000), p. 228.

Leaders of House of Lords since 1828

	Date appointed
Duke of Wellington	1828 (party leader until 1834)
Lord Stanley (14th Earl of Derby, 1851)	1846 (and party leader)
Earl of Malmesbury	1868
Lord Cairns	1869
Duke of Richmond	1870
Earl of Beaconsfield	1876 (and party leader)
3rd Marquess of Salisbury	1881 (and party leader from 1885)
Duke of Devonshire	1902
Marquess of Lansdowne	1903
Earl Curzon	1916
4th Marquess of Salisbury	1925
1st Viscount Hailsham	1930
Marquess of Londonderry	1935
Viscount Halifax	1935
Earl Stanhope	1938
Viscount Caldecote	1940
Viscount Halifax	1940
Lord Lloyd	1941

Leaders of House of Lords since 1828 (cont'd)

	Date appointed
Lord Moyne	1941
Viscount Cranborne (5th Marquess of Salisbury, 1947)	1942
Earl of Home	1957
2nd Viscount Hailsham	1960
Lord Carrington	1963
Earl Jellicoe	1970
Lord Windlesham	1973
Lord Carrington	1973
Lord Soames	1979
Lady Young	1981
Viscount Whitelaw	1983
Lord Belstead	1988
Lord Waddington	1990
Lord Wakeham	1992
Viscount Cranborne	1994
Lord Strathclyde	1998

N.B. Until the Parliament Act (1911) the leaders in the Lords and the Commons were regarded as coequals unless one of them was Prime Minister, or had been Prime Minister, in the preceding Conservative government.

1922 Committee

Founded in 1923 by backbenchers first elected to parliament in the 1922 general election, its initial aim was to help these new MPs find their parliamentary feet. From 1924 the practice of a whip attending the committee's weekly Monday meetings was commenced. Consequently this provided a conduit from backbenchers to leadership and enabled the Whips' Office to use the Committee as a barometer of feeling within the parliamentary party. From February 1926 the membership of the committee became universally open to all Conservative backbenchers. During the 1930s there was a decline in attendances and the committee became little more than a glorified lecture club; however, with the outbreak of war in 1939 a revival in fortunes occurred. First, the committee was prepared to discuss issues of controversy. Second, ministerial briefs provided information that could not be given during parliamentary debates. Third, during the period 1941–42 the committee established its authority to speak for the party as chairman Erskine-Hill led the criticisms of the Churchill coalition. The importance of this was that henceforth the '1922' would be perceived as the voice of the mainstream of the party, rather than any fringe. Furthermore in the post-1945 period it became established practice for the 1922 chairman (and sometimes the entire executive committee) to have regular face-to-face meetings with the party leader. Such meetings have been responsible for encouraging the sacking of ministers, such as Leon Brittan in 1986, and for expressing dissatisfaction with the direction of policy, as with the Poll Tax in 1989, or for even suggesting a leader no longer has the confidence of their party, as Cranley Onslow informed Thatcher after the first leadership ballot in 1990. The chairman of the Committee is responsible for administering the leadership contests.

Chairmen of 1922 Committee

	Tenure
Sir Gervase Rentoul	1923–32
William Morrison	1932–35
Sir Hugh O'Neill	1935–39
Sir Annesley Sommerville (Acting Chairman)	1939
William Spens	1939–40
Sir Alexander Erskine-Hill	1940–44
John McEwen	1944–45
Sir Arnold Gridley	1945–51
Derek Walker-Smith	1951–55
John Morrison	1955–64
Sir William Anstruther-Gray	1964–66
Sir Arthur Vere Harvey	1966–70
Sir Henry Legge-Bourke	1970–72
Edward du Cann	1972–84
Cranley Onslow	1984–92
Sir Marcus Fox	1992–97
Archie Hamilton	1997–2001
Sir Michael Spicer	2001–

Conservative Members of the European Parliament (MEPs)

From the time of Britain's entry into the EEC in 1973 party delegates were sent to Strasbourg and Brussels. Since 1979 there have been direct elections to the European Parliament and Conservative candidates have contested these elections. The outcome of these elections, every five years, has tended to mirror the national election results. (See 4.4 Conservatives and Europe for further details.)

Leaders of Conservative European Delegation

Leader	Date selected
P. Kirk	January 1973
G. Rippon	February 1977
J. Scott-Hopkins	June 1979
Sir H. Plumb	June 1982
C. Prout	April 1987
Lord Plumb	June 1994
T. Spencer	January 1997
Edward McMillan-Scott	September 1997

Source: D. Butler and G. Butler *Twentieth Century British Political Facts* (2000), p. 513

VOLUNTARY

National Union

This is the voluntary side of the organisation created in 1867 as a response to the expansion towards a mass electorate. Originally called the National Union of Conservative and Constitutional Associations it re-titled itself the National Union of Conservative and Unionist Associations in 1912 following the merger with the Liberal Unionists. It is based upon a federal structure (with associations paying an annual affiliation fee) and is intended to represent the views of the local constituency associations and party activists while seeking to promote the formation of local conservative associations, to co-ordinate the recruitment of members and to win elections.

Over the decades its role has evolved. Under the leadership of Lord Randolph Churchill (1883–84) it became subsumed in a power struggle with the leadership of Salisbury. However, it lost and became subjugated to the Principal Organiser (later Chairman) and Central Office. The most visible function of the National Union is its annual conference (see below). The idea of the National Union is to provide a deliberative and advisory platform for party opinion, although in theory the party leadership is free to ignore its advice. However, its officials have frequent and unpublicised contacts with the leadership, ensuring the representation of its views. Nevertheless, its role is reactive rather than proactive: it can register objections or express concerns but it lacks power to initiate. The three principal forums for the National Union are:

Central Council

This is the National Union's governing body. Since 1945 it has met annually. Its function is to stage debates on resolutions from the regional and local organisations and to hear addresses from the party leadership. It is also the forum for the annual election of the National Union's officers. Membership of the Central Council is open to the Party Leader, all constituency association chairmen, treasurers, agents and leaders of the youth, women's and trade union committees as well as MPs, peers, prospective parliamentary candidates and National Union officials. Officials from Central Office can attend in an ex-officio capacity as can representatives from the party in Scotland and Northern Ireland.

Executive Committee

Over the past century this committee's role has evolved from an administrative to a more overtly political one. At the end of the nineteenth century it was a small body meeting about ten times per annum to deal with routine matters. Rule changes in 1924 provided the basis for its current activities such that it would discuss matters of general political and party interest. The Party Leader and other principal members and officials of the party are members as well as the national chairmen from the youth, women and trade union organisations. Membership was increased with delegates appointed from each regional area in proportion to the number of constituencies. The increase in membership has seen a corresponding decrease in the frequency of meetings, to the extent that critics suggest that now it is little more than a talking shop for regional chairmen. Nevertheless, it discusses resolutions forwarded from the local and regional organisations, sending them on to the leadership, if necessary, and even dispatching delegations to discuss particularly vexing matters. Reforms in 1998 replaced the executive with the National Convention which performs the same functions.

Chairmen of the National Union Executive Committee

	Date appointed
John Gorst	1867
Viscount Holmesdale	1868
H.C. Raikes	1869
Viscount Mahon	1875
Lord Claud Hamilton	1876
Earl Percy	1879
Lord Randolph Churchill/Sir Michael Hicks Beach	1884
Lord Claud Hamilton	1885
Ellis Ashmead Bartlett	1886
Sir A.K. Rollitt	1889
F. Dixon-Hartland	1890
H. Bryon-Reed	1891
C.B. Stuart-Wortley	1892
Sir Stafford Northcote	1893
J. Rankin	1894
Sir C.E.H. Vincent	1895
Marquess of Granby	1896
A.H. Smith-Barry	1897
Sir B. Stone	1898
G.W.E. Loder	1899
Lord Windsor	1900
Sir Alfred Hickman	1901
Sir Charles Cave	1902
Francis W. Lowe	1903
Henry Ferryman Bowles	1904
Sir Walter Plummer	1905
Henry Imbert-Terry	1906
Duke of Rutland	1907
Sir Robert Hodge	1908
Sir Thomas Wrightson	1909
Henry Chaplin	1910
Lord Kenyon	1911
Sir William Crump	1912
The chairmanship of the executive is held by the Party Chairman[1] (see table on p. 133)	1912–30
Sir H. Kingsley Wood	October 1930
G. Herbert	March 1932

Chairmen of the National Union Executive Committee (cont'd)

	Date appointed
Sir George Stanley	April 1937
Sir Eugene Ramsden	April 1938
R. Proby	April 1943
N. Colman	April 1946
Anthony Nutting	April 1951
Sir E. Errington	April 1952
Sir Eric Edwards (cr. Lord Chelmer 1963)	February 1957
Sir C. Hewlett	September 1965
(Sir) J. Taylor	July 1971
Sir C. Johnston	July 1976
Sir R. Sanderson (cr. Lord 1985)	July 1981
Sir Peter Lane (cr. Lord 1990)	July 1986
Sir B. Feldman (cr. Lord 1995)[2]	July 1991
R. Hodgson[3]	March 1996

Notes:
1. The formal link between the Party Chairman and the National Union was broken by the revised Rules of the National Union that were established in October 1930.
2. March 1993 the office was renamed 'Chairman of the National Union'.
3. Post abolished March 1998 and replaced with National Convention, the chairmanship of which Hodgson has held since that date.

Annual Conference

The public face of the National Union. It is the annual gathering for the party's rank and file with social functions, debates on motions from the constituencies, and opportunities to see the great and the good of the party. Attendance is open to all members of the Central Council (i.e. constituency chairmen, treasurers, agents and leaders of the youth, women's and trade union committees), MPs, MEPs, peers, prospective parliamentary candidates, local councillors, area and Central Office officials plus a further two representatives from each constituency association (one of whom should be from the youth movement). This means a theoretical attendance as great as 7,000, although the figure is usually nearer 3,000. The first conference was held in November 1867, but conference did not pass its first policy resolution until 1876. It is rare to have balloted votes on motions, with a show of hands usually sufficing. The 'highlight' of the conference is the leader's speech, although leaders have only begun attending the entire proceedings since 1965. The duration of conference has also increased since its early beginnings. In 1900 it met for two days, by 1958 this had increased to four days with this schedule being retained. Many are dismissive of the conference's impact on party policy, suggesting proceedings are far too stage-managed. Balfour is attributed as having taken conference less seriously than the advice of his valet. In the past decade there has been some attempt by academics to reassess the significance of conference in policy formation.

Regional Areas

The regional areas were established in 1886 by the National Union to improve relations between Conservative associations and Central Office in England and Wales. Essentially the regional areas ran at two levels: Central Office regional administrative units and National Union provincial units. Originally there were 10 National Union regions; however, after 1906 they haemorrhaged into over 30 units, often along county lines. The fragmentation and the resultant dissipation of effort encouraged the National Union to form new regional units under rules introduced in 1930. By 1931 8 provincial areas had been created and a further 4 were established in 1937. These provincial areas were identical to the administrative districts covered by the existing 12 Central Office Areas. This regional structure would remain virtually unchanged for 50 years and was the 'classic age' for the provincial organisation. The Provincial Area Council is the ruling body for each region with representatives from the constituency associations and the women's, youth and trade union elements of the party. Cutbacks since the late 1960s reduced staff levels in Central Office area offices and obliged the closure of several offices. In June 1993 the remaining 10 area offices were reduced to 6. The Area Agents were based in the area offices, although they are employees of Central Office rather than the area. Their remit is to provide advice to local agents and to advise on candidate selection. In the event of internal divisions within a local association, or a dispute between an MP and his association, the Area Agent can be brought in to mediate and ensure that the wishes of the party's leadership prevail. The reduction in area offices meant that increasingly the Area Agent was responsible for large swathes of the country, especially in the Midlands (which embraced 108 constituencies from the Severn Estuary to the Humber) and the London and Eastern region (comprising 135 seats). The decision was taken in July 1998 by the party's Management Committee to close all the Central Office regional offices. The National Union decided to retain its regional administrative units, based on 26 'areas', mostly corresponding to two or three counties.

Regional Provincial Areas during the 'classic age' 1930–c.1993

1. *Metropolitan* (The City of London and all London boroughs)
2. *Northern Counties* (Cumberland, Durham, Northumberland and Middlesbrough)
3. *Lancashire, Cheshire and Westmorland*
4. *Yorkshire* (excluding Middlesbrough)
5. *East Midlands* (Derbyshire, Leicestershire, Lincolnshire, Nottinghamshire, Northamptonshire and Rutland)
6. *West Midlands* (Gloucestershire, Herefordshire, Shropshire, Staffordshire, Warwickshire, Worcestershire)
7. *Eastern* (Bedfordshire, Cambridgeshire, Hertfordshire, Norfolk, Suffolk)
8. *Essex and Middlesex*[1]
9. *Kent, Surrey and Sussex*

10. *Wessex* (Berkshire, Buckinghamshire, Dorset, Hampshire, Isle of Wight, Oxfordshire, Wiltshire)
11. *Western* (Cornwall, Devon, Somerset, Avon)
12. *Wales and Monmouthshire*

Note:
1. In 1963 the Essex and Middlesex area was dissolved. Middlesex was moved to Metropolitan to take account of the local government reorganisation of London, and Essex joined Eastern.

Scottish Unionist Association

Scotland has a separate identity and incorporates features from both the English and Welsh National Union regional and national structures. Created in 1882 the Scottish organisation has had its own party agent since 1890 and its own party chairman since 1950. It has its own annual conference, council, executive and subcommittees as well as a regional organisation.

Scottish Party Chairmen since 1950

	Tenure
Hon. James Stuart	1950–62
Rt. Hon. Michael Noble	1962–63
Sir John George	1963–65
Sir John Gilmour	1965–67
Sir Gilmour Menzies-Anderson	1967–71
Sir William McEwen-Younger	1971–74
Rt. Hon. George Younger	1974–75
Russell Fairgrieve	1975–80
Michael Ancram	1980–83
Lord James Goold	1983–88
Michael Forsyth	1989–90
Lord Sanderson	1990–93
Sir Michael Hirst	1993–97
Annabel Goldie	March–July 1997
Raymond Robertson	1997–2001

Party membership

Accurate figures for the party's membership are impossible to achieve because until 1998 the party kept no central membership records. Instead it was the responsibility of local constituency associations to recruit and retain their own membership. Membership has been ill-defined: there was no minimum subscription, and the party's rule book vaguely defines membership as requiring that individuals give generalised support to the policy objectives and candidates of the party. Consequently the figures below should be taken as only estimates. Nevertheless, three key features are apparent. Firstly, total membership has been declining since the 1960s. Secondly, the average age of the membership has been rising to the extent that one academic analysis suggested an average age of 63 years. Thirdly, more than half of the membership is female. The decision was taken in 1998 to create a central register of members.

Conservative Party membership (millions)

1947	1.2
1952	2.8
1970	1.25–1.5
1974	1.5
1982	1.2
1992	0.75
1998	0.35
2001	0.32

Constituency Conservative associations

Background

Conservative associations began emerging as early as 1831, as in Newark, but it was between the years 1832 and 1836 that the phenomenon established itself. Antecedents did exist in the form of political clubs, such as the True Blue Club, but they rarely if ever bore a party label and saw themselves as clubs. By 1837 several hundred Conservative associations existed, although coverage was patchy. As late as 1874 only 44 out of 82 English county divisions had a Conservative association. Many associations experienced a spasmodic beginning. Not unusually a Conservative MP, or peer, lent his name to enable their creation, but the costs of voter registration were expensive and their continued existence owed much to local enthusiasm and the patronage of the local elites. In early days their main roles were registration and canvassing although, on occasions, participation in the selection of candidates and the financing of election contests occurred. The growth of associations mirrored the national party's fortunes thus, with the 1846 split many went into abeyance. This did not signal the end of local Conservative activities during the mid to late 1840s since many re-emerged as protection societies.

Role

The key feature of local Conservative associations is their autonomy within the national party structure to manage their own affairs: to elect officers, appoint agents and select parliamentary and local council candidates. It is an autonomy that the associations jealously guard. During the twentieth century the role of constituency associations evolved in terms of activities and methods rather than organisational structures. Before the First World War they were essentially registration societies. The advent of a mass franchise saw them develop their social, propaganda and campaigning functions as Conservatism attempted to embrace the new electorate. Important matters, particularly candidate selection, were still settled by a select group of leaders of higher social status. From 1945 genuine attempts were made to achieve a mass party membership but since the early 1960s various changes in society have seen a decline in membership and political activism. The advent of technology, targeted mail shots and computers has meant that associations can continue to function with a small core membership and still attain their objectives of propaganda and campaigning.

Officers

These are voluntary positions whose key ones are the chairman, treasurer and president. The chairman is effectively responsible for the day-to-day affairs of the association supported by the agent, treasurer and prospective candidate or MP. With the decline in active members since the 1960s there has been a tendency for the same individuals to rotate between posts. Presidents of the association are honorific posts and usually given to a local peer or retired former MP. The president is expected to lend prestige to fund raising and to take the chair at public rallies, such as the annual general meeting.

Agents

The evolution of the Conservative constituency agent since 1883 has been marked by the growth of professionalism. Before the Corrupt and Illegal Practices Prevention Act (1892) an agent was typically a local solicitor who acted as the election agent, drew his fee, and then returned to his solicitor's duties. As the need to master the complicated rules of registration for voters became imperative, agents quickly formed the National Society of Conservative Agents, their own 'trade union', and devised examinations and grades that became an indispensable element of the party structure. Today the constituency agent is a professional trained in the details of election law and procedure, entrusted with a constituency and expected to ensure the maintenance of the local organisation. Agents' salaries have typically been met by the local constituency, which has led to wide discrepancies between individual salaries and a tendency for only the wealthier 'safer' constituencies to be able to afford the services of an agent. Attempts to make the agent the appointee of Central Office were resisted. With the decline in local constituency revenues and falling membership the numbers of full and part-time agents has dropped very rapidly since the 1992 election to such an extent that many constituencies are now without an agent, or share agents, or only appoint agents in the run up to a general election. Central Office sought to revive its central employment scheme abandoned in 1974 and between January 1995 and October 1996 103 central appointments were made, amounting to one third of all agents now being centrally employed.

Numbers of constituency agents in employment

Year	Number of agents in employment
1937	352[1]
1948	440
1959	506
1960	535
1966	499
1968	409
1974	365[2]
1979	359
1980	330
1982	284
1987	233[3]
1992	299
1993	234
1997	310

1. Plus an additional 99 certified women organisers.
2. Although 189 constituencies were without an agent.
3. Covering 319 constituencies.

Youth movements

Junior Imperial League

Created in July 1906 in the aftermath of the electoral debacle and reached its heyday during the 1920s. Membership was open to 16 to 30 year olds. Unsurprisingly its membership was hit by the advent of war in 1939 and it ceased to function, finally being abolished in 1944.

Young Britons

Was intended for children aged 6 to 16 and sought to promote citizenship, patriotism and Conservative principles in a less overt partisan manner. The inter-war years saw the organisation's heyday with a membership of nearly ½ million.

Young Conservatives (YCs)

Founded in July 1946. By mid-1948 there were 2,219 branches with a membership of 148,988. These branches provided a mix of social and political activities. Members provided ideal canvassers at election times and sometimes candidates for local council elections. During 1980s the over-exuberance of some YCs at their annual conferences provided acute embarrassment to the national leadership. By 1997 it had a membership of approximately 3,000. With a declining membership moves were made to abolish the YCs. The membership decline also had implications for the average age of the membership and the calibre of its leadership. Whereas originally many of the leadership were drawn from the upper end of the 16–30 age band this eventually was confined to the 16–19 band. This had the effect of reducing the influence of the youth group within the local Conservative association and widened the generational gap between YCs and the local association.

Federation of Conservative Students

A group aimed at those potential Conservatives involved in higher education. However, during the 1980s it proved too rebellious an organisation for the party to control and it was disbanded in 1986 and replaced with the *Collegiate Forum* which claimed a membership of 10,000.

Conservative Future

Launched at the October 1998 annual conference, after a 1997 review of youth organisation by party vice-chairman, Archie Norman, it was intended as a replacement for the Young Conservatives. Membership was aimed at the under 30s.

Women's movement

The involvement of women in the organisation of the Conservative party has been a significant feature. As recently as 1993 it was claimed that the Conservative party represented the largest women's movement in the world. However, the party's hierarchy has not always been prepared to acknowledge the importance of the role of women. From the earliest days women were involved in the Primrose League, although they found themselves excluded from the Grand Council, which was an all-male preserve. From 1906 Women's Unionist Associations were created outside the formal party structure, but ran in tandem to the constituencies. The advent of female suffrage obliged the party to recognise the significance of the female activist and voter. In 1928 Central Office began encouraging constituency associations to create their own women's branches with their own officers.

CHRONOLOGY OF ORGANISATION

1830

January — *Political Quarterly* uses term 'Conservative' for the first time in its modern sense. The term quickly gains currency.

1832

Carlton Club formed.

1833

A motion to suppress political unions is moved by Ultra-Tory George Finch, but it only attracts the support of ten Conservatives and is easily beaten.

1834–35

Appearance of Conservative and Constitutional Associations. Often formed independently of the central party normally the result of local enthusiasm and co-operation with the local Conservative aristocracy.

1835–37

Operative Conservative Associations started, especially in West Midlands and North. Provide a political outlet for skilled working class.

1835

May — Francis Bonham proposes to Peel that a committee be created to prepare for a sudden Whig dissolution. Bonham appointed the party's first full-time agent with Sir George Clark, Granville Somerset and Thomas Fremantle as his principal assistants. Somerset appointed to chair a small committee to supervise elections, and assist registration of voters in the provinces. This committee is based at the Carlton Club.

1836

July — *The Conservative*, a monthly newspaper formed. Although no official connection to central party it provides publicity about party meetings nationwide and promotes the establishment of Conservative associations.

1837

December — Scheme to establish a central registration society proposed, but fails to secure support of Bonham.
Spottiswoode appeal launched to raise funds to subsidise petitions against successful Liberal candidates, especially in Ireland. Officially the party leadership distances itself from the proposal.

1846

July — Most agents recruited by Bonham remain loyal to Peelites.

January — Protection Societies headquarters in Old Bond Street provide an alternative HQ for anti-Repeal Conservatives.

1851

Carlton Club revives the election committee including Malmesbury, Salisbury and Stanley. But lacked co-ordination with the constituencies.

1852

Philip Rose (Disraeli's solicitor) appointed principal agent. Declines a salary based upon belief it would lower his legal reputation. Based in Victoria Street.

December — Squabbles at Carlton Club between Protectionists and Peelites. Some Derbyites wish to create a new purely Conservative club.

1853	
March	Disraeli purchases the *Press* to propagate his own vision of Conservatism and to counter influence of *Standard* and *Morning Herald.* The first edition was in May. By July it had a circulation of 2,000. Disraeli sold the paper in 1858. Separate party office, the Central Conservative Society of Ireland, established in Dublin.
1854	
	Russell's Corrupt Practices Act required formal appointment of candidates' agents and the declaration of expenses.
1855	
March	Rose memorandum on state of party organisation and developments since 1853 and potential future developments.
1859	
	Responsibility for the electoral fund transferred from Jolliffe (former Chief Whip) to Colonel Taylor (new Chief Whip).
1863	
	Rival body to the activities of Jolliffe and Rose emerged with formation of National Conservative Registration Association. Without official sanction this association soon collapsed.
1866	
June	Colonel Taylor creates Efficient County Registration Association to centralise the process of county registration and provide a rival to the Liberals.
1867	
April	Conservative Working Men's Association hold conference in London.
November	First meeting of National Union of Conservative and Constitutional Associations.
1868	
September–November	The party's activities during the general election campaign co-ordinated by an Election Committee chaired by Spofforth (Principal Agent).
December	Second conference of National Union attracts only six delegates.
1870	
April	Conservative Central Office created. Located 53 Parliament Street, Westminster. Press agency purchased to ensure the regional press, which now had a range of broadly Conservative sympathetic titles, is provided with favourable copy of party speeches, meetings and reports. Attempts also made to achieve co-operation with *Evening Standard* and *Morning Post.*

1871

June — Bristol hosts the fifth National Union conference, the first which is deemed a 'success' and attracts a good attendance from the party's social elite.

1873

At Disraeli's request a small committee is formed to help ensure that at next election the party properly contests the county seats.

1874

Hints for Candidates, a party handbook, helps ensure that across the country prospective candidates broadly speak the same political rhetoric.

February — Central Office relocates to St Stephen's Chambers, Westminster.

1878

January — Arbuthnot memorandum on reorganisation of party structure. Seeking to reduce tensions between London and the regions he makes 23 recommendations including regional organisations. Plans rejected despite favourable responses from Conservative associations.

1880

April — W.H. Smith chairs Central Committee of enquiry into state of party organisation.

July — Gorst agrees to return as Principal Agent on condition that he will be given political office when the Conservatives next win office.

1882

National Union of Scottish Conservative Associations created.

1883

October — Annual Conference of the National Union held in Birmingham witnesses Lord Randolph Churchill attack the party's leadership.

November — Primrose League founded by Churchill and Drummond-Wolff.

1884

March — National Union's relations with Central Office deteriorate and it is threatened with eviction from St Stephen's Chambers.

July — Party leadership settles its differences with Churchill. Sir Michael Hicks Beach elected chairman of National Union Council. Central Committee abolished. Primrose League officially recognised.

December — First edition of *The Constitutional Yearbook*. It provides salient facts and information for Conservative speakers and journalists. Continues until 1939.

1885

Under the 'democratic reforms' all Conservative Associations automatically affiliated to the National Union and eight provincial unions created.

1886

February — Preliminary version of what by 1888 was to become *National Union Gleanings* shown to Salisbury for approval.

1891

April — Middleton and Wolmer form the Unionist Joint Registration Committee for Ireland.

November — National Society of Conservative Agents formed.

1892

May — Agents' Benevolent Fund launched.

July — Middleton collapses due to overwork.

1895

November — Party agents make representations to Middleton about the new Registration bill. Signals the increased sophistication of party workers.

1896

March — Salisbury presents Middleton with a testimonial cheque for £10,000 and a silver casket.

1904

May — Joseph Chamberlain becomes President of the Liberal Unionist Association ousting Devonshire. New constitution adopted and it becomes a tariff reform caucus.

1906

July — Junior Imperial League founded. National Union adopts new rules giving it central control over literatures and speakers; party funding remains the domain of the chief whip; and the regional organisations are abolished.

1911

February — Unionist Organisation Committee created under chairmanship of Akers-Douglas.

April — Interim Report of Unionist Organisation Committee.

June — Final Report of Unionist Organisation Committee.

1912

May — Conservative and Liberal Unionist parties in England and Wales formally merge.

1919

July — Labour subcommittee of National Union holds first meeting. Aim is to co-ordinate the Unionist Labour Movement.

1921

September — Younger (Chairman) fails to get new party rules approved which would separate the chairmanship of the party from the chairmanship of the National Union and thereby remove potential conflicts of interest.

October — National Union officially separated from Central Office, although 'independence' only nominal.

1922

March — Motion of confidence in Younger proposed by Steel-Maitland withdrawn on understanding that ministers cease attacks on the party chairman.

October — Carlton Club meeting of Conservative MPs. Austen Chamberlain resigns as leader.

1923

April — 1922 Committee holds its first meeting. Founded to support Conservative MPs elected to the House for the first time in the 1922 general election.

1924

February — National Union Central Council make demands for more democratic party system. Fobbed off with an offer to review the National Union's rules and the possibility of a liaison committee between the National Union and leader.

July — Herbert Blain (Principal Agent) successfully persuades National Union to adopt new rules giving the constituency associations the direct basis of representation.

1925

Young Britons established for children aged 6–16 years old.

Joint Examinations Board for Agents created in collaboration between National Union and National Society of Conservative Agents.

National Union rules relegate 'Unionist' to an additional form that was retained only for the party in Scotland and Ireland.

1926

February — 1922 Committee decides to open membership to all Conservative backbench MPs, but retains name.

1927

December — Stanley committee recommends the division of Central Office into three main divisions: organisation under the Principal Agent; publicity and propaganda under Director of Publicity; and personnel and finance under the Office Controller.

1929

July — Bonar Law Memorial College at Ashridge opened as the party's residential educational centre. National Union Central Council, critical of the election defeat, launches questionnaire enquiry into its causes.

November — Joseph Ball, ex-MI5 officer, appointed director of the newly created Conservative Research Department.

1930

Neville Chamberlain elevates status of Principal Agent above other departmental heads in Central Office and changes title to General Director.

July — National Union conference to agree new rules and changes in the party's regional structure, creating Provincial Areas.

1933

National Union agree that in future all appointed agents must hold a Joint Examinations Board certificate.

1935

Standing Advisory Committee on Candidates (SACC) formed.

1936

March — Central Council rejects a motion proposing to change name to 'National' party.

1937

December — Crawford Committee of Inquiry convened to examine the financing of the organisation.

1938

January — Following poor election results, Sir Kingsley Wood forms a committee to consider party organisation in London area.

1939

January — Issue of financial relationship between candidates and constituency parties highlighted by press release that claimed rich candidates were buying seats.

September — Hacking sends letter to all constituency parties suggesting they suspend political activities for the duration of the war.

1941

October — Standing Advisory Committee on Candidates given Central Council authority to examine financial arrangements between candidates and associations and the power to withhold endorsement if these are unsatisfactory.

1943

February — 1922 Committee decides to admit ministers, changing its name to 'Conservative and Unionist Members Committee', although the old title continued to be used.

May — First party conference held since 1937. In Churchill's absence, Eden addresses the floor.

December — Palmer Committee on Youth Organisation reports. This provides the basis for the post-war foundation of the Young Conservatives.

1944

July — New 'Young Conservative' movement for 15–30 year olds announced to replace Junior Imperial League. Launched in July 1946.

October — Party conference cancelled due to flying bombs and the limitations of transport in southern England owing to military operations following the invasion of Europe.

December — New rules on candidates, local association subscriptions and the percentage contributions that associations must make to election expenses announced by Standing Advisory Committee on Candidates.

1945

February — All-party talks agree terms for temporary release of political agents from military and public service for forthcoming election. However a week before the election only 80 Conservative agents had been demobilised.

September — Policy committees to advise front bench in opposition are announced.

December — R.A. Butler announces creation of Conservative Political Centre (CPC).

1946

Throughout year there is widespread internal party discussion about whether to adopt new name for party in wake of 1945 defeat. Suggestions ranged from 'Unionist' to 'New Democratic Party' to 'National Unionist Party'.

1947

May — Woolton–Treviot agreement for merger of Liberal Nationals.

1948

March — Woolton announces the success of the 'Million Fund'

April — Eden launches in Sheffield the campaign to double party membership from one million to two.

June — Young Conservatives hold first conference at Albert Hall.

June — 'Quota scheme' for constituency associations introduced.

1949

May — National Union Executive approve final report of Maxwell Fyfe committee on Party Organisation.

1951	
November	1922 Committee reverts to being a purely backbench forum.
1953	
October	Young Conservatives claim a membership of 140,000.
1954	
October	First televised coverage of party conference.
1957	
June	Colyton inquiry into party organisation. Intended as a second Maxwell Fyfe, but it made very little impact.
1958	
June	Central Office relocates to 32 Smith Square, Westminster.
1963	
June	Selwyn Lloyd report on party organisation agreed basic structure of party was sound, but made a number of recommendations aimed at improving efficiency and command-control structures.
1964	
October	Deputy-chairmanship is given to Michael Fraser with the role of linking the chairmanship with full-time party officials and to co-ordinate policy and organisation. Heath takes chair of the Advisory Committee on Policy, created with the aim of examining specific policy issues to prepare for a future manifesto.
1965	
February	Central Office publishes new rules for formal selection of the leader of the party.
March	CPC is integrated into Central Office.
May	The Chelmer Committee on Party Agents is submitted. Calls made for higher salaries and better training for agents, plus the introduction of subsidies for local constituency associations to enable them to offset the costs of employing an agent.
June	Young Britons, after years of membership decline, finally dissolved.
October	Macleod Committee on Young Conservatives reports to Heath. Argues the need for YCs to become involved in serious political discussions and also to increase involvement in community affairs. Further proposes that the age limit be raised to 35.
1966	
May	Central Office launches an urgent appeal for funds to local constituency treasurers.
October	'Project '67' and 'Action '67' launched at conference to increase party membership and make it more representative

at the constituency level, and recruitment to the Young Conservatives respectively. Neither campaign proved successful in the longer term.

October — Brooke Committee considers the party's organisation in the cities.

1970

July — Lord Chelmer appointed by the National Union executive to investigate the democratisation of the party.

1972

March — The interim report of the Chelmer review committee on candidate selection procedures placed before, and accepted, by the Central Council.

1973

October — Final Report of Chelmer review committee abandoned after debate at annual conference.
Scheme for the central employment of agents introduced.

1974

March — Letter to *The Times* complains of the poor support Petersfield Conservative Association given by Central Office during recent election campaign. Similar letters follow.

November — Special committee, chaired by Lord Home, to review leadership election rules.

December — New leadership rules, as recommended by Home committee, published.

1977

Swinton College closed.
Central Employment of Agents scheme scrapped and agents returned to traditional model of local employment.

1979

Conservative Research Department abolished as well as the Community Affairs Department. The sale of the Old Queen Street property would reduce the party deficit of £2.2m.

1981

Central Office budget cut by 20 per cent. This leads to reduced spending on regional organisation, opinion polling and advertising. The small business unit and trade union section downsized and merged with the Organisation Department.

1982

September — *Newsline* (monthly party newspaper) launched by the Marketing Department to replace the various publications published by Central Office. It eventually secured a paying subscription of 150,000.

December	Central Office adopts US Republican electioneering tactics. Uses computer system to target key voters in critical constituencies. Appeals for funds using direct personalised letters sent to 83,000 voters in 50 constituencies. Saatchi and Saatchi's advertising campaign budget for the party totals £2.4m including £150,000 earmarked for the forthcoming 1983 local elections.
1984	
October	'Grass Roots Campaign' launched at annual conference. Anthony Garner (Director of Organisation) introduces concept of constituency 'annual audit'.
1986	
November	Federation of Conservative Students disbanded against its will after bitter ideological battles within its structure caused embarrassment to the leadership, especially the call by one official that Lord Stockton (Harold Macmillan) should be tried as a war criminal for his role in the repatriation of the Cossacks. Replaced with Conservative Collegiate Forum.
July	Launch of a direct mailing campaign, initially using the British Telecom shareholders list, to seek new members and funds. Five per cent response rate secures £1.5m in donations.
1988	
May	Chairman Peter Brooke launches 'Campaign '88', the first nationally co-ordinated membership recruitment drive for more than a decade.
1989	
June	New party logo adopted upon initiative of Brendan Bruce (Director of Communications). Replaces the existing flame with a torch, to represent freedom.
October	Annual Conference overwhelmingly calls for affiliation of National Union of Conservative Associations of Northern Ireland.
1990	
March	Central Council cuts last formal links with Ulster Unionist Party.
1991	
February	Richard Ryder (Chief Whip) initiates a No. 12 Committee to co-ordinate government and party activity on a day-to-day basis.
1992	
	Sir Malcolm Chaplin forms a committee to recommend a solution to the failing 'quota' scheme.
February	The Fowler review leads to the publication of two reports *One Party* (on the professional organisation) and *Working Together* (on the National Union) and includes proposals for significant

	revision of areas; creation of Board of Management to comprise 15 people drawn from the National Union and parliamentary party, a minority of whom to be appointed by the leader.
March	Meeting of National Union Central Council at Harrogate rejects five points in the reports that infringe on local autonomy.
1993	
January	Norman Fowler (Party Chairman) and John Major (Leader) agree to implement cost-cutting exercise to improve party's poor financial position.
February	Four area offices closed and 61 jobs shed; new Board of Management created to bring together the elected, voluntary and professional wings of the party.
June	Seven members of the Conservative Collegiate Forum resign in protest at the party blocking a Eurosceptic from becoming its national director.
August	New Board of Treasurers appointed.
September	Party officially confirms it has an overdraft amounting to £18.6 million.
October	Norman Fowler launches a £250,000 fund to assist constituency associations with the cost of agents.
1994	
June	Central Office sheds a further 70 jobs.
1996	
January	Party formally ends its associations with Saatchi Cordiant (formerly Saatchi and Saatchi) and engages Maurice Saatchi and M & C Saatchi.
March	Party has a revenue deficit of £7.2m.
1997	
June	Review of Scottish Party organisation to be led by Lord Strathclyde.
1998	
February	William Hague launches *Fresh Start* programme that revised leadership rules and altered rules of National Union. Instead a national convention will meet twice a year. Central Office to be reformed. All foreign donations banned.
July	Board of Management gave approval to closure of regional offices and loss of 40 jobs.
1999	
June	Announced that Andrew Cooper (Director of Political Operations) is to leave in new year and duties to be redistributed among the Directors of Communications, Research and Campaigns.

October	Conference debates a motion calling for the Party Treasurer to be elected by the membership.
2000	
January	Only 20 out of 161 Conservative associations have hit their financial quota targets set by Central Office.
February	Shropshire Conservatives vote on a proposal to rationalise local party organisation by closing their five constituency offices and replacing them with one single campaign office.
June	Party membership stands at 309,000.
September	Renewing One Nation Unit established in Central Office with £200,000 annual budget and three full-time staff. Intended as a think-tank to draw up proposals for tackling poverty and encouraging family life.
2001	
January	Michael Ancram circulates a memorandum to Conservative Associations in Northern Ireland indicating the desire of Central Office that Conservative candidates should only contest seats where the party will not lose its deposit.
February	Internal audit puts party membership at 325,000, an improvement on figures from June 2000. This figure includes 28,500 members who have been recruited centrally.

3.2 PARLIAMENTARY PARTY

PROFILE OF CONSERVATIVE MEMBERS OF PARLIAMENT, 1885–1906

	1885	1886	1892	1895	1900	1906
Landed classes	45.8%	43.3%	46.2%	41.2%	38.5%	40.1%
Industry and commerce	31.1%	29.5%	28.1%	28.3%	32.0%	31.5%
Professional and public service	19.9%	23.2%	20.7%	23.2%	21.3%	19.6%
Others	2.9%	4.0%	4.7%	7.3%	8.6%	8.4%
Total	270	370	298	381	368	143

Source: J.P. Cornford, 'The parliamentary foundations of Hotel Cecil', in *Ideas and Institutions* (1967), ed. R. Robson, p. 310.

PROFILE OF CONSERVATIVE MEMBERS OF PARLIAMENT, 1945–97 NUMERICAL TOTAL (PERCENTAGE)

Profile	1945	1959	1970	1983	1997
Public school[1]	70 (36)	93 (35)	73 (22)	60 (15)	15 (9)
Oxbridge[2]	106 (50)	183 (50)	170 (52)	190 (52)	84 (51)
All-universities	124 (58)	218 (60)	208 (64)	282 (71)	133 (81)
Landowners	11 (5)	38 (10)	31 (10)	19 (5)	5 (3)
Professionals[3]	101 (48)	167 (46)	149 (45)	177 (45)	61 (37)
Business[4]	57 (27)	113 (30)	101 (30)	142 (36)	65 (39)
Miscellaneous[5]	6 (3)	46 (13)	47 (14)	55 (14)	33 (20)
Manual workers[6]	6 (3)	1 (1)	2 (1)	4 (1)	1 (1)
Grand total	213	365	330	397	165

Sourced from: *Nuffield General Election Studies* 1959, 1970, 1983, 1997; J. Ross, *Elections and Electors* (1955), pp. 417, 418, 424, 436.

Notes

1. Eton and Harrow.
2. Oxford and Cambridge Universities.
3. Defined as barrister, solicitor, doctor/dentist, architect/surveyor, civil/chartered engineer, civil servant/local government, teacher (university, adult, school), consultant, scientific research.
4. Defined as company director, company executive, commerce/insurance, management/clerical, general business.
5. Defined as miscellaneous white collar, political/political organiser, publisher/journalist, housewife, student, local administration.
6. Defined as miner, skilled worker, semi/unskilled worker.

Part 4

4.1 CONSERVATIVES AND THE REGIONS

1. CONSERVATIVE GENERAL ELECTION RESULTS BY REGION

Conservative regional general election results (numbers of seats)

Year	No. of seats won England	No. of seats won Wales	No. of seats won Scotland	No. of seats won Ireland	No. of seats won Universities	Total no. of seats won
1832	117	14	10	28	6	175
1835	200	17	15	35	6	273
1837	239	19	20	30	6	314
1841	277	21	22	41	6	367
1847[1]	239	20	20	40	6	325
1852	244	20	20	40	6	330
1857	185	17	14	42	6	264
1859	209	17	13	53	6	298
1865	213	14	11	45	6	289
1868	211	10	7	37	6	271
1874	280	14	18	31	7	350
1880	197	4	6	23	7	237
1885	213	4	8	16	8	249
1886[2]	332	8	27	17	9	393
1892	261	3	19	21	9	313
1895	343	9	31	19	9	411
1900	332	6	36	19	9	402
1906	122	0	10	15	9	156
Jan 1910	233	2	9	19	9	272
Dec 1910	233	3	9	17	9	271
1918[3]	315	4	30	23	10	382
1922	307	6	13	10	8	344
1923	221	4	14	10	9	258
1924	347	9	36	12	8	412
1929	221	1	20	10	8	260
1931	398	6	48	10	8	470
1935[4]	454	17	67	12	9	559
1945	167	4	27	8	4	210
1950[5]	253	4	31	10	—	298
1951	271	6	35	9	—	321
1955	293	6	36	10	—	345
1959	315	7	31	12	—	365
1964	262	6	24	12	—	304

Conservative regional general election results (cont'd)

Year	No. of seats won England	No. of seats won Wales	No. of seats won Scotland	No. of seats won Ireland	No. of seats won Universities	Total no. of seats won
1966	219	3	20	11	—	253
1970	292	7	23	8	—	330
Feb 1974[6]	268	8	21	—	—	297
Oct 1974	253	8	16	—	—	277
1979	306	11	22	—	—	339
1983	362	14	21	—	—	397
1987	358	8	10	—	—	376
1992	319	6	11	0	—	336
1997	165	0	0	0	—	165
2001	165	0	1	0	—	166

Source: F.W.S. Craig, *British Electoral Facts 1832–1987* (1989).
Notes
1. includes Peelites thereafter.
2. includes Liberal Unionists thereafter.
3. includes Coalition Conservatives and Conservatives.
4. includes Liberals National thereafter.
5. The Universities seats were abolished by the 1948 Representation of the People Act.
6. From 1972 Ulster Unionist MPs no longer took the Conservative whip.

Conservative general election regional vote (total percentage of the vote)

Year	% of vote won in England	% of vote won in Wales	% of vote won in Scotland	% of vote won in Ireland	% of vote won in Universities	% of vote won nationally
1832	29.9	53.4	21.0	32.1	76.2	29.4
1835	42.6	63.9	37.2	42.4	—[a]	42.6
1837	48.9	52.8	46.0	41.5	90.1	48.3
1841	53.1	53.2	38.3	40.1	—[a]	50.9
1847[1]	42.1	89.5	18.3	34.0	88.2	42.2
1852	40.5	54.7	27.4	46.3	100.0	41.4
1857	31.7	34.6	15.2	43.6	80.7	33.1
1859	32.9	63.6	33.6	38.9	—[a]	34.3
1865	41.0	26.0	14.6	44.4	76.5	39.8
1868	40.2	37.9	17.5	41.9	55.4	38.4
1874	46.2	39.1	31.6	40.8	—[a]	43.9
1880	43.7	41.2	29.9	39.8	49.2	42.0
1885	47.5	38.9	34.3	24.8	53.7	43.5
1886[2]	52.6	46.1	46.4	50.3	84.7	51.4
1892	51.1	37.2	44.4	20.6	80.9	47.0
1895	51.9	42.2	47.4	26.0	—[a]	49.1
1900	52.4	37.6	49.0	32.2	—[a]	50.3

Conservative general election regional vote (cont'd)

Year	% of vote won in England	% of vote won in Wales	% of vote won in Scotland	% of vote won in Ireland	% of vote won in Universities	% of vote won nationally
1906	44.3	33.8	38.2	47.0	60.6	43.4
Jan 1910	49.3	31.9	39.6	32.7	61.3	46.8
Dec 1910	48.8	33.8	42.6	28.6	58.1	46.6
1918[3]	42.6	11.3	32.8	28.4	54.4	38.4
1922	41.5	21.4	25.1	55.9	54.8	38.5
1923	39.8	21.1	31.6	58.1	58.1	38.0
1924	47.6	28.4	40.8	83.8	57.9	46.8
1929	38.8	22.0	35.9	68.0	55.4	38.1
1931	57.8	22.1	49.5	56.1	18.9	55.0
1935[4]	52.8	27.6	48.7	64.9	60.4	51.7
1945	40.2	23.8	41.1	53.7	25.5	39.6
1950[5]	43.8	27.4	44.8	62.7	—	43.5
1951	48.8	30.9	48.6	59.3	—	48.0
1955	50.4	29.9	50.1	68.5	—	49.7
1959	49.9	32.6	47.2	77.2	—	49.3
1964	44.1	29.4	40.6	63.0	—	43.4
1966	42.7	27.9	37.7	61.8	—	41.9
1970	48.3	27.7	38.0	54.2	—	46.4
Feb 1974[6]	40.2	25.9	32.9	—	—	37.9
Oct 1974	38.9	23.9	24.7	—	—	35.8
1979	47.2	32.2	31.4	—	—	43.9
1983	46.0	31.0	28.4	—	—	42.4
1987	46.2	29.5	24.0	—	—	42.3
1992	45.2	28.6	25.6	5.7	—	41.9
1997	33.7	19.6	17.5	1.2	—	30.7
2001	34.3	21.0	15.6	0.3	—	31.8

Notes

1. includes Peelites thereafter.
2. includes Liberal Unionists thereafter.
3. includes Coalition Conservatives and Conservatives.
4. includes Liberals National thereafter.
5. The Universities seats were abolished by the 1948 Representation of the People Act.
6. From 1972 Ulster Unionist MPs no longer took the Conservative whip.

a. no contests since Conservative and Liberal Unionist candidates unopposed.

2. DEVOLUTION ELECTIONS 6 MAY 1999

Scottish Parliament

Party	Total no. of seats	No. of candidates elected:		% of total vote	
		Direct	Top-up	Direct	Top-up
Conservative	18	—	18	15.6	15.5
Labour	56	53	3	38.8	34.0
SNP	35	7	28	28.7	27.6
Liberal Democrat	17	12	5	14.2	12.6
Others	3	1	2	2.1	10.3

Source: D. Butler and G. Butler, *20th Century British Political Facts 1900–2000* (Macmillan, 2000), p. 459; *http://www.election.demon.co.uk*
Turnout: direct 58.8%; top-up 57.2%.
Each elector had two votes. 73 members were chosen directly (i.e. first-past-the-post), from the existing Scottish Westminster constituencies; 56 were elected on top-up lists from the eight Scottish Euro-constituencies.

Welsh Assembly

Party	Total seats	Total no. of seats won		% total vote	
		Direct	Top-up	Direct	Top-up
Conservative	9	1	8	15.8	16.5
Labour	28	27	1	37.6	35.5
Liberal Democrat	6	3	3	13.5	12.5
Plaid Cymru	17	9	8	28.4	30.6
Others	—	—	—	4.7	4.9

Source: D. Butler and G. Butler, *20th Century British Political Facts 1900–2000* (Macmillan, 2000), p. 460; *http://www.election.demon.co.uk*
Turnout: direct 46.3%; top-up 46.1%.
Each elector had two votes. 40 members were chosen directly (i.e. first-past-the-post), from the existing Welsh Westminster constituencies; 20 were elected on top-up lists from the eight Welsh Euro-constituencies.

3. CHRONOLOGY

1867

October — Disraeli attends a Conservative demonstration in Edinburgh and assures a rally of Scottish Conservative working men that the Conservatives were the 'national party of England'!

1885

August — Salisbury creates Scottish Office and appoints a Scottish Secretary at cabinet rank.

1889

January — Conservatives fare badly in the first Welsh County Council elections.

1893

November — Middleton (Chief Party Agent) acknowledges weakness of party's organisation in Wales and warns that without improvement the party's fortunes in the Principality are 'doomed'.

1895

June — Scottish Standing Committee, only created by the Liberal Government the previous year, is disbanded by the incoming Conservative administration.

1914

May — Younger Scottish Home Rule memorandum circulated to all Scottish Conservative parliamentary candidates acknowledging existence of popular support for Home Rule.

1924

May — First gathering of Welsh Conservative National Women's Council. Claims a total of 17,000 subscribing members.

1930

Scottish Unionist, the party's newsheet, folds after declining circulation.

1932

Elements from Cathcart Conservative Association split to form the Scottish Party because they consider Westminster to be indifferent to Scotland. This becomes a moderate right-wing Home Rule movement.

1934

May — Outrage in Scotland when the president of the Scottish National Party (SNP), Duke of Montrose, drops the Conservative party whip in the House of Lords and takes the Liberal whip.

1935

Scottish Illustrated launched as the new party newsheet. Its content is less overtly partisan.

1937

Decision to reform the government of Scotland is announced. It will relocate to Edinburgh.

1939

Completion of St Andrew's House for the relocation of the Scottish Office.

1951

October — Churchill's new administration appoints a Minister for Welsh Affairs.

1953	
	Balfour report into Scottish government concludes that the Scottish Office should control Scottish affairs.
1955	
May	General election sees over 50 per cent of the vote in Scotland won by the Conservatives.
1965	
	'Conservative' replaces 'Unionist' in the Scottish party's title.
1967	
June	Heath creates Scottish Policy Group to explore possibilities and options for devolved government in Scotland.
1968	
May	Heath's 'Declaration of Perth' when he pledges the party to supporting a Scottish Assembly.
July	Constitutional Committee created with a membership of senior Conservatives, former Scottish ministers and academics. When they report in early 1970 the recommendation is for a directly elected Assembly.
1972	
	Local Government Act for England and Wales.
1973	
February	Government defeat in Commons on Local Government bill for Scotland when five Conservatives vote for an amendment which leads to the survival of Fife as a region.
October	Kilbrandon Royal Commission recommends a Scottish Assembly.
1974	
October	Heath pledges that if re-elected the Conservatives will increase the powers of the Secretary of State for Wales and create a new Select Committee for Welsh MPs.
1976	
September	Heath calls for referendum on whether Scotland wished to remain part of the UK.
December	Shadow Cabinet decide to oppose Labour's devolution bill. Alick Buchanan-Smith (shadow Scottish Secretary) and Malcolm Rifkind (spokesman on Scottish Affairs) resign. At the bill's second reading 27 Conservatives abstain and 5, including Heath, Rifkind and Buchanan-Smith, vote with Labour in defiance of the three-line whip.
1977	
February	Labour government defeated on a guillotine motion on Devolution bills for Scotland and Wales.

1978

January — Labour government suffers serious defeat in the Commons on Scottish devolution bill. Amendments carried requiring minimum 'Yes' vote of 40 per cent of the whole electorate.

March — One third of parliamentary party ignore Thatcher's hostility and vote in favour of proportional representation in the Welsh Assembly.

1979

March — Voters reject Labour's Scottish and Welsh devolution plans.

1985

May — Party fares badly in Scotland's local elections experiencing a backlash against the general rates re-evaluation.

1986

May — Scottish Conservative conference reveals discontent over rates re-evaluation.

1989

April — Poll tax is introduced in Scotland, a year ahead of England and Wales.

May — Rifkind announces reform of business rate in Scotland

1990

January — Enterprise and New Towns (Scotland) bill given second reading. Rifkind condemns plans for a devolved Scottish assembly.

June — Letterbomb sent to Conservative MP, Nicholas Bennet (Pembroke), is defused.

December — Vice-chairman of Scottish Conservatives claims party is considering options for constitutional reform.

1991

May — Conservatives lose Monmouth by-election.

August — Firebomb defused outside the Bangor Conservative Association offices.

September — John Major expresses opposition to devolution in *Western Mail* interview.

October — David Hunt (Welsh Secretary) calls for an EC regional assembly rather than a Welsh assembly.

November — Defeated in Kincardine and Deeside by-election by the Liberal Democrats.

December — The Scottish Conservative party disbands Argyll and Bute Conservative Association.

1992

February — Major calls for a wider discussion on Welsh devolution.

June — Major rejects devolution in Prestwich speech.

1993	
	More devolved administration promised to Scottish Office by Major.
1994	
January	Welsh Secretary, John Redwood, orders Welsh Development Agency to promote Wales as an integral part of United Kingdom and drop the 'Wales in Europe' slogan.
May	Conservatives fare badly in Scottish regional council elections.
November	Scottish Local Government bill becomes law.
December	John Major attacks Scottish Home Rule as 'teenage madness'.
1995	
February	Major warns about 'sleepwalking into devolution' and fears it to be a 'Trojan horse' for independence.
May	Poor Conservative results in Scottish local elections. Only 81 Conservative councillors elected. Lose Kinross and West Perth by-election to SNP – its first ever by-election gain from Conservatives.
September	Major attacks devolution as 'loopy' and proportional representation as alien.
1997	
February	Scottish Conservatives discuss whether to change name of party to Scottish Unionist Party. Stephen Dorrell, government constitutional spokesman, is sacked after suggesting that if a Scottish parliament was ever created by Labour a future Conservative government would abolish it. This contradicts views of the Scottish Secretary, Michael Forsyth.
May	Scotland fails to return a single Conservative MP in the general election. As a consequence no Conservative shadow Scottish spokesman is appointed. Party in Scotland begins an internal audit of its failure.
June	Scottish Conservatives reject devolution and in House of Lords Conservative peers vow to resist the measure.
October	Conservatives agree to support Scottish parliament. Party's financial crisis obliges closure of two of its three Scottish offices.
1999	
March	Hague launches Conservative campaigns for the devolution elections pledging to draw a line under the past and to fight to make the new parliament and assembly work.
April	David McLetchie (leader Scottish Conservatives) launches his party's Scottish election manifesto with an apology for the actions of the Major government.

May	Conservatives regain some lost ground in elections for new Scottish parliament.
August	Nick Bourne is chosen as a replacement leader for the Conservatives in the Welsh Assembly after the resignation of Rob Richards.
2000	
May	Sir Malcolm Rifkind (Scottish Conservatives President) is appointed Scottish spokesman with rights to attend the shadow cabinet. Charged with masterminding the Scottish Conservatives' general election campaign; Scottish Conservatives criticise plans by the Scottish Executive to repeal Section 28.
June	Tasmina Ahmed-Sheikh, a Conservative MSP candidate in 1999, defects to the SNP.
2001	
June	One Conservative MP returned in Scotland, but none in Wales.

4.2 CONSERVATIVES AND IRELAND

CHRONOLOGY

1843

July	Irish Arms bill opposed by 'Young England' quartet.

1844

November–December Cabinet discusses Peel's proposals for Maynooth grant.

1845

January	Peel admits to Gladstone that his proposals for Ireland risk fatally wounding the government.
February–May	Government propose to increase the subsidy to the Catholic Seminary at Maynooth. Measure only carried with the support of the Liberals with nearly 150 Conservatives voting against both first and second readings.

1847

March	Bentinck's Irish railway building bill is opposed by 100 of his own protectionist supporters.

1852

May	Walpole agrees to establish a committee of inquiry into the operation of the Maynooth grant to appease Irish supporters.
December	Disraeli fails to secure Derby's support for Irish land reforms and consequently fails to win Irish Radical support for the minority administration on the eve of the budget vote.

1854

May	Disraeli plays 'Protestant card' during annual debate on Maynooth grant.

1873

March	Gladstone resigns after unexpected defeat for his Irish University Scheme after an alliance between Conservatives and Catholics.

1881

May	200 peers meet at Salisbury's Arlington Street home and pledge 'no surrender' on Gladstone's Land bill.
August	Party's front benches meet at Northcote's house and resolve to abandon resistance to Land bill.

1882

May	Lord Frederick Cavendish, Chief Secretary for Ireland, and T.H. Burke, the Under-Secretary, are murdered in Phoenix Park, Dublin by the 'Invincibles'. New Crimes bill introduced.

1884

May	137 Conservatives support amendment to Reform bill regarding Irish Westminster representation.

1885

August	Carnarvon–Parnell interview to discuss possibility of Irish Home Rule.
November	Parnell and O'Connor urge Irish voters in Britain to vote against Liberals. Contemporaries debated whether it gained the Conservatives an extra 20 seats.
December	Gladstone's commitment to Irish Home Rule becomes public, the so-called 'Hawarden Kite'. It enables the Conservatives to shed their Irish 'allies' and gives them a cause around which to re-unite.

1886

April	Salisbury convenes a meeting of ex-cabinet members to consider tactics for Gladstone's impending Home Rule bill.
May	Salisbury delivers his 'Hottentots' speech to conference deriding the fitness of the Irish for home rule. Deliberately seeks to polarise the debate in order to force the hands of the disaffected Liberals following Lord Hartington's leadership. Randolph Churchill inflames the debate by playing the 'orange card' and declaring 'Ulster will fight and Ulster will be right'.
June	Parnell reveals his version of his discussion with Carnarvon during the furore over Gladstone's Home Rule bill. Causes maximum embarrassment for the Conservatives. However, combination of 250 Conservatives and 93 Liberal Unionists defeat the bill.
August	Salisbury tells Lord Mayor's Banquet that Ireland remains 'the skeleton in our cupboard'.
March	Introduction of Balfour's Irish Crimes bill provokes four Liberal Unionists to return to Gladstone's fold.

1890

November	Opening of new parliamentary session overshadowed by O'Shea divorce case and the discrediting of Parnell.

1891

	Balfour (Chief Secretary in Ireland) encourages tenant land purchases with an assistance budget of £30 million.

1895

October	Balfour (Chief Secretary in Ireland) declares Unionist intent to 'by kindness to kill home rule'.

1903

	'Wyndham's Act' seeks to promote universal sale of estates to tenants. £100 million set aside to assist tenant purchasers.

1905	
July	Government defeated on Estimates for Irish Land Commission, 199–196 votes.
1912	
July	Bonar Law declares the cause of Irish Unionists to be 'the cause of the Empire'. At Blenheim rally supports plans for Ulster resistance.
November	Conservatives inflict defeat on Government amendment to financial resolution of the Government of Ireland bill.
1913	
	Home Rule bill defeated in the House of Lords, but awaits automatic implementation under provisions of the 1911 Parliament Act.
1914	
July	Buckingham Palace conference fails to reach agreement on Ulster's exclusion from Home Rule.
1920	
December	Government of Ireland Act passed partitioning 'Northern Ireland', the 6 northern counties, from 'Southern Ireland', comprising the remaining 26 counties.
1921	
November	Annual conference endorses the Irish settlement only after leadership make, in effect, the vote one of confidence.
1922	
June	IRA assassinates Ulster Unionist MP, Field Marshal Sir Henry Wilson, who is a critic of Lloyd George's Irish policy. Provokes outrage from diehard Conservatives. Bonar Law receives an ovation from Conservative MPs when he expresses his dissatisfaction with the government's Irish policy.
December	Irish Free State comes into existence.
1925	
December	Border Commission confirms the status quo over the Northern Ireland and Irish Free State boundary.
1938	
January	De Valera visits Chamberlain in London for an Anglo-Irish conference that leads to agreements in April on tariffs and ports.
May	Parliament ratifies the Anglo-Irish agreement.
1949	
April	Ireland declares itself a republic and leaves the Commonwealth.
1953	
October	Churchill's leader's speech to the party conference gives strong support to the Northern Irish Unionists.

1956

Beginning of renewed IRA campaign against Ulster.

1959

December — Rab Butler (Home Secretary) attacks the Irish government for failing to stop terrorists after he visits the site of an RUC officer's murder in Rosslea.

1962

Campaign against Ulster called off by IRA.

1970

January — Provisional IRA and the Provisional Sinn Fein formed.

July — IRA bombing campaign begins in Northern Ireland.

1971

February — First British soldier killed in Belfast.

August — Internment without trial introduced in Northern Ireland.

1972

January — 13 people killed in Londonderry 'Bloody Sunday'.

March — Direct rule re-imposed on Northern Ireland as Stormont Assembly dissolved.

1973

March — Ulster referendum: overwhelming majority in favour of retaining links with Britain. White Paper proposes a Northern Ireland Assembly, elected by proportional representation.

September — Heath visits Dublin to meet Irish PM, Liam Cosgrave. This is the first occasion a serving British PM had visited Eire.

December — Sunningdale Agreement establishing a Council of Ireland.

1974

January — Direct rule ended and the beginning of power-sharing experiment. This fails and direct rule re-imposed in May.

1979

March — Airey Neave assassinated at the House of Commons by Irish National Liberation Army.

August — IRA bombing at Warren Point. Lord Mountbatten assassinated in Irish republic.

1980

May — Summit meeting between Irish premier, Charles Haughey, and Mrs Thatcher. A joint communiqué affirms wish of Irish government to secure unity of Ireland but only 'with the consent of a majority of the people in Northern Ireland'.

December — Further summit meeting agrees to initiate joint studies on new institutional structures, citizenship rights, security, and economic and cultural co-operation.

1981

May — Bobby Sands, Sein Fein MP, dies after hunger strike in Maze prison. By October ten IRA prisoners have died in this protest.

November — Summit between Thatcher and FitzGerald, new Irish Premier, leads to establishment of Anglo-Irish Intergovernmental Council to hold regular meetings at ministerial and official levels to discuss matters of common concern.

1982

James Prior (Secretary of State for Northern Ireland) introduces a bill for a Northern Ireland Assembly to resume legislative and executive powers by a process of gradual devolution. Nationalists and Republicans boycott the Assembly.

1983

September — Mass outbreak of IRA prisoners from top security Maze prison.

December — IRA bomb Harrods killing six.

1984

October — IRA bomb destroys the Grand Hotel, Brighton narrowly missing Margaret Thatcher and members of Cabinet but claiming 5 lives and injuring 31.

November — Thatcher and FitzGerald meet for second summit of the Anglo-Irish Intergovernmental Council.

1985

November — Anglo-Irish Agreement signed, by Thatcher and FitzGerald, at Hillsborough. Denounced by Unionists as a sell-out.

1986

February — Ulster Unionist leaders meet Thatcher, but fail to end her support for Anglo-Irish Agreement.

June — Dissolution of Northern Ireland Assembly announced.

1987

November — IRA bomb attack on Enniskillen Remembrance Day parade.

1988

March — Three IRA members shot dead by SAS in Gibraltar. There are accusations of a 'shoot to kill' policy. The government fails, the following month, to stop *Death on the Rock*, a TV documentary on the incident.

October — Douglas Hurd places media ban on broadcasting the voice of republican politicians.

1990

July — Ian Gow, Thatcher's former PPS, assassinated by car bomb.

1991

February — IRA launches a mortar attack on Downing Street.

1992	
June	Inter-governmental Conference meets in London and announces suspension of meeting to allow talks to take place between representatives from Northern Ireland and Irish government.
November	Patrick Mayhew (Northern Ireland Secretary) announces to the Commons that the constitutional talks have been suspended without agreement.
1993	
July	Ulster Unionists save the government from defeat on the Maastricht bill leading to allegations of a 'deal' with John Major.
December	John Major and Albert Reynolds, Irish Taoiseach, give momentum to Northern Irish peace process with their Anglo-Irish Downing Street declaration.
1994	
August	IRA announces first ceasefire.
September	Broadcasting ban on Sinn Fein lifted.
October	Loyalist ceasefire in Northern Ireland.
1995	
February	Northern Irish peace process sees the launch of the Framework document.
November	All-party peace talks breakthrough in Northern Ireland.
1996	
January	U.S. Senator Mitchell's report on the future of Northern Ireland and his proposals for an election are published.
February	IRA's Canary Wharf bomb ends 'first' ceasefire.
May	Northern Ireland assembly elections lead to Unionist majority but with significant Sinn Fein representation.
June	All-party talks begin in Northern Ireland; first ever state visit to UK by an Irish President, Mary Robinson.
1998	
November	Thatcher claims in a review of an Enoch Powell biography that she now has second thoughts about having signed up to the 1985 Anglo-Irish Agreement.
December	Andrew McKay (shadow Northern Ireland secretary) calls for a halt to the early release of terrorist prisoners until the IRA begins decommissioning its weapons arsenal.
1999	
June	Hague questions whether the Northern Ireland ceasefire exists, but reaffirms support for the Good Friday agreement.

October	Lord Tebbit condemns the Patten Report on the future of the Royal Ulster Constabulary (RUC). Nearly 30 Conservative MPs sign a letter to the *Daily Telegraph* warning of the dangers from reforming the RUC without terrorist decommissioning.
November	Conservatives suggest that the preservation of the RUC title will be a manifesto commitment.
2000	
November	A wrecking amendment proposed by Conservative peers succeeds in defeating government plans to allow members of the Irish parliament to stand for elections to the Commons and Northern Ireland Assembly.

4.3 CONSERVATIVES AND EMPIRE

CHRONOLOGY

1843	
January	Conquest of Sind by General Charles Napier.
April–May	Gambia and Natal become colonies.
May	70 Conservative MPs rebels against the bill to lower duty on Canadian corn.
December	Basutoland created British protectorate.
1855	
May	Disraeli moves a motion of censure on Palmerston government's conduct of Crimean war.
1857	
March	202 Conservatives combine with a number of Liberals and Peelites to defeat Palmerston over bombardment of Canton. 39 Conservatives side with Palmerston.
1858	
May	Derby's second administration nearly forced out of office after the publication of a dispatch disapproving of the Indian Governor-General Lord Canning.
1867	
July	British North America Act unites New Brunswick, Nova Scotia, Ontario and Quebec in the Dominion of Canada.
1868	
January–April	Napier expedition to Abyssinia successfully releases British captives and provides a fillip for the Conservative administration.
1872	
April	Disraeli, in Manchester speech, links the party's traditional values of monarchy and empire with social reform.
June	At Crystal Palace, Disraeli claims that the Conservatives are the party of empire.
1874	
March	Ashanti war ended.
1875	
December	Disraeli's government purchases shares in the Suez Canal Company owned by the Khedive of Egypt.
1876	
January	Proclamation of Queen Victoria as Empress of India. Formalised by Royal Titles Act in April.

September	Salisbury (Secretary for India) refers to 'the new British province of Egypt'.
October	Britain and France establish dual control of Egyptian finances.
1877	
April	Transvaal annexed. Carnarvon persuaded Disraeli that this is necessary because the Afrikaners are bankrupt and the Zulus present a military threat.
1878	
March	Derby resigns as Foreign Secretary in opposition to secret plans to occupy Cyprus.
June	Under Cyprus Convention, administration of the island passes to British.
July	Disraeli and Salisbury return from Berlin Congress claiming 'peace with honour'.
October	British forces led by Lytton undertake Afghan expedition enabling Disraeli to assert the following month at Guildhall that Britain's vocation is empire.
December	Ultimatum sent to King Cetewayo of the Zulus.
1879	
January	Beginning of Zulu War in South Africa. British defeated at Isandlwana. Disraeli refuses to recall Sir Bartle Frere (High Commissioner in South Africa) who encouraged the campaign.
July	Defeat of Zulus at Ulundi brings war to an end.
September	Reassertion of Anglo-French control of Egyptian finances. British Afghan mission slaughtered.
October	British troops led by General Roberts enter Kabul.
November	Gladstone's Midlothian campaign denounces the Conservative Party for being 'drunk with imperialism'.
1885	
February	Northcote and Salisbury move motions of censure against Gladstone government over fall of Khartoum.
1887	
April	First Colonial Conference held in London.
1888	
March	Protectorates established over Sarawak, Borneo and Brunei.
October	Cecil Rhodes acquires concession of all mining rights in Matabeleland.
1889	
May	Naval Defence Act based upon concept of 'Two-Power Standard'.
1891	
January	Jameson appointed administrator of South Africa Company.

1894	
November	Joseph Chamberlain memorandum on imperial and social policy.
1895	
December	Border dispute between British Guiana and Venezuela causes crisis in Anglo-American relations. Jameson raid launched in South Africa.
1896	
January	Joseph Chamberlain (Colonial Secretary) repudiates Jameson raid.
September	General Kitchener advances into Sudan.
1897	
May	Milner arrives in Cape Town as High Commissioner.
July	Committee of House of Commons reports on Jameson raid. Chamberlain and Colonial Office absolved of blame, but Rhodes is censured.
1898	
April	British leased Wei-hai-wei naval base in China. This is followed in June by leasing of New Territories near Hong Kong.
June	Anglo-French Convention settled colonial boundaries in West Africa.
September	Capture of Khartoum. 'Fashoda Crisis': confrontation of French and British forces at Fashoda.
1899	
March	Anglo-French Convention resolves spheres of influence dispute concerning Congo and Nile basins.
October	Outbreak of Boer War.
1900	
January	General Roberts arrives in South Africa to replace Buller after succession of British defeats the previous month.
May	Relief of Mafeking.
June	British troops despatched to Peking to quell Boxer rebellion.
October	Conservatives fight 'Khaki' general election.
1902	
May	End of Boer War.
November	Balfour Cabinet decides to include imperial preference on corn duties in next budget.
December	Joseph Chamberlain begins a ministerial tour of South Africa.
1903	
February	Britain agrees to arbitration at The Hague over Venezuela dispute.

May	Joseph Chamberlain announces his support for imperial preference.
1904	
April	'Entente Cordiale' between Britain and France leads to resolution of disputes over Morocco, Siam, Egypt and Newfoundland.
October	Balfour pledges not to introduce imperial preference until after a second general election.
1920	
July	Amritsar debate. Parliamentary party divided with 122 to 93 Conservative MPs voting against government.
1922	
October	Griffith Boscawen (Agricultural Minister) resigns over importation of Canadian cattle.
1929	
November	Baldwin commits Conservatives to the Irwin declaration on India and its policy of bi-partisanship.
1930	
December	Churchill makes public his opposition to Baldwin's India policy. Resigns the following month from the shadow cabinet.
1931	
December	Churchill's amendment critical of the Government's India policy secures the support of 44 Conservative backbenchers.
1932	
August	Baldwin leads the British delegation to the Imperial Conference at Ottawa.
1933	
February	National Union Central Council gives narrow approval for Indian policy.
June	Special meeting of Central Council accepts Baldwin's Indian policy.
October	Conference accepts amendment approving Indian policy by 737 to 344 votes.
1934	
October	Conference narrowly supports Government's India policy. Result was 543 votes to 520 with nearly 700 abstentions.
December	Special meeting of Central Council approves Baldwin's India policy by 712 majority.
1935	
February	India bill given second reading despite rebellion of 80 Conservative MPs.
1935	
August	Government of India bill finally passed.

1936	
June	National Union Central Council reject the idea of returning ex-German colonies.
October	Conference rejects calls from leadership and adopts a motion flatly rejecting the return of former German colonies to Hitler.
1948	
October	Addressing party conference Churchill speaks of three circles: the Commonwealth, Europe and the English-speaking nations (America). Argues Britain is the common denominator linking the three circles and this provides Britain with an opportunity to forge a new role for herself.
1949	
October	Beaverbrook and *Daily Express* launch policy of Empire Free Trade.
1952	
January	Commonwealth finance ministers' conference in London to co-ordinate policy of the sterling area.
October	Mau Mau revolt in Kenya.
1953	
October	Conference carries a motion urging renegotiation of GATT to enable imperial preference.
December	Government suspends negotiations with Egypt over Suez Canal Zone after pressure from Conservative backbenchers.
1954	
	Colyton (Minister for Colonies) declares Cyprus could 'never' expect full independence.
July	'Suez Group' of Conservative backbenchers threatens to vote against government in the event of a withdrawal from the Suez Canal Zone.
October	Final agreement on Britain's withdrawal from Suez Canal Zone.
1956	
October	Anglo-French forces launch attack on Suez Canal Zone, following Nasser's nationalisation of canal in July. Operations suspended after one week because of international, especially American, pressure.
December	Anglo-French forces formally withdraw from Suez Zone; Government survives a vote of confidence.
1957	
March	The Cypriot, Archbishop Makarios, is released.
May	Macmillan allows British ships again to use Suez Canal. 14 Conservative MPs abstain when Labour move a motion of censure.
July	Federation of Malaya Independence Act is given royal assent.

1958	
January	Macmillan begins a Commonwealth tour.
June	British plan for Cyprus rejected by Greek government.
1960	
February	Macmillan delivers his 'winds of change' decolonisation speech to South African Parliament.
1961	
February	Robin Turton's early day motion (EDM) critical of the Macmillan government's plans for a major increase in African representation in the Northern Rhodesian legislature secures 101 Conservative signatures.
September	Monday Club holds its inaugural meeting and discusses 'The situation in Africa'. The club's objective is to discredit the Government's African policy.
November	Commonwealth Immigrants bill introduced, ending principle of free entry to Britain of Commonwealth citizens.
October	Conservative Political Centre Conference in Rhyl debate a motion calling upon the Government to compensate settler farmers in Kenya.
December	Conservative rebels table a motion urging the Government to cease contributions to the United Nations' peacekeeping force in the event of the failure to achieve a ceasefire in Katanga.
1962	
March	30 Conservatives support an EDM calling for protection of Commonwealth interests as a precondition of EEC membership.
July	EDM calls for 'definite assurances for Commonwealth trade' in EEC negotiations.
October	Conference calls for imperial preference.
December	47 Conservative MPs sign an EDM urging government to fight for Commonwealth concessions over negotiations to join EEC. Conservative peers use a debate on Central African Federation to attack the Government's negotiations with the Federal Government.
1963	
May	Rumours abound at Westminster that Macleod (Party Chairman) and Boyle (Education Minister) will resign if Southern Rhodesia is granted independence under white minority rule.
1965	
October	Lord Salisbury and Patrick Wall move an amendment at Party Conference deploring likelihood of Rhodesian sanctions.
December	50 Conservatives defy leadership policy of abstention and vote against sanctions against Rhodesia.

1968

June — Conservative peers defy Heath and succeed in defeating the Mandatory Sanctions Order against Rhodesia that was due for renewal.

1978

November — 116 Conservative backbenchers defy leadership and vote for an end to sanctions against Rhodesia.

1979

September — Lancaster House conference on Rhodesia convenes. Agreement reached in December.

1982

April — Argentina invades the Falklands Islands and South Georgia. Thatcher dispatches a naval task force to recapture the islands.

June — Port Stanley, the Falklands' capital, is surrendered to British forces.

1984

December — Britain and China agree the return of Hong Kong to China in 1997.

1985

October — Thatcher resists demands at Commonwealth conference for imposition of sanctions against South Africa's apartheid policies.

1986

July — Geoffrey Howe (Foreign Secretary) travels to South Africa to explore possibilities of reform.

August — Thatcher still resisting demands to impose economic sanctions against South Africa.

1992

April — Chris Patten, former Conservative Party Chairman, appointed Britain's last Governor of Hong Kong.

1994

September — John Major speaking in Leiden refers to the importance of Britain's relationship with her Commonwealth in making Britain a power of importance.

1997

July — Hong Kong is returned to China.

2001

March — On Commonwealth Day, the Conservatives attack the behaviour of the Mugabe regime in Zimbabwe.

4.4 CONSERVATIVES AND EUROPE

1. DIRECT EUROPEAN ELECTIONS SINCE 1979

	Total no. of Conservative candidates	No. of Conservative MEPs elected	Total vote	% Share of total vote
June 1979	78	60	6,504,481	50.6
June 1984	78	45	5,426,866	40.8
June 1989	78	32	5,331,098	34.7
June 1994	84	18	4,248,531	27.8
June 1999*	84	36	3,578,217	35.8

Compiled from: T.T. Mackie (ed.), *Europe Votes* 1979, 1984, 1989 and 1994
* From 1979 to 1994 British MEPs were elected from single-member constituencies. The European Parliamentary Elections Act 1999 introduced a system of regional list proportional representation, with nine English regions returning between four and eleven members each, Scotland eight and Wales five.

2. CONSERVATIVE PARTY REFERENDUM ON THE EUROPEAN CURRENCY, 1998

William Hague in September 1998 announced his intention to poll paid-up party members on his policy of ruling out joining the European single currency until at least the end of the next Parliament. The following result was released 5 October 1998:

	Total number of votes	Percentage share of vote
Yes	170,558	84.4
No	31,492	15.9
Total of returned forms	202,674	

Source: Statistics taken from *Daily Telegraph*, 6 October 1998.
Total number of ballot forms sent: 344,157 (although the Post Office failed to deliver 8,000)
Total number of ballot forms returned: 202,674 (58.9%)

3. CHRONOLOGY

1945

November — Duncan Sandys talks in Brussels of a 'United States of Europe', but vague as to meaning.

1946

September — Churchill makes speech in Zurich advocating European Union.

1947

January — 39 Conservative MPs support the establishment of a European federation within the framework of the United Nations Organisation.

April — United Europe Movement created with Duncan Sandys as chairman. Inaugural meeting held at Royal Albert Hall and addressed by Winston Churchill.

1948

March — 60 Conservative MPs sign a pro-federalism early day motion on Western Union that was tabled by Boothby. Unusually the Commons debates the motion in May.

May — Churchill, and other British MPs, attend Congress in The Hague that calls for the creation of a European Parliament.

July — Herbert Willams (MP for Exeter and chairman of National Union) denounces Churchill's pro-European policy, likening it to a Colorado beetle undermining British trade. The party chairman reprimands him.

1949

February — 61 Conservatives support an early day motion calling for political union and a trading area.

October — For the first time at Conference Europe becomes a specific issue. Sandys tables a motion, but instructed to tone down its pro-Europeanism by the chairman of the 1922 Committee.

1950

July — After the Labour government's rejection of the Schumann Plan Harold Macmillan and David Eccles publish their plans for a non-supranational coal–steel institution.

1951

November — Anthony Eden declares Britain could never join a European army. This statement would be criticised in retrospect by pro-European Conservatives such as Boothby, Macmillan and Kilmuir.

1952

January — Anthony Eden speaking at Columbia University indicates that Britain could never join a federal Europe.

March	'Eden Plan' launched seeking to improve links between European 'Six' and other European nations.
May	The European Defence Community (EDC) created. Eden signs, on behalf of Britain, a 50-year mutual security treaty with the new organisation.
1955	
June	Conservative cabinet agrees to send a junior representative to the Spaak Committee. This represents a policy change with Britain abandoning the principle of non-involvement in discussions with the Six.
1956	
July	Macmillan and Thorneycroft advocate 'Plan G'. Proposes a free trade area involving the non-Six countries of Europe and the Six.
November	Macmillan makes public plans for a free trade area but significantly places emphasis on the 'three circles', with American and the Commonwealth as important as Europe.
1957	
January	Selwyn Lloyd launches his 'Grand Design'. It aims to tie together with institutional links the EEC, WEU and the Council of Europe. The Six perceive it as another British attempt to disrupt the EEC.
March	Treaty of Rome signed creating the European Economic Community (EEC). Britain is not involved.
1958	
November	France formerly rejects British proposals for a European Free Trade Area.
1959	
November	Agreement reached between non-EEC countries to form European Free Trade Area (EFTA). Ratified by House of Commons the following month, with the Labour party abstaining.
1961	
July	Britain announces her intention to join the EEC. Edward Heath dispatched to undertake the entry negotiations.
August	Government easily win vote agreeing to formal application to join EEC: 313 to 5. Labour abstained, as did 25 Conservatives. The five opponents were 4 Independent Labour MPs and Conservative Anthony Fell. Anti-Common Market League is founded.
October	Party conference debates a pro-negotiation motion. Of the 42 motions on EEC received only 5 were in favour, 4 were directly opposed and the remainder expressed a variety of anxieties and concerns.

1962

March — 30 Conservatives support an EDM calling for protection of Commonwealth interests as a precondition for EEC membership.

July — Internal Conservative opposition to EEC entry is signalled when 49 backbenchers sign a motion critical of Britain's application.

October — Llandudno conference receives only 31 motions on EEC. 3 are opposed, 19 support government policy and the remainder display varying shades of anxiety.

December — 47 Conservative MPs sign an EDM urging government to fight for Commonwealth concessions even at the risk of breaking off EEC talks.

1963

January — De Gaulle (French President) vetoes Britain's application for EEC membership.

1966

October — Conference vote on a British application for EEC membership is won 1,452 to 475 votes.

1967

May — Although the Conservative front bench supports a Labour government motion approving Britain's second EEC entry application, 26 Conservatives rebel.

1969

October — Enoch Powell critical of attempts to join EEC because of threat to parliamentary sovereignty.

1970

June — Negotiations begin over Britain's entry to EEC 12 days after election victory.

October — Rippon's party conference speech argues that EEC membership would strengthen Britain's world position and allow greater aid to the Commonwealth.

1971

June — EEC negotiations concluded.

July — Heath rejects the need for a referendum on EEC entry. He tells the National Union's Central Council that the Commons will decide, but not with a free vote.

October — Annual conference accepts the government's terms for EEC entry with a substantial majority, 2,474 to 324.

The Commons approves the terms of Britain's EEC membership by 356 to 244. The rebellion of 39 Conservative MPs is more than counteracted by the connivance of the Labour pro-Europe rebels with the government's whips.

1972

February — Rebellion by 15 Conservative MPs fails to prevent second reading of bill for entry into EEC being carried 309 to 301.

July — 16 Conservative MPs vote against and 4 others abstain as a Commons vote carries the final reading of the EEC entry bill. The passage of the bill has taken 300 hours of parliamentary debate time.

1973

January — Britain joins the EEC.

1975

January — Labour government announce the holding of a referendum in June to confirm British membership of the EEC. Majority of Conservative frontbenchers support the 'Britain in Europe' campaign. A number of backbenchers are involved in the 'No' campaign, the 'National Referendum Campaign'.

February — Margaret Thatcher elected Conservative leader with the support of all the party's Eurosceptic MPs. She maintains a low profile during referendum campaign, considering it to be 'Ted's issue'.

April — Labour government survives a vote on the EEC largely due to Conservative and Liberal support.

June — Referendum gives two to one majority for remaining in EEC.

1977

December — Labour government's proposal for proportional representation for European Parliament elections rejected on a free vote. 61 Conservatives voted in favour but 198 were opposed.

1979

November — Attending Dublin EC Council Thatcher attacks the size of Britain's EC budget contribution.

1980

May — Deal struck over reducing British contribution to EC budget.

1983

June — Thatcher urges upon EC the need for a long-term solution to Britain's excessive budgetary contribution.

1984

June — Revision of Britain's contribution to EC budget agreed at Fontainebleau.

1985

December — Luxembourg summit agrees Common European Act.

1986

February — Single European Act signed by Thatcher, which increased the centralised authority of the Community's institutions.

1987

July — Single European Act comes into force.

1988

July — Leon Brittan sent to Brussels as EU Commissioner.

September — Thatcher proclaims her Eurosceptic vision for the European future in a speech in Bruges.

1989

May — Edward Heath alleges that Central Office are seeking to discredit him and prevent him speaking in the European election campaign.

June — The poor result in the European elections leads to criticisms of the campaign's tone; Britain agrees to enter the Exchange Rate Mechanism (ERM) at Madrid summit. Conservative MEPs begin attempts to join Christian Democrat group in the European Parliament.

1990

July — Nicholas Ridley tells a journalist that the ERM was a German attempt to take over the whole of Europe. He is obliged to resign.

October — John Major (Chancellor) oversees Britain's joining the ERM. Rome Summit of EU agrees timetable for monetary union in spite of Thatcher's clear opposition.

November — Geoffrey Howe (Foreign Secretary) quits the cabinet and then uses his resignation speech to criticise Thatcher's European policy. This precipitates a leadership challenge.

1991

March — Speaking in Bonn, Major wishes Britain at 'the heart of Europe'.

June — Leaked Bruges Group memorandum attacks drift of government's European policy; Thatcher makes a speech critical of European Union in Chicago.

October — Selsdon Group manifesto includes a call for the virtual withdrawal of Britain from EU – obliges several ministers to resign from group.

December — Britain signs the Maastricht treaty but secures an 'opt-out' from the social chapter.

1992

May — 22 'Eurosceptic' Conservative MPs vote against Maastricht treaty bill.

June — The Danes 'No' vote to the Maastricht bill gives fresh encouragement to Eurosceptics. 82 MPs sign an early day motion calling for a 'fresh start' on Europe.

August	Lamont affirms Government's intention to remain in the ERM without devaluation.
September	With sterling under threat from currency speculators Major's government seeks to defend the pound with £10bn. However, the momentum proves unstoppable, and after a desperate last-ditch bid to control the money markets with a huge rise in interest rates, the Chancellor is obliged to withdraw Britain from the ERM. Nicknamed 'Black Wednesday'.
October	Norman Tebbit makes a vigorous Eurosceptic speech to the Annual Conference.
November	The Maastricht paving motion passes the House of Commons 319–316 despite resistance from Conservative 'Eurosceptics'.
1993	
July	Government defeated in vote over Maastricht bill, 324–316. 23 Conservative MPs voted against the government. Despite winning the confidence vote divisions over Europe are not healed by the revelation of Major's off-camera reference to senior right-wing Cabinet colleagues as 'bastards'.
August	Maastricht treaty is finally ratified despite last-minute attempt by Lord Rees-Mogg to mount a legal challenge.
1994	
January	Britain accepts the Ionnanian compromise on blocking minority in EU Council of Ministers.
March	Tony Marlow, the maverick Eurosceptic, openly calls for John Major's resignation following Major's reversal on European blocking minority.
November	Major survives a confidence vote on European Communities (finance) bill 330–303. Whip withdrawn from 8 Eurosceptic backbenchers.
1995	
October	Michael Portillo (Defence Secretary) uses the party conference platform to attack the EU and reaffirm the independence of UK defence policy.
December	Government defeated on EU fisheries 'take note' motion. 3 Conservatives vote against and 7 abstain.
1996	
June	78 Conservative MPs support a call for a referendum on Europe.
September	Six senior Conservatives (Brittan, Carrington, Heath, Howe, Hurd and Whitelaw) send letter to *The Independent* arguing that for Britain to rule out membership of the single European currency would be 'to betray our national interest'.

1997

January	Cabinet publicly agree EMU entry in 1999 'unlikely'.
October	Shadow cabinet meeting agrees to reject EMU for ten years. Peter Temple-Morris (pro-European MP for Kidderminster) admits in a press conference that he will leave the Conservative party at the next election unless it moderates its Eurosceptic stance; while Paul Sykes (millionaire Eurosceptic Conservative donor) warns party that he will not give any further funds unless Hague recommits to his pledge not to accept the single currency for ten years.

1998

January	Senior pro-European Conservatives write to *The Independent* urging Britain to prepare to join single European currency: 'This is the right policy for our country, and it is one we shall continue to commend with conviction to the Conservative party and the nation as a whole.'
September	Hague calls ballot of Conservative party membership over European single currency.
August	Former MPs Nicholas Budgen and Tony Marlow threaten to stand on anti-Federalist ticket against official Conservative candidates in 1999 Euro-election. Both men threatened with expulsion from party if this course of action is undertaken.
October	Result of internal party referendum on the single European currency announced. Support given to Hague's stance.
December	Conservative peers help defeat the European Elections Bill for sixth time. Labour government obliged to use Parliament Act to force legislation through.

1999

May	John Stevens and Brendan Donnelly (former Conservative MEPs) launch their breakaway pro-European Conservative Party's European election campaign in protest at Hague's Eurosceptic stance.
June	Relative Conservative success in European elections. Adrian Rogers, the right-winger and Conservative candidate for Exeter in 1997, resigns from party after he is threatened with expulsion for having written a letter to the *Daily Telegraph* urging Conservative supporters to vote for the UK Independence Party.
July	Tory MEPs agree to join centre-right coalition, the Group for EPP and Conservative Allies, in the European parliament. The row over Europe continues as Kenneth Clarke writes in *The Times* that he is in 'broad agreement on the big issues of Europe' with the Blair Labour government.

August	Sir Julian Critchley and Tim Rathbone (former Conservative MPs) expelled from party for backing breakaway pro-European Conservative candidates in the European elections. Several others Conservatives are cleared of breaking party loyalties.
2000	
February	Hague begins 'Keep the Pound' campaign with a nationwide tour speaking from the back of a truck.
November	Conservative leaders condemn plans for Britain to commit forces to Europe's Rapid Reaction Force. Consider it to be a European Army and threat to British sovereignty. Provokes counter-attack from pro-European Conservatives like Howe and Hurd. East Midlands MEP and former chairman of the Conservative group in the European Parliament, Bill Newton Dunn, defects to Liberal Democrats condemning Hague's hostility to Europe.
December	Ian Taylor, with the backing of the party leadership, survives a deselection attempt by Eurosceptics in his Esher Conservative Association.

4.5 CONSERVATIVES AND WOMEN

1. CONSERVATIVE WOMEN CANDIDATES AND MPS

Women were not admitted to parliament until the passage of the Sex Disqualification Removal Act in 1919. The vote had been granted to women in 1918, but only for those aged 30 or more. Women were allowed the vote at the age of 21 in 1928.

	Conservatives				All parties			
	Candidates	% of total candidates	MPs	% of total MPs	Candidates	% of total candidates	MPs	% of total MPs
1918	1	0.2	—	—	17	1.0	1	0.1
1922	5	1.0	1	0.3	33	2.3	2	0.3
1923	7	1.3	3	1.2	34	2.4	8	1.3
1924	12	2.2	3	0.7	41	2.9	4	0.7
1929	10	1.7	3	1.2	69	4.0	14	2.3
1931	16	3.1	13	2.8	62	4.8	15	2.4
1935	19	3.2	6	1.4	67	5.0	9	1.5
1945	14	2.2	1	0.5	87	5.2	24	3.8
1950	28	4.5	6	2.0	126[1]	6.8	21	3.4
1951	29	4.7	6	1.9	74	5.6	17	2.7
1955	32	5.1	10	2.9	89	6.5	24	3.8
1959	28	4.5	12	3.3	81	5.3	25	4.0
1964	24	3.8	11	3.6	90	5.1	28	4.6
1966	21	3.3	7	2.8	81	4.7	26	4.1
1970	26	4.1	15	4.5	99	5.4	26	4.1
1974 (Feb.)	33	5.3	9	3.0	143	6.7	23	3.6
1974 (Oct.)	30	4.8	7	2.5	161	7.1	27	4.3
1979	31	5.0	8	2.4	216	8.4	19	3.0
1983	40	6.3	13	3.3	280	10.9	23	3.5
1987	46	7.3	17	4.5	329	14.2	41	6.3
1992	63	9.9	20	6.0	571	19.3	60	9.2
1997	69	10.3	13	7.9	672	18.0	120	18.2

Complied from: D. Butler and G. Butler, *Twentieth Century British Political Facts* (2000); J. Lovenduski *et al.*, 'The Party and Women', in *Conservative Century* (1994), p. 626; M. Pugh, *The Evolution of the British Electoral System, 1832–1987* (1988), p. 22; C. Rallings and M. Thrasher, *British Electoral Facts 1832–1999* (2000).

Notes:

1. Florence Horsbrugh (Con.) is only counted once. She was defeated at Middleton and Peebleshire but subsequently elected for Manchester Moss Side where polling had been postponed due to the death of the Conservative prospective candidate.

2. CONSERVATIVE VOTING ON WOMEN SUFFRAGE 1911–17

	Conservative	Total Commons vote
1911 Conciliation Bill		
For	53	255
Against	43	88
1912 Conciliation Bill		
For	63	208
Against	114	222
1913 Dickinson's Representation of the People Bill		
For	28	221
Against	140	268
1917 Representation of the People Bill		
For	140	387
Against	45	57

Source: M. Pugh, *Women's Suffrage in Britain 1867–1928*, p. 28.

3. CHRONOLOGY

1869 Municipal Franchise Act grants the vote to a number of women ratepayers in local election.

1870 Married Women's Property's Act. Further acts in 1874 and 1882. Propertied women able to vote for School Boards.

1875 Propertied women allowed to vote for Poor Law Boards.

1883 Primrose League formed. 49 per cent of its membership was female.

1885 Exclusion of women from the Primrose League Grand Council obliges them to form the Ladies' Grand Council.

1886 Repeal of Contagious Diseases Act.

1887 National Union vote in favour of votes for women.

1888 Propertied women able to vote in County Council elections.

1894 Married women allowed to qualify as occupiers of property but not for the same property as their husbands.

1888 Salisbury declares himself in favour of female political equality.

1900 1,147 women have been elected to the boards of Poor Law Guardians.

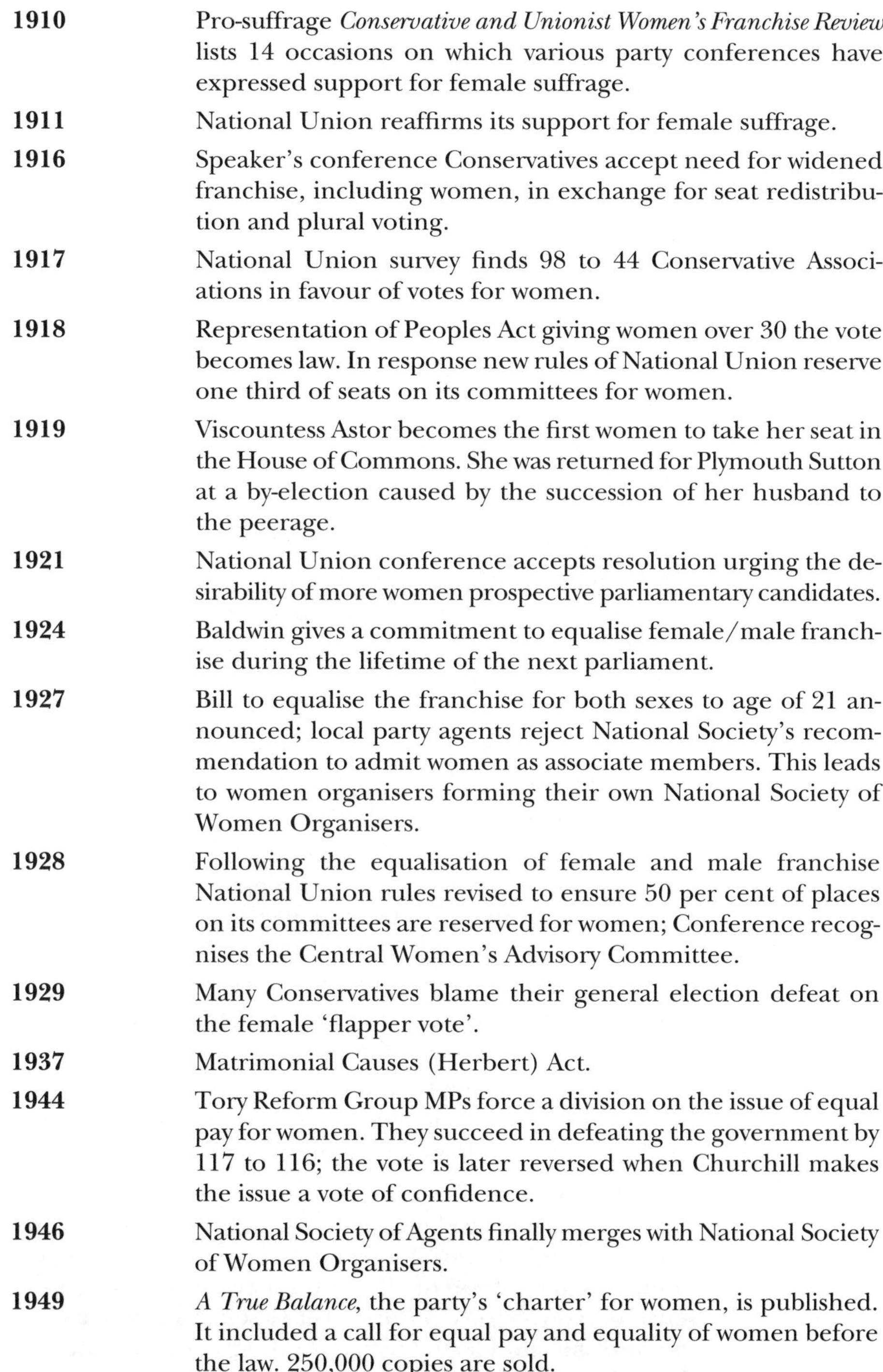

1910 Pro-suffrage *Conservative and Unionist Women's Franchise Review* lists 14 occasions on which various party conferences have expressed support for female suffrage.

1911 National Union reaffirms its support for female suffrage.

1916 Speaker's conference Conservatives accept need for widened franchise, including women, in exchange for seat redistribution and plural voting.

1917 National Union survey finds 98 to 44 Conservative Associations in favour of votes for women.

1918 Representation of Peoples Act giving women over 30 the vote becomes law. In response new rules of National Union reserve one third of seats on its committees for women.

1919 Viscountess Astor becomes the first women to take her seat in the House of Commons. She was returned for Plymouth Sutton at a by-election caused by the succession of her husband to the peerage.

1921 National Union conference accepts resolution urging the desirability of more women prospective parliamentary candidates.

1924 Baldwin gives a commitment to equalise female/male franchise during the lifetime of the next parliament.

1927 Bill to equalise the franchise for both sexes to age of 21 announced; local party agents reject National Society's recommendation to admit women as associate members. This leads to women organisers forming their own National Society of Women Organisers.

1928 Following the equalisation of female and male franchise National Union rules revised to ensure 50 per cent of places on its committees are reserved for women; Conference recognises the Central Women's Advisory Committee.

1929 Many Conservatives blame their general election defeat on the female 'flapper vote'.

1937 Matrimonial Causes (Herbert) Act.

1944 Tory Reform Group MPs force a division on the issue of equal pay for women. They succeed in defeating the government by 117 to 116; the vote is later reversed when Churchill makes the issue a vote of confidence.

1946 National Society of Agents finally merges with National Society of Women Organisers.

1949 *A True Balance*, the party's 'charter' for women, is published. It included a call for equal pay and equality of women before the law. 250,000 copies are sold.

1950	Conference adopts principle of equal pay.
1955	Conservative government introduces equal pay in the public sector.
1958	Women admitted to the House of Lords.
1970	Equal Pay Act designed to prevent discrimination between men and women doing equal work.
1974	Dame Irene Ward retires as a Conservative MP. To date she is the longest serving woman MP having represented Wallsend 1931–45 and Tynemouth 1950–74 (Feb.). She contested 12 elections.
1979	Margaret Thatcher becomes Britain's first female Prime Minister.
1984	Amendment to 1975 Sex Discrimination Act entitles women to equal pay with men when doing work which is the same, broadly similar, or of equal value.
1987	Sex Discrimination bill prepared to bring 1978 Act in line with EEC directives, including one relating to the right of women to continue working to the same age as men.
1989	Anne Widdecombe's Abortion (Amendment) bill that intended to reduce the time allowed to seek an abortion to 18 weeks is talked out of the House of Commons.
1990	Angela Rumbold (Minister for Education and Science) rejects tax incentives for childcare. Major is criticised for not appointing any women to his first cabinet.
1991	Major launches Opportunity 2000, which promotes equality for women in the work place. Child Support Act sets up Child Support Agency to secure maintenance from errant fathers.
1992	Teresa Gorman's Representation of the People (Amendment) bill introduced under the Ten Minute Rule to give two seats to each constituency (one for male candidates and one for females) receives a first reading.
1995	Backbench protests oblige the Government to abandon plans to give people living together the same rights as married couples in cases of domestic violence.
2000	Current Conservative female MPs are to act as mentors for women candidates seeking selection to stand for parliament. The think tank, Centre for Policy Studies, publish a report urging the imposition of all-women shortlists for those Conservative Associations that have yet to select a candidate for the next general election; Julie Kirkbride becomes the first sitting Conservative MP to give birth since Lady Tweedsmuir in 1949.

4. CONSERVATIVE WOMEN CABINET MINISTERS

1953–54	Florence Horsbrugh: *Education Secretary*
1970–74	Margaret Thatcher: *Education Secretary*
1979–90	Margaret Thatcher: *Prime Minister*
1982–83	Lady Young: *Chancellor of the Duchy of Lancaster 1981–82; Lord Privy Seal 1982–83*
1992–97	Virginia Bottomley: *Minister for Health 1992–95; Minister for National Heritage 1995–97*
1992–97	Gillian Shephard: *Minister for Employment 1992–93, Minister for Agriculture, Fisheries and Food 1993–94; Education Secretary 1994–97*

4.6 CONSERVATIVES AND THE TRADE UNIONS

CHRONOLOGY

1871

October — Senior Conservatives meet leading trade unionists to consider social reforms.

1875

August — Conspiracy and Protection of Property Act allows peaceful picketing and eliminates conspiracy from trade disputes unless they are illegal. Employers and Workmen Act limits the penalty for breach of contract to civil damages.

1896

January — Conciliation Act gives powers of mediation in industrial disputes.

1897

August — Workmen's Compensation Act offends many natural Conservative supporters.

1901

July — Taff Vale verdict removes the legal protection attached to trade union funds.

1905

Unemployed Workmen Act is a belated attempt to win over Labour party voters.

1906

March–May — Conservatives condemn the Liberal government's Trade Disputes Act as class legislation and as a surrender to union power.

1914

June — Unionist Social Reform Committee publish *Industrial Unrest.* The pamphlet argues that the state has a legitimate role in industrial relations both in terms of defending the consumer and national interest and in mediating between unions and employers.

1918

February — Unionist Labour Movement and Labour Sub-Committee (in May) founded to organise against socialism and syndicalism and to promote 'patriotic labour'.

1919

September — Industrial Courts Act creates a permanent arbitration tribunal to resolve disputes, but the scheme is voluntary.

1925

March — Conservative F.A. Macquisten's private member's bill, which proposes to replace 'contracting out' of the trade union political levy with 'contracting in', rejected by Baldwin.

October — Conference rejects Baldwin's trade union policy and unanimously supports a motion urging abolition of the political levy.

1926

February — National Union Central Council passes a motion urging abolition of political levy.

May — General Strike. Baldwin portrays the strike as an attack on constitutional democracy. Strike collapses after nine days.

1927

February — Baldwin makes a rare appearance at National Union Executive meeting as it debates the trade union question.

May — Trade Disputes and Trade Union Act declares sympathetic strikes and lockouts illegal; introduces 'contracting in' for the political levy, bans the closed shop and forbids civil service unions from affiliating to outside organisations like TUC.

1931

October — Baldwin declares, during a radio broadcast, that the general election is about whether government gets its authority from parliament or is controlled by the TUC.

1932

October — Conference accepts Harold Macmillan's motion for the creation of National Councils to represent different industrial sectors.

1935

October — Addressing conference Baldwin dwells on the legitimacy of the trade union movement and argues it is derived from 'Englishness'.

1937

April — Factory Act provides the first full-scale review of industrial work practices since 1901. It is welcomed by the TUC for increasing health and safety provisions.

1938

March — Walter Citrine, TUC general secretary, has secret talks at Number Ten about the rearmament programme.

October — Holidays with Pay Act extends the practice of holidays with pay for workers.

November	Chamberlain government shies away from introducing compulsory national service for fear of antagonising the unions whose support is critical for the rearmament programme.
1939	
July	TUC delegation about employment upset after it receives a frosty reception from Neville Chamberlain.
September	Chamberlain tells TUC that reform of trade union law must depend on the unions' conduct during wartime.
1940	
October	1922 Committee warns Churchill government not to amend the 1927 Trade Disputes Act.
1941	
September	Party group to meet TUC to discuss possible amendment of 1927 Trade Disputes Act.
1943	
February	Bevin's Catering Wages bill, that sought to extend state regulation to this previously unorganised, low-wage industry, carried against considerable Conservative opposition.
1944	
May	White Paper on Employment Policy sanctions government intervention to secure and create jobs and monitor wage levels.
1947	
March	Party's trade union organisation revived with aim of increasing trade unionist support for the party, explaining the party's policies to the union movement and encouraging non-socialist union members to contract-out of the political levy.
May	*Industrial Charter* emphasises Conservative governments' role in providing legal protection for unions and welcomes the participation of the unions in public policy formulation.
1951	
October	Walter Monckton appointed Minister for Labour with instructions not to antagonise the union movement.
1961	
July	Wage freeze imposed without consulting the trade unions.
1962	
	National Economic Development Councils (NEDCs) bring trade unions into 'corporatist' fold to examine questions of economic management.
1963	
May	Internal party report proposes reforms that would deprive unofficial strikers of social security benefits and advocates pre-strike ballots.

1965	
August	Internal party committee recommends the revision of union immunities. This is enshrined the following month in the policy statement *Putting Britain Right Ahead.*
1968	
March	*Fair Deal at Work* policy statement published. It argues for trade unions to operate in a legal framework that protects the public interest. Advocates cooling-off periods before strikes occur, the registration of unions and stricter definition of a trade dispute.
December	Industrial Relations bill published. Within two weeks it has secured its second reading.
1971	
February	Mass TUC demonstration against Industrial Regulation bill.
August	Industrial Regulation Act provides for the regulation of unions, obliging formal registration, collective agreements and placing restrictions on trade union immunities, the closed shop and secondary action. Also creates the National Industrial Relations Court. Legislation is neutralised by union non-compliance and is ignored by employers.
1972	
August	Intervention of official solicitor required to release those dockers (the 'Pentonville Five') imprisoned under Industrial Regulation Act.
November	Attempts to negotiate voluntary policy of wage restraint between TUC and CBI fail, obliging government to take a U-turn and impose a 90-day freeze on pay and policies.
1974	
February	National Union of Miners calls a national strike after attempts by government to negotiate terms for wages and overtime fail. Heath dissolves Parliament and fights general election on issue 'who governs?'
1976	
February	Thatcher addressing the Conservative Trade Unionist conference calls for a strong, responsible union movement.
1977	
January	TUC 'inner cabinet' meets Conservative front bench. Meeting fails to lift mutual hostility on both sides.
September	Thatcher proposes off-the-cuff, while speaking on television, the use of referendums to resolve industrial disputes.
November	Keith Joseph's 'stepping stones' report on political economy proposes utilising public hostility to tame the unions whom he identifies as the main stumbling block preventing Britain's economic recovery.

1978

Ridley report on privatisation has a secret annex that proposes strategies to deal with trade union unrest. It provides the model for ending the 1984–85 coal dispute.

1979

January — Thatcher party political broadcast seizes initiative over trade union reform by proposing no-strike agreements in essential industries and the taxation of welfare benefit for strikers. Labour government survives a Commons vote of confidence on its handling of industrial relations.

December — Government introduces Employment bill.

1980

April — Government faces rebellion on the closed shop.

May — One-day strike opposing government trade union legislation receives only limited support.

August — Employment Act imposes restrictions on picketing and the closed shop.

1982

October — Employment Act lifts trade union immunity from civil actions and further restricts the closed shop with compensation for workers sacked after refusing to join closed shop.

1983

June — Conservative election manifesto promises further legislation to force trade unions to hold strike ballots and regarding payment of the political levy.

1984

January — Government ban on trade unions at Government Communications Headquarters (GCHQ).

March — Beginning of the year-long miners' dispute.

April — Government wins on union right to contract in to political levy, although 42 Conservatives vote against.

July — Trade Union Act introduces secret ballots for strikes and election of union officials and imposes the need for a ballot on the political levy.

1988

May — Employment Act imposes postal ballots for union leadership elections and the political levy vote. Also failure to hold a secret ballot on strike actions makes the strike illegal.

October — Trade unionists at GCHQ are sacked.

1989

Employment Act restricts the rights of union lay officials, limits cases going before full industrial tribunals and removes restrictions on employment of women and children.

1990

November — Employment Act further restricts the closed shop, makes unions liable for civil damages for unofficial strikes and secondary action. Enables employers to selectively dismiss unofficial strikers.

1991

December — Britain secures 'opt-out' from Maastricht treaty's social chapter with its implications for equal opportunities, working conditions and workers' rights.

1992

Trade Union and Labour Relations (Consolidation) Act brings together all collective employment rights, including trade union finances, elections, dismissals and time off.

1993

July — Trade Union Reform and Employment Rights Act enables public services to seeks injunctions to prevent unlawful industrial action. The automatic deduction of union dues by an employer is rendered unlawful without written authorisation. All ballots must now be postal and subject to independent scrutiny with employers being granted 7 days' notice of industrial action.

1994

March — Stephen Dorrell becomes first Conservative minister to address a TUC forum for over 20 years. His speech emphasises the need for pay restraint in the public sector.

1997

January — Ban on unions at GCHQ is lifted.

4.7 CONSERVATIVES AND SOCIAL REFORM

CHRONOLOGY

1838	
February	13 Conservative MPs vote in favour of repealing the Poor Law.
1839	
Autumn	Peel resists the secularisation of national education.
1841	
March	101 Conservative MPs vote against the 5-year renewal of the Poor Law.
1844	
March	95 Conservative MPs support an amendment to the Factory Bill that proposes a 10-hour day for textile workers. The amendment is reversed four days later after Peel threatens resignation.
June	Factory Act introduces 12-hour day for women.
1848	
July	Public Health bill gains support for majority of free-trade Peelites but opposed by 56 per cent of protectionists opposed to its centralising features.
1850	
February	Disraeli tables a parliamentary motion seeking to relieve agricultural poverty by reducing Poor Law levies.
1871	
October	Leading Conservatives promote a seven-point social programme, the 'New Social Alliance'.
1872	
April	Disraeli speaking in Manchester links the Conservatives with social reform.
June	Disraeli's Crystal Palace speech speaks of 'the elevation of the condition of the people'.
1873	
March	Conservatives combine with Catholics to defeat Gladstone's Irish University Scheme.
1874	
August	Factory Act introduces maximum 56-hour working week.

1875

June	Artisans Dwellings Act.
July	Cabinet decision to abandon merchant shipping legislation reversed. Legislation become law the following March.

1886

January	Salisbury's minority administration defeated on 'three acres and a cow' amendment to the Address.

1889

November	Salisbury argues at party conference for free elementary education.

1890

March	Salisbury urges party not to prejudge elementary education issue until the government has published its proposals.

1891

March	J.S. Sandars, in a briefing document for Balfour, argues the 8-hour day in mining would raise wages and other employer costs.

1892

July	Party's *Campaign Guide* critical of 8-hour day.
September	Joseph Chamberlain advocates legislation to restrict working hours for shop workers.
November	Chamberlain calls for programme of social reform including compensation for industrial injuries and old age pensions.

1895

July	Party's *Campaign Guide* proposes a contributory pensions scheme.

1897

August	Workmen's Compensation Act.

1902

March	Balfour cabinet agrees to introduce an Education bill that will include rate support, abolish School Boards and transfer power to local authorities. Not passed until December.

1905

August	Unemployed Workmen Act passed. Unemployed registers formed under control of local government boards. Expenses to be defrayed by voluntary contribution.

1906

December	Liberal Education bill is defeated by Conservative majority in Lords.

1909

November	Conservatives in Lords reject Lloyd George's 'People's Budget'.

1911

	Conservatives vote for the National Insurance bill.

1921

July — Christopher Addison (Minister without Portfolio) resigns over government's abandonment of social reform.

1922

February — 'Geddes Axe' cuts public spending.

1923

February — Government majority reduced to 22 on a motion calling for universal pensions.

1924

June — *Looking Ahead*, a Conservative policy document, emphasises social reform.

1925

December — Contributory pensions introduced and the minimum age to qualify is reduced from 70 to 65 years of age.

1927

August — Unemployment Insurance Act reforms system and reduces benefits.

1929

March — Local Government Act abolishes Poor Law guardians.

1935

January–February — Conservative backbenchers combine with Labour and Liberals to object to the equalisation of social security payments.

1938

July — National Union Central Council less than enthusiastic about slum-clearance plans and demands a revision of the compensation rates for property owners.

November — Bill introduced to extend holiday pay to all workers.

1939

June — National Union Central Council calls for programme of public works to generate employment.

1941

July — Post-War Problems Central Committee formed to devise policy for post-war reconstruction.

1942

December — Beveridge Report published.

1943

March — Tory Reform Committee established by Conservative backbenchers favourable to Beveridge Report.

1944

March — Tory Reform Group MPs manage to win a division on the issue of equal pay for women.

August — Butler Education Act passed raising age of school leavers.

1945

June — Family Allowances bill enacted.

1947

May — *Industrial Charter* published.

1948

June — *Agricultural Charter* published.

1950

October — Annual conference agrees to the specific target of a future Conservative administration building 300,000 new houses.

1954

July — All food rationing ended.

1959

National Insurance Act enables 'contracting-out' of state pensions.

1961

February — Increase in NHS prescription charges announced.

1965

October — *Putting Britain Right Ahead* makes new pledges on social security.

1970

October — Free school milk ended. Publication of Family Income Supplements bill.

1971

March — Barber's budget increases pensions and welfare benefits, part of which is paid for by increased National Insurance contributions.

November — Plans for cost-related prescription charges dropped.

1973

July — Tax credit scheme announced to give mothers £2 per week per child, together with tax changes intended to help poorer families.

1974

October — Sir Keith Joseph causes outrage when speaking about birth control in poor families.

1980

August — Housing bill enables council tenants to purchase their homes.

1982

March — 13 Conservative MPs defy whip and vote to reverse the Government's decision to reduce unemployment benefit.

1984

December — Plans to increase parental contributions to student grants withdrawn after pressure from Conservative backbenchers.

1985

June — Green paper on social security suggests end to income-related pensions and introduction of 'family credit'.

1988

Social Security Act alters eligibility for income support and pattern of benefit contributions.

July — Education Act introduces national curriculum, testing and option for schools to leave local education authority control.

November — Government proposes loan scheme for students.

1989

January — Plans to introduce market forces to NHS outlined in white paper *Working for Patients.*

May — Thatcher government rejects EC Social Charter.

1990

National Health Service and Community Care Act enables hospitals to 'opt out' and become self-governing trusts; allows general practitioners to control own budgets; and reorganises system of local community care giving local authorities responsibility for care of elderly people in the community.

1991

July — Major launches Citizen's Charter.

December — Maastricht Treaty. Britain secures an opt-out from the social chapter.

1992

March — Labour's 'Jennifer's ear' party political broadcast attacks the Conservative's NHS provision.

1993

April — Major government launch 'Care in Community' programme.

October — Major launches 'Back to Basics' crusade. Assumption is made that this speech, following as it does a series of attacks on single mothers by ministers, is the clarion call for a new moral social agenda.

1994

February — Free vote in House of Commons agrees to lower homosexual age of consent to 18.

April — VAT on fuel comes into force (at 8 per cent).

1995

Completion of 'internal market' in NHS under terms of 1990 Act.

1999

April — Peter Lilley suggests that the NHS and education are too important to entrust to the private sector and free-market economy.

2000

July — Conservative peers block repeal of Section 28 on the promotion of homosexuality.

4.8 CONSERVATIVES, IMMIGRATION AND RACE

1. CHRONOLOGY

1885

Autumn — The Conservative agent in Whitechapel lodged 1,800 objections to names on the electoral register: alleged that they are foreigners with no right to vote.

1888

House of Commons select committee on emigration and immigration (foreigners) is established; also House of Lords committee under chairmanship of Lord Dunraven is created to investigate the sweating system.

1892

July — All Conservative election candidates in the East End of London, except for C.T. Ritchie, advocate immigration controls. Ritchie loses his seat.

1894

July — Salisbury's Aliens bill introduced. Aims at excluding from UK entry destitute eastern European immigrants and revolutionary/political extremist exiles. Fails to get past a second reading.

November — Chamberlain memorandum on imperial and social policies proposes restrictions on alien immigration.

1901

British Brother's League (BBL) formed as an anti-alien alliance between East End of London workers and backbench Conservatives like Howard Vincent and W.E. Evans-Gordon.

1902

January — BBL rally – addressed by several Conservative MPs.

1903

February — Immigration Reform Association formed with active participation from Conservative backbenchers.

November — Immigration Reform Association holds a mass rally.

1904

April — Balfour government's first alien bill introduced seeking to implement the recommendations of the Royal Commission on Alien Immigration (which reported August 1903). Attracts considerable parliamentary hostility and is eventually abandoned.

1905	
August	Aliens Act seeks to restrict entry of eastern European immigrants, particularly Jewish. Its definition of aliens is more rigorous than the 1904 bill although still intent on excluding undesirables and the destitute.
1919	
October	Amendment to Alien restriction bill carried on report stage against the Lloyd George coalition government.
1937	
June	The Mayor of Cheltenham, Daniel Lipson, wins the Cheltenham by-election as an Independent Conservative after the Cheltenham Conservative Association refuse to adopt him as a parliamentary candidate because he is Jewish.
July	Parliamentary debate on immigration hears a number of Conservatives, including Winston Churchill, call for tighter controls.
1938	
February	National Union approve a motion expressing concern at alien entry into Britain. This is forwarded to the Home Secretary.
November	Following the Nazi Kristallnacht pogrom against German Jews the 1922 Committee inform Chamberlain that there should be no further gestures of appeasement to Germany; but National Union's labour subcommittee pass a resolution expressing concern at the level of alien entry into Britain.
December	Deputation of Conservatives to Home Office to express disquiet at levels of Jewish immigrants entering Britain.
1939	
Autumn	Mounting calls from Constituency Associations for the internment of aliens.
1940	
January	Leslie Hore-Belisha sacked from War Office. Provokes claims of anti-semitism at the highest levels of the government.
June	In aftermath of Dunkirk evacuation Churchill government agrees to the introduction of full-scale internment of aliens.
1943	
February	Significant Conservative support for an EDM calling for the rescue of European Jewry.
1955	
February	Cyril Osborne, MP for Louth and a fervent opponent of non-white immigration, fails to introduce a private member's bill controlling immigration.
1958	
Summer	Rioting and racial tensions in Nottingham and Notting Hill, London.

October	Conference urges restrictions upon commonwealth and colonial immigrants despite the calls for restraint from R.A. Butler.
1960	
July and November	Deputations of Conservative MPs lobby Colonial Office for restrictive entry legislation.
October	No provision is made at the annual conference for a debate on immigration, despite seven 'pro-restriction' motions being received.
1961	
January	Harold Gurden (MP Birmingham Selly Oak) organises backbench meetings to urge for immigration control. Deputation sent to Home Secretary.
February	Cyril Osborne's private member's bill on immigration receives no government sanction and fails to progress.
July	Conservative parliamentary Commonwealth and Home Committees of opinion that immigration control 'should be taken urgently'.
October	Conference again calls for restrictions on immigration.
1962	
July	The Commonwealth Immigrants Act introduced. This seeks to restrict immigration by introducing a voucher system for entry.
1964	
October	Peter Griffith unexpectedly wins the Smethwick general election ousting the Labour shadow foreign secretary. Griffith had campaigned on an overtly anti-immigrant platform.
1968	
April	24 left-wing Conservatives abstain when a Conservative amendment during the second reading of the Race Relations bill is debated. Enoch Powell dismissed from the shadow cabinet by Edward Heath. This follows his 'rivers of blood' speech to an audience of Conservatives in Birmingham.
October	Conference pledges itself to restrict immigration and adopt measures to relieve concentration of migrants despite wishes of leadership.
December	Conservative Political Centre surveys its 412 constituency groups and finds that 327 want all immigration stopped and a further 55 favour a five-year ban on new immigrants and stricter rules concerning immigrants' dependants.
1969	
October	Conference carries, by 1,349 to 954, a motion urging the earliest implementation of restrictive immigration policies.

1970	
June	Only 26 per cent of Conservative candidates mention immigration in their election addresses.
1971	
February	Immigration bill published. It aims to tighten entry controls and becomes law in January 1973.
1972	
September	Monday Club 'Stop Immigration' rally in Central Hall, Westminster attracts participation from the extremist National Front.
October	Conference backs government policy on Ugandan Asians, 1,721 to 736, but only after the intervention of Conservative youth groups and the Young Conservative leader, David Hunt. Plymouth Drake Conservative Association punish Hunt for challenging Powell's conference motion by dropping him as their prospective parliamentary candidate. Anthony Reed-Herbert resigns from party over the outcome of the conference vote and joins the National Front.
November	Government plans to change the immigration rules are defeated by 275 to 240, with 7 Conservative MPs voting against and a further 49 abstaining.
1973	
February	Ugandan Asians granted entry to Britain provoking protests from party activists that the leadership was disregarding their wishes.
October	Conference takes view that no further large-scale immigration should be allowed.
1976	
January	Andrew Rowe appointed director of Conservative Central Office Department of Community Affairs that targets minority groups in electorate. Later an Ethnic Minorities Unit was established with the aim of educating party members on the growing electoral importance of Asian and West Indian votes.
1977	
Autumn	John Moore MP nominated as the Conservative representative (and joint chairman) on the Joint Committee Against Racialism. Thatcher vetoes his involvement despite objections from the National Union. A compromise is reached by appointing the non-parliamentarian Conservative, Shelagh Roberts, to serve on the committee. Federation of Conservative Students launch anti-racism campaign.

1978

January	Thatcher speaking on television referred to feeling of 'swamping' by immigrants.
April	Willie Whitelaw, speaking in Leicester, proposes a quota system to reduce immigration and a compulsory register of dependants.

1979

January	Anglo-West Indian Conservative Society formed.
April	Manifesto for general election commits party to a nationality law that will define British citizenship and rights of abode, will establish a register of dependants for Commonwealth immigrants who have already entered Britain and establish a quota system for entry from non-European Community countries.
November	Anglo-Asian Conservative Society, founded by Narindar Saroop, Conservative councillor for Kensington and Chelsea, says that the party's immigration proposals are ill-judged.

1980

October	Conference welcomes the impending British Nationality Law.

1981

March	British Nationality bill introduced. On becoming law it suspends the 1948 Nationality Act. Widely denounced as 'racist'. Only fulfils first pledge of 1979 manifesto to define British citizenship and rights of abode.
April	Scarman Commission appointed to consider inner-city riots. It blames widespread deprivation of inner-city areas and sense of discrimination among Black and Asian youths. Reports in December.

1982

December	Government defeated over plans to restrict the entry of immigrant spouses into Britain after a rebellion by 23 Conservative backbenchers.

1983

April–June	Controversy caused by Conservative general election poster which pictures a West Indian man and the slogan 'Labour Says He's Black. Tories Say He's British.'

1988

	Immigration Act further tightens entry control. Claims to UK citizenship now have to be established before travelling.

1989

February	Douglas Hurd addressing Birmingham Muslims urges them not to break the law over the Salman Rushdie *Satanic Verses* affair.

October	BBC programme 'Dispatches' alleges Conservative anti-Semitism played a role in the campaign against Edwina Currie after her salmonella gaffe in 1988.
December	Norman Tebbit attacks the issuing of UK passports for Hong Kong citizens in *Evening Standard* article.
1990	
February	John Taylor adopted as Conservative candidate in Cheltenham after a bitter race-fuelled selection contest; Norman Tebbit leads a deputation of over 80 Conservative MPs who signed a letter declaring their unwillingness to support the Government's bill allowing 225,000 Hong Kong citizens the right to settle in Britain.
April	44 Conservative MPs rebel against second reading of Hong Kong Citizenship bill.
November	Thames Television documentary alleges racial discrimination in the recruitment of secretaries by the Association of Conservative Clubs and Central Office.
December	Cheltenham rebels try to overturn the selection of John Taylor. This leads to the expulsion of Bill Galbraith from the party for racist remarks about Taylor.
1991	
February	Cheltenham Conservatives vote 406 to 164 to support John Taylor's candidature as prospective parliamentary candidate.
June	John Major calls for an urgent clampdown on illegal immigration into EC at Luxembourg summit.
November	Asylum bill published. It increases the burden of proof on refugees seeking asylum.
1992	
February	Government abandons its Asylum bill.
October	Asylum and Immigration bill presented to House of Commons. Intended to help speed up refugee cases and appeals.
1993	
May	Winston Churchill MP makes a speech attacking immigration and alleging that over 50 per cent of the population in some cities are from ethnic minorities.
1995	
February	Charles Wardle (junior minister Department of Trade and Industry) resigns over European immigration rules.
November	Brian Mawhinney (Minister without Portfolio) has paint thrown over him on College Green by an Asylum bill protestor. Alan Duncan effects a citizen's arrest.

1997

July — Major government's ruling that prevented asylum seekers from finding jobs while appealing against a refusal to grant refugee status is ruled unlawful in the High Court.

October — Hague rebukes Lord Tebbit for criticising the development of a multi-cultural society in Britain.

1998

November — Thatcher, in a review of a biography of Enoch Powell, claims that she had opposed his sacking by Heath in 1968.

1999

April — Hague, addressing an audience of Asian millionaires, announces the creation of a 'cultural unit' at Conservative Central Office. Indicates his desire for more Conservative ethnic minority candidates.

2000

February — Shaun Woodward (Conservative defector) uses his first Commons speech as a Labour MP to attack the Conservative front bench's indifference to the Race Relations Amendment bill, which is a response to the recommendations of the Stephen Lawrence Inquiry.

April — Hague proposes that all new illegal immigrants should be held in detention centres. UN High Commissioner for Refugees accuses Hague of breaking an all-party commitment not to encourage prejudice with inflammatory language on asylum issues. This is in reference to the party's local election manifesto that pledges to stop bogus asylum seekers and to cut the tax burden of paying for refugees.

October — Hague attempts to woo potential ethnic voters by addressing various ethnic minority organisations and praising their religious beliefs particularly regarding morality and family values.

2001

March — John Townend's (retiring MP for Yorkshire East) remarks about the undermining of 'Anglo-Saxon society' by mass immigration sparks a row about race and politics. Hague resists calls to remove the whip from Townend.

April — A number of Conservative MPs, led by Portillo, boycott the Campaign for Racial Equality's 'race' election pledge. This causes embarassment for Hague who had previously committed the party to the pledge.

Townend is forced to retract his comments, after Lord Taylor (the Conservative's only black peer) threatens to quit the party and accuses Hague of 'weak leadership'. Laurence Robertson (MP for Tewkesbury) is also forced to retract his support for Townend's comments.

2. CONSERVATIVE PARLIAMENTARY CANDIDATES FROM ETHNIC MINORITIES

	Candidates		MPs	
	Conservative	All Parties	Conservative	All Parties
1979	2	5	0	0
1983	4	18	0	0
1987	6	29	0	4
1992	8	22	1	6
1997	9	39	0	9

Source: Adapted from C. Rallings and M. Thrasher, *British Electoral Facts 1832–1999* (2000).

4.9 CONSERVATIVES AND IDEOLOGY

There is no one text, or philosopher, that can be held up as the gospel of Conservative ideology. Conservatives seek to argue that their politics are based upon pragmatism rather than ideology. The tendency is to express a belief in the Conservative 'temperament' rather than a Conservative 'philosophy'. This distinction is important and leads to two outcomes. Firstly, by presenting themselves as non-ideological Conservatives are able to attack other political doctrines by characterising ideology as a negative and restrictive mode of thought. This provoked J.S. Mill to label the Conservatives 'the stupid party' in 1861. Secondly, the belief in pragmatism is considered a source of strength for it enables the party to reinvent itself under different leaders and different political contexts. As Iain Macleod declared at the 1962 party conference: 'There is no new Conservatism, only a restatement of old beliefs in modern terms.'

If not ideologically rigid, Conservatism does revolve around certain core tenets: the defence of institutions (state, monarchy and church) and traditions; the preservation of society; and the safeguarding of the individual. These core values have been articulated in the writings of Conservative thinkers such as Bolingbroke, Michael Oakeshott, Quintin Hogg, Richard Law and F.A. Hayek. Although the modern Conservative party emerged in the 1830s, historians of political ideas, such as Professor Bob Eccleshall, argue that the emergence of a recognisable Conservative creed can be traced back to the seventeenth-century Restoration.

DEFENCE OF INSTITUTIONS AND TRADITIONS

Conservatism is essentially a defensive creed that is wary of change. It is accepted that society is evolutionary, but change either wholesale or for change's sake is dangerous and anathema. This does not eliminate a willingness to reform abuses and was a fundamental element of Robert Peel's *Tamworth Manifesto*. However, Conservatives believe that a long historical evolutionary process has created the key elements of society – monarchy, parliament, cabinet, courts and rule of law. These elements, or institutions of state, have stood the test of time and their continued defence is an absolute necessity.

PRESERVATION OF SOCIETY

Respect for the institutions of state promotes order and discipline in society. Order provides the fabric within which the individual fulfils his or her potential. Conservatives are wary of planning, particularly state planning; however the development of the individual must be as a citizen and not at the expense of the state. Consequently emphasis is placed upon public duty and citizenship. If necessary this will oblige limited state intervention and oblige sacrifices from the citizen, for example conscription. In other words the preservation of the state from external and internal challenges is essential if the conditions for individual fulfilment are to be guaranteed.

SAFEGUARDING OF THE INDIVIDUAL

The individual is central to Conservative thinking. It is considered crucial to provide the conditions that will encourage the individual to play a role conducive to society – this usually entails intervention to remove restrictions as with Thatcher's 'rolling back the state'. The belief in property ownership reflects a rationale that this promotes stability, provides independence for the owner and offers a bulwark against the encroachment of an over-mighty state. At the other end of the spectrum the state undertakes a role in social provision, but at a level necessary to promote the return to self-dependence.

4.10 CONSERVATIVE FACTIONS, REBELS AND DEFECTORS

CONSERVATIVE FACTIONS, GINGER GROUPS AND PRESSURE GROUPS

Aims of Industry

Established in late 1942 it was a Conservative propaganda front organisation run by Collin Brooks with start-up funding from Lord Perry. Opposed the 1945–51 Labour government's nationalisation programme. Secured 78,000 column inches of newspaper space in 1947, and was able to provide local constituency parties with cartoons, illustrations and articles for local publications. In 1949 AOI provided 4,000 cinema shows attended by nearly half a million people. With encouragement from Central Office it intervened in marginal by-elections, such as Bradford in 1949, promoting the anti-nationalisation message. Renamed Aims by the mid-1960s it had a staff of 40 and at the 1983 general election spent £250,000.

Anti-appeasers

Label applied to small grouping of Conservative MPs opposed to Neville Chamberlain's policy of appeasement, which came into being during the summer of 1938. Main group followed the lead of Anthony Eden, who had resigned as foreign secretary in 1938, while a smaller number looked to Winston Churchill. Variously labelled the Glamour Boys or Edenites by the whips' office the groupings lacked formality and had a very limited impact upon the government's foreign policy.

Anti-Common Market League

Founded in 1961 to oppose Britain's moves to join the European Common Market. Led by Sir Derek Walker-Smith and Robin Turton, the leadership of these older parliamentarians gave the campaign considerable weight in parliament and the constituencies. The League was the first of nearly 80 European ginger groups that were spawned within the Conservative party between 1961 and the 1992 Maastricht treaty.

Anti-Socialist League

An example of the proliferation of 'legion of leagues' that emerged during the Edwardian period seeking to counter the 'Socialist menace'. Although non-party, membership was overwhelmingly Conservative. That the Conservative party sought to harness public interest in, and support for, its values and interests is seen as innovative. Alternatively, it has been suggested that the presence of Conservatives in such organisations was evidence of the grass roots' frustration with their party's inability to represent their concerns.

Anti-Waste League

A pressure group that objected to the increases in taxation and urged tighter control of public expenditure. Instigated by the *Daily Mail* and *Daily Express* and their proprietors Lords Rothermere and Beaverbrook. The League ran four candidates in by-elections in 1921 against official Conservative candidates (Wrekin, Dover, Hertford and St George's Westminster). Attracted strong middle-class support and showed the threat that independents could pose on the anti-spending message. Faced with pressure from the Conservative back benches, the Lloyd George coalition government responded by creating the Geddes Committee to consider public expenditure. Although the anti-spending threat had receded by June 1921 it marked the beginning of the end of the Coalition.

Blue Chip Dining Club

Formed by new intake of 'intellectual' MPs when the party returned to power in 1979. Members included William Waldegrave, Chris Patten and John Patten. The group established a reputation for being 'wet' especially with its 1981 publication that called for more government aid to industry.

Bow Group

Founded in 1950 by a group of university friends, it secured Central Office backing in 1952 before re-launching itself in 1957. By 1960 its membership stood at around 800. Its journal *Crossbow* and its publications provided a platform for younger thinking Conservatives to expound their views, although it was made clear that the contents of these publications did not represent either a Party or a Group view. Many members subsequently moved on to ministerial posts, such as ex-chairman Geoffrey Howe and Enoch Powell. Commonly perceived as being left of centre because of its emphasis on social policy and human rights it has always been committed to the principle of sound finance.

British Housewives' League

Independent organisation, receiving tacit Conservative support during 1947, that attacked the Labour government's handling of the food shortages and its interventionist policies. The right-wing journalist Dorothy Crisp chaired the League. She had co-authored with Oliver Stanley *The Re-birth of Conservatism* (1931). The 'consensus' collapsed in 1948 when the League criticised the 'totalitarian' stance of the Conservatives on the right of an individual to contract out of the NHS.

British Workers' League

Founded by Lord Milner in 1917, one of the few Unionists of the period keen to exploit divisions within the Labour movement, as a front organisation that supported the wartime coalition. Led by Victor Fisher, it sought to provide a standard for 'patriotic labour' to rally to. Urged social reform within a broad imperial policy and attacked the official Labour leaderships for unwillingness to castigate pacifists and militants. Re-named the National Democratic Party for 1918 coupon election and, despite hostility from local Unionist associations, succeeded in winning 11 seats. These were all in Labour strongholds unattractive to Unionists and Coalition Liberal candidates. Lacking an organisation it blurred into the ranks of the coalition majority thereafter.

Bruges Group

Anti-federalist grouping taking their name from Thatcher's September 1988 Bruges speech where she infamously declared that her governments had 'not successfully rolled back the frontiers of the state only to see them re-imposed at a European level'.

Budget Protest League

Formed by Walter Long in June 1909 to take to the country the Unionists' objections to Lloyd George's People's Budget. It was an example of the proliferation of single-issue protest groups that had affiliations to the Unionist party. In the short term helped re-unite the party, although critics wondered why the Party could not articulate the concerns of the various protest leagues.

CAFE

see **Conservatives Against a Federal Europe**

Canningites

Often described as a 'party', their action between 1801 and 1827 hardly justifies the label. There were no obvious connections of kinship or patronage that bound the group together. The inner core had formed friendships at Eton and Christ Church, Oxford. They numbered between 15 and 30 and were inclined to act independently and in contradiction to one another. When Canning chose to resign in 1820 he took the decision without consulting any of the Canningites.

Carlton Club revolt, 1922

Party meeting on 19 October 1922 that voted to abandon the coalition with Lloyd George, obliging his resignation as Prime Minister. This event destroyed the leadership ambitions of Austen Chamberlain after he had argued in favour of retaining the coalition.

Cecil Club

Founded in 1883 by H.C. Raikes and T.E. Kebbel it met every Tuesday night of the parliamentary session to bring together the Conservative and political literary circles. It represented a deliberate attempt to advance the intellectual antecedents of Conservatism to the nation.

Centre for Policy Studies

Formed in 1974 by Keith Joseph with the dual purpose of research and lobbying, the CPS sought to promote free enterprise and was responsible for the political growth of monetarism. It was sponsored by private business funds with donations from 17 CBI member firms and was independent of party funding. The think tank acted as speechwriter and policy developer for Joseph. It succeeded in converting a sceptical shadow cabinet to previously unpopular policies that would prove electoral assets in future years, such as trade union reform. Furthermore it proved the training ground for a succession of Thatcherite policy advisers: Ralph Harris, Alfred Sherman, Hugh Thomas and Alan Walters. It strongly supported the monetarist policies of Thatcher's first administration, but found its influence declining in the late 1980s as their source of ideological patronage dissipated – e.g. Joseph's retirement, Howe's move to the Foreign office and Thatcher's resignation.

Centre Forward Group

Launched by Francis Pym, following his sacking as foreign secretary in 1983, this was short-lived grouping of 'wets' in the parliamentary party during the 1980s who tried to swim against the Thatcherite tide. Meetings only attracted an average attendance of six MPs and the group was finally disbanded in 1987.

Cliveden Set

Mythical belief that leading 1930s politicians gathered at Cliveden House, home of Waldorf and Nancy Astor, to devise means of appeasing Nazi Germany. Coined by the left-wing journalist Claud Cockburn, the phrase entered the popular anti-appeasement vocabulary of the era. The reality was that the Cliveden parties were part of a declining nineteenth-century phenomenon of the political house party that mixed lavish hospitality with discussion of the issues of the day.

Confederacy, The

Founded in 1905 to press the Conservative party into accepting tariff reform. It was one of the most diehard of the tariff-reform agitators. Membership deliberately sought to exclude 'manufacturers'.

Conservative Constitutional Club

Founded in 1882 by Lord Abergavenny to rival the National Liberal Club, the Constitutional Club quickly found premises in Regent Street in 1883. It claimed a membership of 4,560 and catered for a mainly provincial and non-'West End' clientele. Party managers were wary of it, fearing the possible creation of a regional power base, and consequently refused to provide financial assistance.

Conservative Way Forward Group

Formed after Thatcher's resignation from office in order to promote the ideals she represented. Although membership is not restricted to the parliamentary party, until 1997 it claimed between 80 and 100 MPs as members. There is considerable overlap with membership of the '92 Group.

Conservatives Against a Federal Europe (CAFE)

Launched in 1995 around 'The Whipless Nine', the organisation claimed in 1999 it had 4,000 members. It is an influential Eurosceptic pressure group comprising mainly Conservatives. Lord Lamont (former Chancellor of the Exchequer) is chairman with Lord Pearson of Rannoch and Lord McAlpine (former party treasurer who defected to the Referendum Party in 1997) as Presidents.

diehard

Right-wing party man unyielding in defence of his 'true blue' principles, especially during the Edwardian period.

ditchers

Diehard Conservative opponents to the 1911 Parliament Act prepared to 'die in the last ditch' rather than concede the principle of parliamentary reform.

Empire Crusade

A movement that tried to impose the policy of Empire free trade upon the Conservative party, 1929–31. The press barons Beaverbrook and Rothermere supported the campaign. Mutated from being a newspaper stunt to a propaganda organisation to a fully-fledged single-issue political party. The 'crusade', so labelled by the *Daily Mirror*, contested a series of by-elections: Twickenham, East Islington, South Paddington and St George's. The result was usually to split the Conservative vote, except when they secured victory in South Paddington. In early days received encouragement from pro-tariff Conservative MPs and attracted support from disgruntled Conservative activists, especially in southern England and the agricultural east Midlands.

European Movement

Established, in July 1948, in succession to Winston Churchill's United Europe Movement. It has become the leading pro-European pressure group and draws support from across the political spectrum. In 1969 it merged with the Britain in Europe organisation.

Eurosceptic

Term applied to those individuals who express distrust at the moves towards closer European Union. The phrase has only become current since the 1980s.

Fair Trade Movement

A protectionist publicity league that drew considerable support from Conservative borough MPs at the end of the 1870s and in the 1880s.

Forty Thieves, the

Belittling label given to an informal group of Conservative diehard backbenchers with banking and industrial interests. Sometimes known as the 'Industrial group' these politicians were very right-wing, inarticulate, poorly regarded and intent upon implementing protectionism.

Fourth Party

Ginger group of four Conservative MPs created to harass the Commons leadership of Sir Stafford Northcote and largely succeeded in doing so, 1881–84. The membership comprised John Gorst, Drummond Wolff, Lord Randolph Churchill and (for a time) A.J. Balfour.

Free-Fooders

Supporters of free trade who joined the Free Food League in 1903 opposing Joseph Chamberlain's calls for the introduction of tariffs. The dispute left the Conservative party, at all levels, deeply divided.

Fresh Start Group

Single-issue Eurosceptic grouping opposed to the passage of the European Communities (Amendment) Bill – to ratify the Maastricht treaty – in 1992 and 1993. Their name was taken from a June 1992 early day motion (EDM) that called for a 'fresh start' on the issue of Europe. The EDM gathered 69 signatures. The group operated with an informal whip and claimed a membership of 80. Rumours that they were preparing to become a general-purpose faction grouping proved baseless. The extremely poor reception experienced by John Major when addressing the group in June 1995 on Europe was one of the factors that encouraged his decision to initiate the 1995 leadership election contest.

Guy Fawkes group

A grouping that emerged with the 1979 parliamentary intake and from a contemporary viewpoint drew together MPs from the party's left including Stephen Dorrell, David Mellor, Robin Squire and John Major. Name taken because their first meeting was held on 5 November.

Halsbury Club

Diehard organisation founded in 1911 with Lord Selborne as its first elected chairman and including Milner, Austen Chamberlain, Willoughby de Broke, F.E. Smith and Leo Amery among its members. As a response to the 1911 Parliament bill the party's leadership were fearful that it might exacerbate divisions within the party and possibly provide a platform to displace Balfour.

Hedgers

Conservatives reluctantly prepared to compromise over the passage of the 1911 Parliament Act.

Imperial South Africa Association

Founded in 1896 as a propaganda and lobbying organisation promoting British rule in South Africa. The organisation attracted strong support from Conservative activists and claimed 50 Conservative and 11 Liberal Unionist MPs as members.

India Defence League

Created in June 1933 with the merger of the India Defence League and the Indian Empire Society. Dedicated to resisting the Government of India bill, the IDL was supported by the *Daily Mail* and *Morning Post*. Rudyard Kipling and Sir Edward Carson were vice-presidents. Faced with resistance from the National Union executive and the party's leadership the IDL sought to capture the support of the grass roots; this it successfully managed to achieve, especially in the southern English rural constituencies, which often had ex-officers and retired colonial civil servants among their elected Association officers.

Industrials, The

see **Forty Thieves**

Institute of Economic Affairs

Founded in 1955 by Antony Fisher (a Conservative businessman) and Oliver Smedley (a Liberal free-trader) the IEA was intended to be a non-partisan promoter of free enterprise and challenger of the Keynesian consensus. By the mid-1960s, under the direction of Ralph Harris and Arthur Seldon it was increasingly influential with Conservative figures such as Keith Joseph, John Biffen, Enoch Powell and Geoffrey Howe. It was the last that introduced Margaret Thatcher to the IEA when she required expertise on welfare economics. From 1963 the IEA was helping Powell with his speeches giving the organisation valuable publicity. Additional publicity was derived from the editorial support of the *Daily Telegraph* during the 1964–74 editorship of Maurice Green. In the early 1970s as Labour moved leftwards, the IEA helped win converts to the 'new right' such as Lord Chalfont, Patrick Cormack and Paul Johnson.

Liberal Unionist Party

Rejected Irish Home Rule in 1886 consequently splitting from the Gladstonian Liberal party. They supported the Salisbury 1886–92 Administration and joined in government in 1895. Comprised both radicals, like Joseph Chamberlain, and Whigs, like Hartington. Retained own party structure until formally merged with Conservatives in 1912. There were strong regional associations with the West Midlands and Scotland.

Liberty and Property Defence League

Founded in 1882 by Lord Elcho this League sought to resist the advance of collectivism. By 1891 the League proclaimed that it had resisted 386 parliamentary bills.

Lollards

Dining club that was the Conservative left wing's equivalent to the '92 Group. The name was derived from their original meeting place, a flat in Lollards tower at Lambeth Palace, residence of the founding member and former Conservative MP for Wokingham 1959–79, Sir William van Straubenzee. Peter Temple-Morris, who later organised the Heseltine 1990 leadership bid, became a key figure.

Middle Class Alliance

Launched at a formal lunch in the House of Commons in May 1956 the MCA quickly gathered a membership of 50,000 derived from the professional and salaried electorate and owners of small businesses. Many were associated with the Conservative Party, consequently they were viewed as a pressure group within the party. Henry Price, MP for West Lewisham, was the chairman. A key theme of the MCA was the belief that public expenditure, and by consequence taxation, was too high and adversely affected the middle-class and natural Conservative voter. Conservative Central Office's view was that the MCA should be discouraged but not antagonised. A sudden collapse in membership and the resignation of Price led to closure of the organisation in March 1957. Thatcher supporter, John Gorst, revived the ideas of the MCA in 1975.

Milk Street Mafia

Press reference to the 1922 Conservative backbench committee under the chairmanship of Edward du Cann, a critic of Heath, at a time when the Committee was trying to convey to Heath the party's desire that he should submit himself to a leadership contest. The nickname arose after press photographers snapped members of the '22 leaving a private meeting at the Milk Street offices of the merchant bank of which du Cann was chairman.

Monday Club

Founded in 1961, and taking its name from the day of Macmillan's 'winds of change' speech, it focused its activities around matters of colonial and foreign affairs, holding monthly meetings and dinners. Consequently it drew support from diehard Conservatives, many of whom had been active with the 'Suez group' in the 1950s and the 'Katanga lobby' in the early 1960s. By 1968 it claimed that it had 1,000 national and 3,000 local members as a result of its establishing study groups and local branches in universities and constituencies. Part of its intended mission was to counter the influence of left-wing Conservative groups, such as the Bow Group, and moderate Conservatives on the immigration issue. Influence waned during 1970s as its ideas became mainstream among the leadership.

National Democratic Party

see **British Workers' League**

National League for Opposing Women's Suffrage

Formed in 1911 by an amalgamation of the Women's National Anti-Suffrage League and the Men's League for Opposing Women Suffrage. Lord Cromer was president and was succeeded in 1912 by Lord Curzon and Lord Weardale. Dissolved in 1918.

National Service League

Founded in 1902 this pressure group sought to promote the adoption of conscription on the continental model. In November 1905 Lord Roberts accepted the presidency and rapidly transformed the NSL's fortunes. Membership rose from 10,000 in 1907 to 62,000 in 1910 to a claim of 270,000 on the eve of the First World War. Roberts also moderated the demands of the NSL proposing instead the mandatory training of all young men into a home defence militia. Despite 130 MPs pledging themselves to the NSL in February 1910 the Conservative leadership refused to adopt NSL policy.

Next Five Years Group

Cross-party movement that preached the virtues of economic planning during the 1930s. Founded by Lord Allen of Hurtwood it included Harold Macmillan, Arthur Slater and Geoffrey Crowther. Its best known publication was *The Next Five Years* (July 1935), but the group made a limited impact upon the National Government's core economic thinking: the defence of sterling and balanced budgets.

Nick's Diner

Dining club hosted by Nicholas Scott in 1970s that sought to stop Heath lurching rightward. Membership was exclusively 'wet'. The group celebrated its 30th anniversary in July 2000 with a dinner.

Ninety-Two ('92) group

Right-wing dining club, which claimed a membership of about one hundred MPs in 1992. Name is taken from the address (92 Cheyne Walk) of one of its founder members, Sir Patrick Wall. Legend credits the group with engineering the election of suitable members to the internal parliamentary party's subject committees and the 1922 Committee. The importance of the group was seen during the 1995 leadership election when both contestants – Major and Redwood – sought to address a meeting of the group. The group provided one of the centres of internal opposition to the leadership of John Major under the chairmanship of Sir George Gardiner, MP for Reigate.

No Turning Back Group

Small group of Thatcherite MPs active since the 1980s and committed to maintaining the Thatcherite agenda. Rocked by the resignations of Portillo and Maude in October 2000.

One Nation Group

Backbench dining and discussion group formed by members of the 1950 Parliamentary intake. Its début publication *One Nation* is one of the celebrated statements of Conservatism from this period and heralded the vanguard of paternalistic left-wing Conservatism. The name 'One Nation' sought to echo their Disraelian heritage dating back to his 1845 novel *Sybil* that described the polarisation of Victorian society into rich and poor. Early members included Carr, Macleod, Powell and Heath. Many of its members went on to hold key positions in the party and in government, giving rise to an assumption that the Group enjoyed unprecedented behind-the-scenes access and influence within the party at least until the 1970s.

Peacock's tail

Tiny group of Conservative MPs, led by G.M.W. Sanford and including Cranborne, who fought against Disraeli's 1867 Reform Act.

Peelites

Those Conservatives who in 1846 favoured the repeal of the Corn Laws and consequently free trade. A minority grouping around Robert Peel, they included many of the Conservatives brightest stars, including Gladstone. Flirted with the Whig governments from 1846. The split became entrenched during the July 1852 general election, as the Protectionist Party became the party of Protestantism and challenged several leading Peelites. The Beresford bribery scandal accentuated the distrust between the two Conservative wings, as did the rhetoric of Disraeli. When in 1853 the Peelites (Liberal Conservatives as they called themselves) joined the Aberdeen Whig government, liberal conservatism had come to mean more than adherence to free trade and religious toleration, as also a willingness to support reform of parliament and the civil service were important new characteristics. Formally merged with Liberals in 1859.

People's League for the Defence of Freedom

Founded by Edward Martell, many of its leaders had been Liberal candidates and officeholders even though the PLDF operated on the extreme right of the political spectrum campaigning on the single issue of trade union reform. Emerging at the same time as the Middle Class Alliance, Conservative party organisers kept a close watch on the PLDF's activities recognising that while it had failed to attract much support from senior party figures its message appealed to disaffected activists and the middle-class electorate.

Post-war Problems Committee

Party policy committee established in 1941 with Rab Butler as chairman. With a membership comprising the parliamentary, professional and voluntary wings of the party, the committee's remit was to research and report on aspects of national life. Given the nature of the committee's composition many of its proposals were compromises that failed to rival the 1942 Beveridge report.

Progress Trust

Formed in 1943 as a 'libertarian' counterweight to the Tory Reform Group, the Trust evolved from being solely dedicated to the defence of the Conservative's laissez-faire approach to social reform to protecting the principles of paternalism and hierarchy. Membership was selective comprising approximately 20 members, with weekly meetings and monthly dinners with cabinet ministers as guest speakers. The chairman had immediate access to the Chief Whip and Number 10. As a result an impression emerged during the late 1940s that it was even more influential that the 1922 Committee. By the mid-1950s it was influencing the agenda and tone of political debate among the party's other official backbench committees.

Reveille

Launched in 1910 by Henry Page-Croft, this semi-secret society, which had a membership of about 100 with at least the support of 50 MPs and peers, had wide-ranging aims: tariff reform, a strong Navy, a revised scheme of national insurance led by market forces, reform of Poor Law, reform of land ownership and an Imperial policy. Membership overlapped with the Confederacy and was indicative of the declining support for the leadership of Balfour.

Selsdon Group

Collection of neo-liberal Conservative MPs who dissented from Heath's policies in 1973 and harked back to the perceived Mecca aspired to by the 1970 Selsdon Park conference.

Suez Group

Well-organised faction of approximately 40 MPs with a hard core of about 28. They also drew upon a wider grouping of 'sympathisers' among the parliamentary party. Leading members were Charles Waterhouse and Julian Amery. Traditional view is that those affiliated to the group were the Tory 'old guard' or backwoodsmen. However, the senior positions held by many in the party structure placed these men and their beliefs centrally within the party. The group was anti-Israeli (for the most part), suspicious of American policy and designs in the Middle East and contemptuous of the United Nations Organisation.

Tariff Reform League

Formed in 1903 to champion Joseph Chamberlain's calls for the introduction of tariffs. Closely allied with the Liberal Unionist party, the TRL formed local branches in the constituencies. In its first three months of existence it spent £50,000 and by 1904 had an annual income of £140,000. Conservative party managers were reluctant to link their party machine formally to the TRL, but many local constituency associations passed resolutions of support, despite Balfour's attempts to steer a middle course of compromise.

Tory Reform Group

Formed in 1943 this grouping of left-wing Conservatives was led by Peter Thorneycroft, Quintin Hogg, Hugh Molson and Viscount Hinchingbrooke. Their founding aspiration was to persuade the party of the need for social reform and to accept the Beveridge report. It attracted 41 MPs as members, met weekly, produced pamphlets and retained paid research staff. Although they made little impression upon the party's leadership, and attracted considerable animosity from right-wingers, TRG helped contribute to the climate that would shape post-1945 party thinking. In recent times TRG has undergone a renaissance and during the early 1990s drew on the support of about 40 MPs from the left of the party. Membership is not confined to MPs and peers. It is also pro-European.

Tory Strasbourgers

Nickname given to a small core of Conservative pro-Europeans, whose ranks were swelled by the 1950 intake of MPs. They attended Council of Europe meetings in Strasbourg. The experience tended to confirm these individuals' pro-European position, as Duncan Sandys and Robert Boothby found, and enabled them to judge issues in ways other than strictly national terms. They were most influential while the Conservatives were in opposition 1945–51, when it suited the leadership to use the issue of Europe as a weapon against Labour, but they proved surprisingly impotent once Churchill returned to office in 1951. Their presence in Strasbourg helped transform the Council of Europe from an inter-governmental debating forum into a venue for discussion of political integration.

Ulster Unionists

Supporters of the Act of Union between Britain and Ireland. Label applied by Lord Randolph Churchill to those who sought to prevent the inclusion of Ulster in Home Rule proposals. In 1912 the Conservative party adopted the title Conservative and Unionist Party when it formally absorbed those Liberals opposed to Home Rule. Ulster Unionists were the governing party in the devolved Northern Ireland parliament 1920–72; its MPs took the Conservative whip until 1972 and its Ulster Unionist Council was affiliated to the National Union until 1975.

ultras

1820s nickname (taken from the equivalent party of the extreme right in France) for High Tories who resisted the repeal of the Test Acts, Catholic Emancipation and electoral reform.

Union Defence League

Led by Walter Long the UDL opposed Irish Home Rule. However, it distanced itself from the party leadership's stance on the issue 1911–14.

Union of Britain and India (UBI)

Moderate group created by Central Office to support the India bill. Diehards opposed to the bill complained that the party organisation was too partisan upon an issue that split the party. Hampered by a lack of press support and the difficulty in recruiting leaders of sufficient calibre.

Unionist Business Committee

Active 1915–16, this informal backbench group advocated a more vigorous pursuit of the war effort. Successfully harried the Asquith Liberal government and the coalition, but influence diminished once Bonar Law allied the Unionists with Lloyd George.

Unionist Organisation Committee (UOC)

Chaired by Akers-Douglas, a former Chief Whip, the creation of the UOC was announced 1 February 1911. It comprised nine members chosen to represent all strands of the party. Consequently 'rebel' factions found themselves well represented. The committee's creation was in response to mounting pressure for a wholesale review of the party's organisation. Acting rather in the style of a Royal Commission, holding formal meetings, retaining a paid staff and publishing its evidence and findings, the Committee was quickly able to present Balfour with a series of recommendations that overhauled the whole of the party's structure and created the form that is recognisable today.

Unionist Social Reform Committee

A backbench group, chaired by F.E. Smith, seeking to promote a Conservative social policy 1911–14, which enjoyed tacit support from Central Office, but never official recognition from the leadership. Its influence carried into the 1920s by which time a number of its former members were ministers and responsible for social reform.

United Empire Party

The political wing of the Empire Crusade. First formed 18 February 1930, disbanded 8 March and then re-launched 3 April.

Whole Hoggers

Label applied to those Conservatives favourable to tariff reform from 1903. After the 1906 electoral debacle they represented the majority of the parliamentary party.

YMCA

Nickname for group of left-wing Conservative backbenchers in the 1924–29 parliament. Considered too earnest and left-wing by their party leadership the group included Harold Macmillan, Gerald Loder, Noel Skelton and Robert Boothby. Their 1927 publication *Industry and the State* urged greater state intervention in both economic and social spheres.

Young Englanders

Quartet of Conservatives (Benjamin Disraeli, George Smythe, Lord John Manners and Alexander Baillie-Cochrane) who shot to prominence for their localised expression of distrust for Peel's policies. Claimed to represent opposition to liberalism in religion and utilitarianism and middle-class liberalism in politics and economics. An irritant rather than political force, their significance lay in the emergence of Disraeli. His hostility to Peel was motivated by ambition and annoyance at not being offered political office in 1841.

CONSERVATIVE REBELS AND DEFECTORS SINCE 1900

1903

John Gorst (Cambridge University) declares himself an independent supporter of free trade. He is defeated at 1906 election by official Conservative candidate. Subsequently joins the Liberal Party.

1904

January — Winston Churchill (MP for Oldham) resigns whip in support of free trade. Defects to Liberals in April.

March — John E.B. Seely (MP for Isle of Wight) becomes independent supporter of free trade and submits himself to a by-election in April, but is unopposed. He contests the 1906 and January 1910 elections in Abercromby as a free trader against Conservative opposition before joining the Liberal party in March 1910.

April — Ivor Guest (MP for Cardiff) and John Dickson-Poynder (MP for Chippenham) defect to Liberals over free trade.

1905

March — Ernest Hatch (MP for Gorton) becomes independent in defence of free trade. Retires in January 1906.

1906

February — Austin Taylor (MP for East Toxteth) joins Liberals having only contested (although unopposed) the seat the previous month as a Conservative.

1907

February — Rowland Hunt (MP for Ludlow) has whip withdrawn for a month after he attacked Balfour's leadership on the tariff reform issue during a parliamentary debate. He was a long-term supporter of tariff reform.

1917

September — Henry Page Croft (MP for Christchurch) and Richard Cooper (MP for Walsall) form National Party, dissatisfied with the continuation of the Coalition and feeling the Conservatives are not being 'Tory' enough, especially in face of upsurge in trade union activity during 1917. Both men subsequently elected in 1918 election. Cooper retires in 1922, but Page Croft returns to Conservative whip in 1923.

1920

October — Oswald Mosley (Harrow) becomes an Independent before joining the Labour Party in May 1924.

1927

October — Robert Newman (MP for Exeter) becomes Independent after failing to secure re-selection. This provokes the withdrawal of the whip. Re-elected as an Independent in May 1929 against an official Conservative candidate.

1928

July — Sir Basil Peto (MP for Barnstaple) has whip withdrawn after he moved, without warning, an amendment against the government's Naval Prize bill. Peto had already resisted the Racecourse Betting bill earlier in the month (voting eight times with Labour).

1931

February — William Allen (MP for Belfast West) joins Mosley's New Party.

March — Sir William Wayland (MP for Canterbury) has the whip withdrawn for a month after he publicly supported the Empire Crusade candidate in the St George's by-election.

1934

June — James Lockwood (MP for Shipley) becomes Independent after failing to secure re-selection. Defeated in November 1935 by official Conservative candidate.

1935

May — Frederick Astbury (MP for West Salford), Linton Thorp (MP for Colne and Nelson) and Alfred Todd (Berwick-upon-Tweed) become Independents. Joseph Nall (MP for Manchester Hulme) and the Duchess of Atholl (MP for Kinross and West Perth) resign whip, but return in November and September 1935 respectively. All five wrote to Baldwin expressing dissent over India and the 'socialist' nature of domestic reforms.

1936

June — Harold Macmillan (MP for Stockton-on-Tees) resigns National whip in opposition to abandonment of sanctions against Italy, but importantly retains the Conservative whip. Restored in July 1937.

1938

April — Duchess of Atholl (MP for Kinross and West Perth), deselected by her local Conservative Association, becomes Independent. Loses by-election in December.

1942

May — A.S. Cunningham-Reid (MP for St Marylebone) has whip withdrawn because of his advocacy for a 'People's Movement' that sought to improve war efficiency and was planning to create constituency committees. This caused a split in the St Marylebone Conservative Association with a rival organisation being created that received official Central Office sanction for the 1945 election and successfully defeated Cunningham-Reid's independent candidature.

1948

November — Eric Gandar Dower (MP for Caithness) becomes an Independent. During the 1945 election campaign he had announced his intention to seek re-election after the defeat of Japan but, as a result of pressure from his Caithness Conservative Association, he failed to do this until he decided to resign his candidature and the Conservative whip. Remained an Independent until 1950.

1954

June — John Mellor (MP for Sutton Coldfield) and Henry Legge-Bourke (MP for Isle of Ely) resign whip in protest at withdrawal from Suez Canal zone. Restored July and October 1954 respectively.

1956

November — Cyril Banks (MP for Pudsey) becomes independent after criticising the Government's Suez policy, but retakes whip December 1958. Retires 1959 after local party refuse to re-select him as candidate.

1957

May — Eight Conservative MPs resign whip in protest at Macmillan's decision to allow British ships again to use the Suez Canal. Patrick Maitland (Lanark) has whip restored in December; while John Biggs-Davidson (Chigwell), Anthony Fell (Yarmouth), Viscount Hinchingbrooke (South Dorset), Henry Turner (Oxford), Paul Williams (Sunderland South) and Frank Medlicott (Central Norfolk) do not return to fold until mid-1958. Victor Raikes (Garston) and Angus Maude (South Ealing) resign seats October 1957 and April 1958 respectively.

1959

January — Sir David Robertson (MP for Caithness and Sutherland) becomes Independent after his private member's bill for Scottish Highlands was 'talked out'. Re-elected October 1959 as an Independent, but without Conservative opposition.

1961	
October	William Duthie (MP for Banffshire) becomes Independent in opposition to the Sea Fish Industry bill but returns to whip in November 1963.
1962	
	Frank Medlicott (formerly MP for Central Norfolk) joins Liberal Party and subsequently becomes its party treasurer 1969–71.
1964	
January	Donald Johnson (MP for Carlisle) becomes an Independent after being deselected by his local party in December 1963. He had failed to support the Macmillan government over the Profumo vote of confidence, allowing the *Daily Express* to photograph him playing golf at the time of the division. This act of public disloyalty and personality clashes contributed to the deselection. He unsuccessfully contested the seat as an Independent in 1964 election.
1966	
July	Geoffrey Hirst (MP for Shipley) becomes an Independent Conservative until his retirement in 1970. He felt the party was not clear on its intentions, especially concerning the Prices and Incomes Bill.
November	Humphry Berkeley (MP for Lancaster until October 1964) resigns from party having lost his seat in the general election. He was critical of the party's failure to welcome the 1965 Race Relations Act. Joins Labour party in July 1970 and unsuccessfully contests North Fylde upon its behalf in October 1974.
1974	
June	Enoch Powell resigns from the Party having declined to stand as a Conservative candidate in the February 1974 general election in protest at Heath's EEC policy. Shortly joins the Ulster Unionists and becomes their MP for South Down in October 1974.
August	Christopher Hollis (former MP for Devizes, 1945–55) joins the Liberal Party.
1981	
March	Christopher Brocklebank-Fowler (Norfolk North West) becomes only Conservative MP to defect to SDP. Defeated in 1983 election by official Conservative candidate.
1984	
December	Lord Alport is stripped of the Conservative whip in the House of Lords after speaking and voting for the opposition on what was considered to a censure motion of the government's economic policy.

1994

November — Nicholas Budgen (Wolverhampton South West), Michael Carttiss (Great Yarmouth), Christopher Gill (Ludlow), Teresa Gorman (Billericay), Tony Marlow (Northampton North), Richard Shepherd (Aldridge-Brownhills), Teddy Taylor (Southend East) and John Wilkinson (Ruislip Northwood) have whip withdrawn for failing to support the Major government on the European Communities (finance) bill. The whip is restored in April 1995. Richard Body (MP for Holland with Boston) resigns whip in support of eight fellow Conservatives. Retakes party whip in April 1996.

1995

October — Alan Howarth (MP for Stratford) defects to Labour claiming the Conservatives have abandoned one-nation values and moved too rightward.

December — Emma Nicholson (MP for Devon West and Torridge and a former Deputy Party Chairman) defects to Liberal Democrats.

1996

June — John Gorst (Hendon North) claims to be 'free from whip' in protest at hospital closures in his constituency. Formally resigns whip in December.

October — Lord McAlpine (former Party Treasurer) defects to Referendum Party.

1997

March — George Gardiner (MP for Reigate) having been deselected by his local Conservative association announces his defection to Goldsmith's Referendum Party.

September — Hugh Dykes (MP for Harrow East until defeated in May 1997) defects to Liberal Democrats. As a pro-European he considers the failure of Kenneth Clarke to secure the party leadership the final straw.

November — Peter Temple-Morris (MP for Kidderminster) resigns whip before joining Labour in June 1998. A former supporter of Heseltine he had become disillusioned with the rightward shift of the party since 1997 and particularly its European policy.

1999

June — Adrian Rogers (Conservative candidate for Exeter in 1997 election) defects to UK Independence Party.

December — Shaun Woodward (MP for Witney – one of the Conservatives' safest seats) defects to Labour. Disgruntled at his sacking from the shadow front bench because of his refusal to support the preservation of Clause 28.

2000

August	Ivan Massow, the gay millionaire and someone once considered by Central Office as a potential candidate for London Mayor, defects to Labour blaming intolerance.
June	Tasmina Ahmed-Sheikh, a Conservative MSP candidate in 1999, defects to Scottish National Party (SNP).
November	Bill Newton Dunn (East Midlands MEP) defects to Liberal Democrats in opposition to Hague's European policy.

2001

April	Charles Wardle (MP for Bexhill and Battle) has whip withdrawn for favouring an independent candidate as his successor rather than the official Conservative choice.
June	Anthony Nelson (MP for Chichester until 1997) defects to labour because of the Conservatives' Eurosceptism.

Part 5

BIOGRAPHIES OF LEADING CONSERVATIVES

5. BIOGRAPHIES OF LEADING CONSERVATIVES

Aberdeen (George Hamilton Gordon), 4th Earl of (1784–1860): ambassador extraordinary, Vienna 1813; British representative Treaty of Paris 1814; Chancellor of Duchy of Lancaster 1828; Foreign Secretary 1828–30, 1841–46; Secretary for War and Colonies 1834–35; from 1846 leader of Peelite faction in House of Lords; 1852–55 Prime Minister over a coalition of whigs and Peelites; resigned 1855 when Roebuck's motion for a committee of enquiry into the conduct of the Crimean War was carried. Succeeded as Earl of Aberdeen 1801.

Acland-Hood Sir Fuller Alexander (1853–1917): Conservative MP 1892–1911; whip 1900–02; Chief Whip 1902–11. As the Chief Whip he devoted his energies to resisting the 'internal' threat from Joseph Chamberlain, rather than concentrating on modernising the party machinery and subsequently incurred considerable criticism. Created 1st Baron St Audries, 1911.

Akers-Douglas Aretas (1851–1926): Unionist MP 1880–1910; Unionist whip 1883–85; Unionist Chief Whip 1886–92; First Commissioner of Works 1895–1902; Home Secretary 1902–05; created Viscount Chilston 1911. Typifying the country squirearchy, Akers-Douglas was at the heart of British politics during its transition towards a mass electorate with modern political machinery. An active party organiser he became chairman of the 1911 Unionist Organisation Committee.

Alport Cuthbert James McCall (1912–98): Conservative MP 1950–61; Director Conservative Political Centre 1945–50; Assistant Postmaster-General 1955–57; Parliamentary Under-Secretary for Commonwealth Relations 1957–59; Minister of State for Commonwealth Relations 1959–61; created Baron Alport 1961; High Commissioner for Rhodesia and Nyasaland 1961–63. 'Cub' played a crucial role in reviving Conservative fortunes post-1945 and then as a minister overseeing Britain's withdrawal from Empire. A founding member of the 'One Nation Group' he later criticised Thatcherism and became the only peer to lose the party whip for dissent in 1984.

Amery (Harold) Julian (1919–96): Conservative MP 1950–66, 1969–79; Diplomatic Corps and Military Special Service career 1939–45; various under-secretaryships 1957–60; Secretary of State for Air 1962–64; Minister of Public Buildings and Works 1970–72; Minister of State for Foreign and Commonwealth Affairs 1972–74; son of Leo Amery. Leading figure with the Suez Group despite being a supporter of an expanded Commonwealth and advocate of European Union. By nature a 'plotter', whose exploits with the Balkan resistance during the Second World War were legendary, he was never quite accepted into the inner circles of the party. Created Baron Amery of Lustleigh, 1992.

Amery Leopold Stennett (1873–1955): Conservative MP 1911–45; First Lord of the Admiralty 1922–24, Secretary of State for Dominions and Colonies 1924–29, Secretary of State for India 1940–45, journalist and writer. A protectionist and campaigner for imperial unity, it was suggested that Amery could have been prime minister if only he had been half a foot taller and shortened his parliamentary speeches by half an hour! His demand, 'in the name of God, go' (quoting Cromwell), that Neville Chamberlain resign in May 1940 provided a lead for disaffected Conservatives.

Astor (Nancy) Viscountess (1879–1964): Conservative MP 1919–45 becoming the first woman to sit in Parliament. She was never a serious candidate for ministerial office being regarded as more personality than substance. Her weekend gatherings at Cliveden House gained notoriety in the 1930s because of a belief that they were used to further the government's policy of appeasement.

Baldwin Stanley (1867–1947): Conservative MP 1908–37; Financial Secretary to the Treasury 1917–21, President of the Board of Trade 1921–22; Chancellor of Exchequer 1922–23; Party Leader 1923–37; Prime Minister 1923–24, 1924–29, 1935–37; Lord President of the Council (effectively deputy Prime Minister) 1931–35; created 1st Earl Baldwin of Bewdley 1937. A moderate Conservative anxious to guide Britain from the political middle ground, Baldwin became the first Prime Minister to be recognisable to the electorate both in sight and sound. Leadership characterised by periods of lethargy and 'drift' balanced by his tenacity to hold on to office and through his adroit handling of the General Strike and Abdication crisis. Reputation unfairly tarnished by 'guilty men' association with failure to prepare for the Second World War.

Balfour Arthur James (1848–1930): Conservative MP 1874–1922; President of the Local Government Board 1885; Secretary for Scotland 1886; Chief Secretary for Ireland 1887–91; Leader of the Commons and First Lord of the Treasury 1891–92, 1895–1902; Prime Minister 1902–5; Party Leader 1902–11; member of Committee of Imperial Defence which enabled him to attend war cabinets 1914; First Lord of the Admiralty 1915–16; Foreign Secretary 1916–19; Lord President of Council 1919–22, 1925–29; supported Lloyd George coalition 1922; nephew of 3rd Marquess of Salisbury whom he served as parliamentary private secretary 1878–80. With a reputation as an able administrator and intelligent politician his premiership and leadership proved disappointing. Particularly troubled by tariff reform he gave an impression of indecision and indifference threatening the party's very survival. Accusations of ineffectuality and nepotism persuaded Balfour to resign the leadership. As foreign secretary 1916–19 he was responsible for the Balfour declaration on Palestine. Created 1st Earl of Balfour, 1922.

Ball Joseph (1885–1961): MI5 1919–27; Director of Publicity, Conservative Central Office 1927–30; Director, Conservative Research Department 1930–39; Deputy Chairman of National Publicity Bureau 1934–39; Deputy Chairman, Security Executive 1940–42, responsible for enforcing the 18B Regulations. A close ally of Neville Chamberlain, Ball secretly masterminded the purchase of the journal *Truth* for party propaganda purposes. A shadowy figure considered one of the *éminence grise* of official conservatism.

Barber Anthony (1920–): Conservative MP 1951–64, 1965–74; Government whip 1955; PPS to Harold Macmillan 1958; Junior Treasury minister 1959–62; Minister of Health 1963–64; Party Chairman 1967–70; Chancellor of the Duchy of Lancaster 1970; Chancellor of Exchequer 1970–74; Life Peerage 1974. Involved in the early negotiations to join the EEC, then untimely death of Macleod propelled Barber to the Treasury. His tax cutting and liberalising economic policies fuelled inflation and forced the introduction in November 1972 of a statutory prices and incomes policy. This brought the Heath government into conflict with the miners.

Beaconsfield (Benjamin Disraeli), 1st Earl of (1804–81): MP 1837–76; Leader Protectionist MPs 1849; Chancellor of Exchequer and Leader of Commons 1852, 1858–59, 1866–68; Leader Opposition MPs 1849–52, 1852–58, 1859–66; Prime Minister 1868, 1874–80; Leader Conservative party 1868–81; Anglicanised Jew who combined writing with politics. He championed protectionism helping to destroy Peel and was motivated by personal ambition to reach 'top of greasy pole'. This explains, in part, his support for the 1867 extension of the franchise. His associating the Conservatives with social reform was more rhetorical than practical and in many respects his 1874–80 administration was a disappointment. Ingratiated himself with Queen Victoria who found his brown-nosing and flattery vastly preferable to the dourness of Gladstone.

Beaverbrook (William Maxwell Aitken), 1st Baron (1879–1964): proprietor of *Daily Express, Sunday Express, Evening Standard*; Conservative MP 1910–16; Ministry of Information 1918–19; Minister of Aircraft Production 1940–41; Minister of Supply 1942–45. He was never a 'natural' Conservative appearing to have no loyalty or attachment to the party and had a reputation for mischief. Thus excluded from the inner loop of high politics for most of the inter-war years. He consoled himself with his media empire, which he frequently used to hijack political issues.

Biffen John (1930–): Conservative MP 1961–79; various opposition spokesmen positions including Shadow Cabinet 1976–77, 1978–79; Chief Secretary to Treasury 1979–81; Minister for Trade 1981–82; Lord President 1982–83; Lord Privy Seal 1983–87; Life Peerage 1997.

Birkenhead (Frederick Edwin Smith), 1st Earl of (1872–1930): Conservative MP 1906–19; Solicitor General 1915; Attorney-General 1915–19; as Baron Birkenhead, Lord Chancellor 1919–22; coalition supporter 1922; India Secretary 1924–28. As a leading Conservative supporter of Lloyd George's coalition he felt unable to serve under Bonar Law.

Bonar Law Andrew (1858–1923): Conservative MP 1900–10, 1911–23; junior minister 1902–5; Party Leader 1911–21 resigning due to ill health, returned after speaking against Lloyd George Coalition at Carlton Club, October 1922; Colonial Secretary 1915–16; Chancellor of Exchequer and member, War

Cabinet 1916–19; Lord Privy Seal 1919–21; Prime Minister 1922–23. Born in Canada of Ulster parentage and raised in Scotland, this mix of cultures profoundly affected his politics. Gave outspoken support for Ulster Unionists in Home Rule crisis 1912–14.

Boothby Robert (1900–86): Conservative MP 1924–58; PPS to Churchill 1926–29; Parliamentary Secretary, Ministry of Food 1940–41; British delegate to Council of Europe 1949–55; long-term lover of Dorothy Macmillan (wife of Harold Macmillan). Initial promise never fulfilled despite close association with Churchill. Boothby's future political career was dogged by scandal. Created Baron Boothby, 1958.

Boyle Edward (1923–81): Conservative MP 1950–70; various junior posts 1951–56, 1957–62; resigned in protest at invasion of Suez Canal zone 1956; Minister of Education 1962–64; shadow cabinet 1964–69; a liberally inclined Conservative, Boyle specialised in matters concerning education and opposed demands for stricter immigration controls. Created Baron Boyle of Handsworth, 1970.

Brooke Henry (1903–84): Conservative MP 1938–45, 1950–66; early career in local politics; entered parliament in one of the Munich by-elections; Financial Secretary to Treasury 1954–57; Minister of Housing and Local Government and Minister for Welsh Affairs 1957–61; Chief Secretary to Treasury 1961–62; Home Secretary 1962–64 where his Labour opponents dubbed him the 'most hated man in Parliament'. According to Lord Denning, who was conducting an wide-ranging inquiry into the Profumo affair and associated scandals, Brooke was one of only two ministers untainted by the suggestion of scandal or impropriety. The handling of the Profumo case had caused Brooke to consider resignation. His wife, Barbara, was very active in the party organisation. Created Baron Brooke of Cumnor, 1966.

Buchan-Hepburn Patrick (1901–74): Conservative MP 1931–50, 1950–57; PPS to Oliver Stanley 1931–39; Deputy Chief Whip 1945; Chief Whip 1948–55; Parliamentary Secretary to Treasury 1951–55; Minister of Works 1955–57; created Baron Hailes 1957; Governor-General of the West Indies 1958–62. As Chief Whip, he represented the last of the old guard, seeking to retain a sense of military discipline among the parliamentary party ever conscious of the limited size of Churchill's majority.

Butler Richard Austen (Rab) (1902–82): Conservative MP 1929–65; junior minister, India Office (1932–37), Ministry of Labour (1937–38), Foreign Office (1938–41); President of Board of Education 1941–45, passed Education Act 1944; chairman of Conservative Research Department 1945–64; Chancellor of Exchequer 1951–55; Lord Privy Seal 1955–59; Party Chairman 1959–61; Home Secretary 1959–62; Minister responsible for Central African Federation 1962–63; First Secretary of State and deputy Prime Minister 1962–63; Foreign Secretary 1963–64. Twice passed over for the office of Party Leader, despite having frequently deputised for Eden, because of lingering association with 1930s appeasement and later because of the personal enmity of Macmillan.

Spent last years as Master of Trinity College, Cambridge. Created Baron Butler of Saffron Waldron, 1965.

Cairns (Hugh MacCalmont), 1st Earl (1819–1885): MP 1852–66; Solicitor-General 1858–59; Attorney-General 1866, judge 1866–68; Lord Chancellor 1868, 1874–80; the Ulsterman, low church and ultra-Protestant in perspective, was throughout the 1870s a key figure in the inner circles of the Conservative leadership. He was a member of the triumvirate with Derby and Disraeli. He was an intelligent politician, with an unfair reputation for rigidity; he briefly led the House of Lords 1868–69. Nicknamed 'Great Cat' by Salisbury.

Canning George (1770–1827): MP 1794–1822, 1823–27; junior minister Foreign Office 1796–99; President of the India Board 1799–1800, 1816–21; Paymaster-General 1800–1; Treasurer of the Navy 1804–6; Foreign Secretary 1807–9, 1822–27; Leader of House of Commons 1822–27; Prime Minister and Chancellor of Exchequer 1827. Regarded as a liberal in his conduct of foreign affairs. As Prime Minister, Canning managed to hold together a Tory–Whig coalition. This collapsed shortly after his death.

Carrington (Peter), 6th Baron (1919–): Conservative peer, succeeded to title 1938; Opposition Whip, House of Lords 1947–51; junior office 1951, 1954; High Commissioner to Australia 1956; First Lord of Admiralty 1959; Minister without Portfolio and Leader of Lords 1964–70; Defence Minister 1970–74; Party Chairman 1972–74; Minister for Energy 1974; Foreign Secretary 1979–82, resigning after invasion of Falklands by Argentina.

Cecil Lord Robert (Edward Algernon Robert Gascoyne-Cecil) (1864–1958): Conservative MP 1906–10, 1911–23; junior ministerial office 1915–18; Lord Privy Seal 1923–24; Chancellor of the Duchy of Lancaster 1924–27; President, League of Nations Union 1923–45; winner Nobel Peace Prize 1937. Leading inter-war supporter of collective security and the League of Nations. He masterminded the 1934–35 Peace Ballot. Created 1st Viscount Cecil of Chelwood, 1923.

Chamberlain (Arthur) Neville (1869–1940): Conservative MP 1918–40; Minister for National Service 1917; Minister of Health 1924–29; Party Chairman 1930–31; Director of Conservative Research Department 1929–40; Chancellor of Exchequer 1931–37; Prime Minister 1937–40; Lord President 1940. He proved to be a controversial prime minister. His critics suggest he failed to resist the aggression of Hitler which caused the Second World War; to others, and increasingly historians, he recognised the weaknesses of both Britain's economy and defences and sought to mediate while rearming. His achievements at the Ministry of Health have been positively re-evaluated. A true political professional who exercised firm leadership, expected loyalty, personalised debate and was dismissive of his critics.

Chamberlain (Joseph) Austen (1863–1937): Liberal Unionist MP 1892–1906, Conservative MP 1906–37; held a succession of posts including Chancellor of Exchequer 1895–1905, 1919–21; unsuccessful bid for Party Leadership 1911; Secretary of State for India 1915–17; war cabinet 1918–19; Party Leader and

Lord Privy Seal 1921–22, resigned Party Leadership after Carlton Club meeting, 1922 and refused to served under Bonar Law; Foreign Secretary 1924–29 where his achievement was the signing of the Locarno treaty for which he won the Nobel Peace Prize; First Lord of Admiralty 1931. Son of Joseph Chamberlain and half-brother of Neville, the monocled Austen, with a passion for orchids, spent the remainder of the 1930s an increasingly disgruntled (if still widely respected) backbencher.

Chamberlain Joseph (1836–1914): MP 1876–1914 (Radical 1876–86, then Unionist); Mayor of Birmingham 1873–75 where he pioneered slum clearance; Liberal President of Board of Trade 1880–85; President of Local Government Board 1886; leader Liberal Unionists 1891–1906 after breaking with Gladstone over Irish Home Rule; Colonial Secretary 1895–1903 where became a champion for tariff reform and imperial federation. He resigned to lead the tariff reform cause, however a stroke in 1907 ended his political career prematurely.

Churchill Lord Randolph Henry Spencer (1849–1895): Conservative MP 1874–75, 1885–95; India Secretary 1885–86; Chancellor of Exchequer 1886–87. A political intriguer who sought to harness the forces of 'Tory Democracy' for his own ends, but whose decline was even more meteoric than his rise to political prominence. His resignation from government in 1887, in response to increased expenditure, prematurely ended his political career.

Churchill Winston (1874–1965): Conservative MP 1900–4, Liberal MP 1904–22 (crossed to Liberals in defence of free trade), Conservative MP 1924–64; junior office 1905–8; President of Board of Trade 1908–10; Home Secretary 1910–11; First Lord of the Admiralty 1911–15, but obliged to resign over role in disastrous Dardanelles campaign; Minister of Munitions 1917–19; Secretary of State for War and Air 1919–21; Secretary of State for Colonies 1921–22; Chancellor of Exchequer 1924–29; resigned from Conservative shadow cabinet 1931 over protectionism and India; First Lord of the Admiralty 1939–40; Prime Minister 1940–45, 1951–55. Son of Lord Randolph Churchill, Winston's reputation has reached mythical proportions in the popular imagination because of his combative and imaginative wartime leadership; however it is recognised that his achievements before 1939, especially his opposition to the National government's liberal India policy and his stance on the Abdication, were ignoble. His period as peacetime premier was without distinction, especially following his stroke in 1953.

Clarke Kenneth (1940–): Conservative MP 1970– ; Whips' Office 1972–74; opposition spokesman 1974–79; junior minister, Transport 1979–82, Health 1982–85; Paymaster-General 1985–87; Chancellor of the Duchy of Lancaster 1987–88; Health Secretary 1988–90; Education Minister 1990; Home Secretary 1990–93; Chancellor of Exchequer 1993–97; the 'Hush-Puppy'-wearing Chancellor and Europhile closely follows the declining fortunes of his football team, Nottingham Forest, and is a keen bird-watcher. Contested the 1997 leadership election as the centre-left candidate but, despite having as

Chancellor successfully restrained inflation and secured economic growth, his Europeanism disadvantaged his claim to Major's mantle.

Cooper (Alfred) Duff (1890–1954): Conservative MP 1924–29, 1931–45 after winning the St George's by-election which rescued Baldwin's embattled leadership; junior office 1928–29; Financial Secretary to Treasury 1934–35; Secretary of State for War 1935–37; First Lord of the Admiralty 1937–38; Ministry of Information 1940–41; Chancellor of the Duchy of Lancaster 1941–43; British representative with Free French 1943–44; Ambassador to Paris 1944–47; a colourful political character, with a fiery temper, whose expectations (and his wife's) were never fulfilled, especially following his resignation over the 1938 Munich agreement. In retirement he devoted himself to writing historical works and his memoirs, some of the most engaging for his political generation. Created 1st Viscount Norwich, 1952.

Cranbrook (Gathorne Hardy), 1st Earl of (1814–1906): Conservative MP 1856–78; Home Secretary 1867–68; President of Poor Law Board, 1868; Secretary for War 1874–78; Secretary for India 1878–80; leading Conservative figure in the House of Commons, even a potential candidate for leader in the early 1870s, who achieved his status through his own abilities rather than his aristocratic connections. Created Earl of Cranbrook in 1878, but found it difficult to rival the established Conservative peer leaders.

Croft Henry Page (1881–1947): Conservative MP 1910–40; under-secretary War Office 1940–45; a leading protectionist and imperialist, Croft was chairman of the Tariff Reform League 1913–17, and the Empire Industries Association (EIA) 1928–45; a leading 'diehard' and principal organiser of the National Party, a breakaway right-wing faction 1917–22. Created Baron Croft 1940.

Cross (Richard Assheton), 1st Viscount (1823–1914): MP 1857–62, 1868–86; Home Secretary 1874–80, 1885–86; India Secretary 1886–92; Chancellor of the Duchy of Lancaster 1895; Lord President of the Council 1895–1900. Charged with enacting the Disraelian vision for social reform, Cross found the 1874 Conservative administration under-prepared for legislating. Cross and his colleague W.H. Smith were nicknamed 'Marshall and Snelgrove' by Lord Randolph Churchill in reference to their urban middle-class business antecedents.

Cunliffe-Lister Philip (1884–1972): Conservative MP 1918–35; junior office 1920–22; President of Board of Trade 1922–24, 1924–29, 1931; Colonial Secretary 1931–35; Secretary of Air 1935–38; Minister resident, West Africa 1942–44; Minister of Civil Aviation 1944–45; Chancellor of the Duchy of Lancaster 1951–52; Commonwealth Secretary 1952–55; changed surname from Lloyd-Greame 1924, created 1st Viscount Swinton 1935; the acceleration in the air defence programme that Swinton oversaw from 1935 was crucial in preparing the RAF to fight the Battle of Britain; in the post-war years he concentrated on party organisation and oversaw the creation of the Conservative college at Swinton, his Yorkshire family home.

Curzon (George Nathaniel), 1st Marquess (1859–1925): Conservative MP 1886–98; Viceroy of India 1898–1905; Lord Privy Seal 1915–16; President of Air Board 1916; Lord President of the Council 1916–19, 1924–25; Foreign Secretary 1919–24; leader of House of Lords 1916–24; despite being a strong supporter of the Lloyd George coalition he was given office under Bonar Law and was widely tipped as his successor. Nicknamed the 'Purple Emperor' by Balfour.

Davidson John Colin Campbell (1889–1970): Conservative MP 1920–23, 1924–37; Chancellor of the Duchy of Lancaster 1923–24, 1931–37; junior Admiralty minister 1924–26; Party Chairman 1926–30. Davidson worked behind the scenes never achieving cabinet status but gaining a reputation as an *éminence grise.* Reorganised the party machine, both in terms of finance and organisation, and worked closely with Baldwin. Sacrificed in 1930 to satiate Baldwin's critics. Succeeded as 2nd Viscount Davidson, 1937.

Deedes William (Bill) (1913–): Conservative MP 1950–74; journalist; junior minister, Housing 1954–55, and Home Office 1955–57; Minister without Portfolio 1962–64; editor of *Daily Telegraph* 1974–1986. Created Baron Deedes 1986.

Derby (Edward George Geoffrey Smith Stanley), 14th Earl of (1799–1869): MP 1820–44 (Whig); junior whip 1827; junior minister 1827–28; Chief Secretary for Ireland 1830–33; Secretary of State for War and Colonies 1833–34; crossed to join Conservatives (Derby's Dilly); Secretary of State for Colonies 1841–45, resigning in protest at the repeal of Corn Laws; leader Protectionist peers 1846; failed to form government 1851; Prime Minister 1852, 1858–59, 1866–68, all of which were minority governments. The decision to take office stemmed from a desire to establish the Conservative party as a credible party of government.

Derby (Edward George Villiers Stanley), 17th Earl of (1865–1948): Conservative MP 1892–1906; junior whip 1895–1900; junior minister War Office 1900–3; Postmaster-General 1903–5; Secretary of State for War 1916–18, 1922–24; Ambassador in Paris 1918–20; styled Lord Stanley 1893–1908, succeeded as 17th Earl 1908. Exercised considerable political influence in his fiefdom of Lancashire. He manipulated rank and file party opinion in the North West in 1912–13 and 1924, effectively deploying Lancashire hostility to protection and 'food taxes' in order to pressurise the party leadership to give way.

Derby (Edward Henry Stanley), 15th Earl of (1826–1893): Conservative (then later Liberal) politician. His early ministerial posts included Colonial Secretary, 1858 and Secretary for India, 1858–59. Declined the Greek Crown, 1863. Foreign Secretary, 1866–68, 1874–78. Resigned over Eastern Question 1878. Left Conservative Party, 1879. Liberal Colonial Secretary, 1882–85. Leader of Liberal Unionists in the Lords, 1886–91.

Devonshire (Spencer Compton Cavendish), 8th Duke of (1833–1908): Whig MP 1857–68, 1869–91 (Liberal Unionist from 1886); Liberal Cabinet minister 1866, 1868–74; Leader Liberal MPs 1875–80, Liberal Unionists MPs 1886–91; Leader Liberal Unionist Party 1886–1906; Lord President of the Council

1895–1903 resigning in defence of free trade; President of Board of Education 1900–2; Leader of Lords 1902–3; widely known, while Marquess of Hartington, as 'Harty-Tarty'.

Disraeli Benjamin – *see* Beaconsfield, 1st Earl of

Du Cann Edward (1924–): Conservative MP 1956–87; junior minister Board of Trade 1963–64; opposition spokesman Trade and Shipping 1964–65; Party Chairman 1965–67; chairman 1922 Committee 1972–84 where he provided a focus for opposition to Heath; chairman of various select committees including Expenditure 1971–73 and Treasury and Civil Service 1979–83; President, National Union 1981–82.

Dugdale Thomas (1897–1977): Conservative MP 1929–59; PPS to Cunliffe-Lister 1931–35, Baldwin 1935–40; junior minister, Treasury 1937–40, 1941–42; Minister for Agriculture 1951–54 resigning over the Crichel Down affair. Passed over by Churchill for the position of Chief Whip, he became Party Chairman 1942–44 during which time he tried to persuade the leadership of the need to prepare for peacetime reconstruction. Created 1st Baron Crathorne, 1959.

Eden (Robert) Anthony (1897–1977): Conservative MP 1923–57; junior minister, Foreign Office 1931–33; Lord Privy Seal 1933–35; Minister for League of Nations Affairs 1935; Foreign Secretary 1935–38, resigning over Chamberlain's apparent concessions to Italy over Abyssinia and remaining on the back benches as an unconvincing critic of appeasement; Dominions Secretary 1939–40; Foreign Secretary 1940–45, 1951–55; Prime Minister 1955–57 resigning after the fiasco of the Suez invasion. Always interested in foreign policy, Eden had little time for domestic affairs. A highly strung individual, the failure of his anti-appeasement methods against Nasser led historians to begin re-evaluating the viability of Chamberlain's 1930s foreign policy. Created 1st Earl of Avon, 1961.

Elliot Walter (1888–1958): Conservative MP 1918–23, 1924–45, 1946–50, 1950–58; despite voting to continue the coalition, Junior Minister, Scottish Health 1923–24, 1924–26, Scotland 1926–29; Financial Secretary to Treasury 1931–32; Minister for Agriculture 1932–36; Scottish Secretary 1936–38; Minister of Health 1938–40; lifelong political association with Scotland. Kept doubts about Chamberlain's appeasement policy private.

Erskine-Hill Alex (1894–1947): Conservative MP 1935–45; chairman of 1922 Committee 1940–44 during which time the committee became the focus for party discontent with Churchill's wartime leadership.

Eyres-Monsell Bolton Meredith (1881–1969): Conservative MP 1910–35; whip 1911–21; junior minister, Admiralty 1921–23; Chief Whip 1923–31 during which time he sought to contain Baldwin's critics; First Lord of the Admiralty 1931–36 where he sought to improve the defence provisions of the Navy and oversaw the 1935 Anglo-German Naval treaty. Succeeded as 2nd Viscount Monsell, 1935.

Gathorne Hardy – *see* Cranbrook, 1st Earl of

Gilmour, Ian (1926–): Conservative MP 1962–92; junior minister, Defence 1970–72, 1974; Lord Privy Seal 1979–81. A member of One Nation Group until 1992, he was also a past editor of *The Spectator*. One of the 'wets' Thatcher sacked from her cabinet after they sought to oppose her cuts in public expenditure and challenged her economic policy. Created Baron Gilmour, 1992.

Goderich Frederick John Robinson, 1st Viscount – *see* Ripon, 1st Earl of

Gorst Sir John Eldon (1835–1916): Conservative MP 1866–68, 1875–92, 1892–1906; creator of Central Office in 1870, he must claim some credit for the 1874 electoral success particularly because of his concentration on the boroughs which had traditionally been neglected by the party; excluded himself from potential cabinet office by rebelliousness over labour questions; a founder of the 'Fourth Party' and the Primrose League. Increasingly disillusioned with the failure to implement 'tory democracy', he resigned from the party in 1903 in support of free trade. Solicitor General 1885–86; junior minister Education 1895–1902.

Goschen George Joachim (1831–1907): MP 1863–86 (Liberal), 1887–1900 (Liberal Unionist); as a Liberal held office as President of the Poor Law Board 1868–71 and First Lord of the Admiralty 1871–74; as a Liberal Unionist he was Chancellor of Exchequer 1887–92; and First Lord of the Admiralty 1895–1900. Created 1st Viscount Goschen, 1900.

Gower Robert Patrick Malcolm (1887–1964): civil servant; assistant to Bonar Law and Austen Chamberlain 1917–22, and Bonar Law and Stanley Baldwin when they were Prime Ministers 1922–24; deputy Director 1928 and Director Publicity, Conservative Central Office 1929–39.

Hacking Douglas (1884–1950): Conservative MP 1918–45; junior minister Home Office 1925–27, Home Office 1933–34, War Office 1934–35, Dominions 1935–36; vice-chairman, National Union 1930; Party Chairman 1936–42 where he began an overhaul of organisation which laid the foundation for the post-war party. Created 1st Baron Hacking, 1945.

Hague William (1961–): Conservative MP 1989– ; junior minister Social Security 1993–95; Welsh Secretary 1995–97 where he met his future wife Ffion; Party Leader 1997–2001; having first shot to national prominence with his address as a teenager to the 1975 party conference Hague has become the youngest Party Leader since 1832. He was faced with the mammoth task of reviving the party's fortunes after the annihilation of 1997, when he failed to win the June 2001 election he announced his resignation.

Hailsham (Quintin Hogg), 2nd Viscount (1907–): used 1963 Peerage Act to renounce hereditary title, granted life peerage as Baron Hailsham of St Marylebone 1970. Conservative MP 1938–50, 1963–70; leading member of wartime Tory Reform Group; author *The Case for Conservatism* (1947); First Lord of the Admiralty 1956–57; Minister of Education 1957; Party Chairman 1957–59; Lord President of the Council 1957–59, 1960–64; Leader of House of Lords 1960–63; Minister for Education 1964; shadow cabinet 1964–70; Lord

Chancellor 1970–74, 1979–87. He first shot to national prominence narrowly winning the 1938 Oxford 'Munich' by-election. A darling of the annual conference, he always had an eye for the photo opportunity. Ambitions for leadership thwarted by candidacy of Home, 1963.

Halifax (Edward Wood), 3rd Viscount (1881–1959): Conservative MP 1910–25; President of Board of Education 1922–24, 1932–35; Agriculture Minister 1924–25; Viceroy of India 1925–31; Secretary for War 1935; Lord Privy Seal 1935–37; Lord President 1937–38; Foreign Secretary 1938–40; Ambassador to Washington 1941–46; succeeded as 3rd Viscount Halifax 1934; the politician who sought to appease Gandhi and Hitler and who could have become the Party Leader in May 1940 had he not decided to step aside in favour of Churchill.

Halsbury (Hardinge Giffard), 1st Earl of (1823–1921): MP 1877–85; Solicitor-General 1875–80, Lord Chancellor 1885–86, 1886–92, 1895–1905; created Baron 1885, 1st Earl 1898. Aged 80 he was leader of the 'ditchers' in 1911 who resisted the Liberal attack on the House of Lords.

Hartington Marquess Duke of – *see* Devonshire, 8th Duke of

Heath Edward (1916–): Conservative MP 1950–2001; Whip 1951–59, including Chief Whip 1955–59; Minister of Labour 1959–60; Lord Privy Seal 1960–63, charged with conducting the (unsuccessful) negotiations for Britain's entry into EEC; Minister for Trade 1963–64; Party Leader 1965–75; Prime Minister 1970–74; first Party Leader to be elected using a ballot, the method also used to remove him. Premiership characterised by industrial strife, the three-day week and U-turns on economic policy. Since 1975 he has remained a vocal supporter of European integration and a cantankerous critic of his successors. Outside politics retained a passion for classical music and yacht racing.

Heathcoat Amory Derick (1899–1981): Conservative MP 1945–60; junior minister, Pensions 1951–53, Board of Trade 1953–54; Minister of Agriculture 1954–58; Chancellor of Exchequer 1958–60; clash of wills with Macmillan over economic policy and the credit squeeze of June 1960. Retired following month to Lords after Cabinet reshuffle. Created 1st Viscount Amory, 1960.

Herbert Hon. Sidney (1810–61): MP 1832–61; junior minister 1834–35, 1841–45; Secretary of State for War 1845–46; Peelite 1853–55; Colonial Secretary 1855 resigned; Secretary of State for War (Liberal) 1859–61.

Heseltine Michael (1933–): Conservative MP 1966–74, 1974–2001; parliamentary secretary, Transport 1970, Environment 1970–72; junior minister, Department of Trade and Industry 1972–74; Environment Secretary 1979–83, 1990–92; Defence Secretary 1983–1986 when he famously stormed out of a Cabinet meeting discussing the sale of Westland Helicopters and resigned; a hate figure for Thatcherites after he challenged Thatcher for the Party Leadership in 1990 and because of his Europeanism; President, Board of Trade 1992–95; Deputy Prime Minister 1995–97. His political nickname was Tarzan, hence the title for his memoirs, *Life in the Jungle* (2000).

Hicks Beach (Sir Michael), 1st Earl St Aldwyn (1837–1916): Conservative MP 1864–1906; served under Disraeli, Chief Secretary for Ireland 1874–78, 1886–87; Colonial Secretary 1878–80; Chancellor of Exchequer 1885–86, 1895–1902; President Board of Trade 1888–92; free trader from 1903; allegedly the model for a character in *The Prisoner of Zenda.* Created Viscount (later Earl) St Aldwyn. Salisbury is attributed with having said that he would have been a very good Home Secretary: 'He'd hang everybody'.

Hill Dr Charles (1904–91): Liberal and Conservative MP 1950–63; junior minister, Food 1951–55; Postmaster-General 1955–57; Chancellor of the Duchy of Lancaster 1957–61; Minister of Housing and Local Government 1961–62; later chairman of Independent Television Authority 1963–67, and Board of Governors BBC 1967–72; a media specialist, his broadcasting activities earned him the nickname 'Radio Doctor' a reference to his earlier medical career. Created Baron Hill of Luton 1963.

Hoare Samuel (1880–1959): Conservative MP 1910–44; Air Minister 1922–24, 1924–29, 1940; Secretary of State for India 1931–35 during which time he successfully steered the 1935 Government of India Act through parliament despite the active hostility of Churchill and other right-wingers; Foreign Secretary 1935 although resigned after the political outcry surrounding the Hoare–Laval pact; First Lord of Admiralty 1936–37; Home Secretary 1937–39; Lord Privy Seal 1939–40; Ambassador to Spain 1940–44; an ambitious and able politician who saw himself as a potential successor to Baldwin. He became one of Chamberlain's inner cabinet 1938–39. Created 1st Viscount Templewood, 1944.

Home (Alexander Frederick Douglas-Home, Viscount Dunglass), Baron (1903–95): 1963 used Peerage Act to disclaim hereditary peerage, created life peer 1974; Conservative MP 1931–45, 1950–51, 1963–74; PPS to Neville Chamberlain 1935–40; Scottish Minister 1951–55; Minister for Commonwealth Relations 1955–60; leader of House of Lords 1957–60; Foreign Minister 1960–63; Party Leader 1963–65; Prime Minister 1963–64; Foreign Minister 1970–74 when he oversaw Britain's EEC entry; the compromise choice of the 'magic circle' in 1963, Home became Party Leader and Prime Minister (despite his association with appeasement). Narrowly lost 1964 general election, questions arose as to whether another leader with a more 'modern', less aristocratic, image might have won. Decided that party should introduce a leadership ballot. Styled Viscount Dunglass 1918–51, succeeded as 14th Earl of Home 1951, created Baron Home of the Hirsel 1974.

Howe Geoffrey (1926–): Conservative MP 1964–66, 1970–74, 1974–92; Solicitor-General 1970–72; Minister for Trade 1972–74; shadow spokesman 1974–79; Chancellor of Exchequer 1979–83; Foreign Secretary 1983–89; Lord President of Council and Deputy Prime Minister 1989–90; his period as Chancellor helped Thatcher stamp her monetarist economic agenda upon her party, but angered at exclusion from war cabinet during Falklands conflict. The cost of reducing inflation was depression and the highest levels of unemployment since the 1930s. Increasingly concerned at Thatcher's European policy. His devastating resignation speech attacking Thatcher provided a lead to disgruntled Conservatives, especially Heseltine, which ultimately led to her downfall. Created Baron Howe of Aberavon, 1992.

Hurd Douglas (1930–): after diplomatic career, Conservative MP 1974–83; opposition spokesman, Europe 1976–79; junior minister, Foreign Office, 1979–83, Home Office 1983; Minister for Northern Ireland 1984–85; Home Secretary 1985–89; Foreign Secretary 1989–97; the Eton and Cambridge educated Hurd, who was placed third in the 1990 leadership election, proved a supreme loyalist during the turbulent Major years. Saw his role as a politician to be 'the public servant'. He was a traditional moderate Conservative. Created Baron Hurd, 1997.

Irwin – *see* Halifax, 3rd Viscount

Joseph Sir Keith (1918–95): Conservative MP 1956–87; Minister of State, Board of Trade 1961–62; Minister for Housing and Local Government and Welsh Affairs 1962–64; Social Services Secretary 1970–74; Industry Secretary 1979–81; Education Secretary 1981–86; more effective as an intellectual force than a political minister. He founded the Centre for Policy Studies in 1974 that promoted free market values and which became formative influence on 'Thatcherism'. Stood aside from 1975 leadership contest in favour of Thatcher. Created Baron Joseph, 1987.

Joynson-Hicks Sir William (1865–1932): MP 1908–10, 1911–29; junior minister 1922–23; Paymaster-General 1923; Financial Secretary to Treasury 1923; Minister of Health 1923–34; Home Secretary 1924–29; evangelical and puritanical churchman. Created 1st Viscount Brentford, 1929.

Lamont Norman (1942–): Conservative MP 1972–97; junior minister, Energy 1979–81, Trade and Industry 1981–85, Defence 1985–86; Financial Secretary to Treasury 1986–89; Chief Secretary to Treasury 1989–90; Chancellor of Exchequer 1990–93; the chancellor with the 'hawk-like' eyebrows who quipped '*Je ne regrette rien*' as the depression impacted upon middle England. Fell out of favour with Major as the crisis over the pound and Europe took its toll. He became an increasingly bitter and Eurosceptical critic from the backbenches after being sacked. Publication of memoirs in 1999 deliberately coincided with Major's and continues the hostility between the two men; life peerage 1998.

Lansdowne (Henry Charles Keith Petty-Fitzmaurice), 5th Marquess of (1845–1927): Liberal Unionist from 1886; Under-secretary for War 1872–74; Under-secretary for India 1880; Governor-General Canada 1883–88; Viceroy of India 1888–94; Secretary for War 1895–1900; Foreign Secretary 1900–5; leader of Unionists in House of Lords from 1903, subsequently involved in negotiations over 1911 Parliament Act; Minister without Portfolio 1915–16; misjudged political mood when in 1916 he wrote a letter suggesting the need for a negotiated peace with Germany. Subsequently left the party.

Lawson Nigel (1932–): Conservative MP 1974–92; opposition whip 1976–77; opposition Treasury spokesman 1977–79; Financial Secretary to Treasury

1979–81; Energy Secretary 1981–83; Chancellor of Exchequer 1983–89; as chancellor oversaw economic policies that eased the monetarist policy of his predecessor, Geoffrey Howe, but fuelled the boom in house prices which proved troublesome for his successors, and who oversaw Britain's entry into the ERM. Resigned in 1989 in disagreement with the role of Thatcher's policy advisers, especially Alan Walters. Has suffered a roller-coaster reputation, widely praised as architect of Conservative victory in 1987 but held responsible for the deepening recession from 1989. Created Baron Lawson of Blaby 1992.

Liverpool (Robert Banks Jenkinson), 2nd Earl of (1770–1827): MP 1790–1803; Foreign Secretary 1801–4, 1809; Home Secretary 1804–6, 1807–9; Secretary for War and Colonies 1809–12; Leader of Lords 1804–6, 1807–27; Prime Minister 1812–27; the longevity of his premiership was due both to Liverpool's own political skills and the collective talent of his cabinets.

Lloyd (John Selwyn Brooke), Baron Selwyn-Lloyd (1904–78): Conservative MP 1945–76; junior minister, Foreign Office 1951–54; Minister of Supply 1954–55; Minister of Defence 1955; Foreign Secretary 1955–60; Chancellor of Exchequer 1960–62 who initially relaxed economic controls only to reverse these with the 1961 pay pause. Sacked in the 'night of the long knives'; compiled 'Selwyn Lloyd Report' into party organisation 1963; Lord Privy Seal 1963–64; shadow cabinet 1964–66; Speaker of House of Commons 1971–76; criticised for role in Suez crisis and then charged with mending the Atlantic alliance. Constantly in the shadow of Macmillan.

Long Walter (1854–1924): Conservative MP 1880–92, 1893–1921; parliamentary secretary Local Government Board 1886–92; President, Board of Agriculture 1895–1900; President, Local Government Board 1900–5; Chief Secretary for Ireland 1905; Colonial Secretary 1916–19; First Lord of the Admiralty 1919–21; forever a thorn in the flesh of successive leaders from Balfour to Lloyd George, failed to become leader in 1911. Created 1st Viscount Long, 1921.

Lyttelton Oliver (1893–1972): Conservative MP 1940–54, when created 1st Viscount Chandos; President, Board of Trade 1940–41; Minister of State Resident in Cairo 1941–42, with seat in War Cabinet 1941–45; Minister of Production 1942–45; President Board of Trade 1945; Colonial Secretary 1951–54. Reputedly offered nine ministerial posts by Winston Churchill although three of these only ever materialised. He was a member of the party committee that produced *The Industrial Charter*, a document he considered to favour free enterprise.

Macleod Iain (1913–70): Conservative MP 1950–70; Conservative Research Department 1948–50; Minister of Health 1952–55; Minister of Labour and National Service 1955–59; Colonial Secretary 1959–61; Party Chairman and Leader, House of Commons 1961–63; editor *The Spectator* 1963–65 where he wrote an article criticising the 'magic circle' that selected Home as leader; consequently refused office under Home, 1963; shadow cabinet 1964–70; Chancellor of Exchequer 1970; premature death contributed to the problems of the Heath government.

Macmillan Harold (1894–1986): Conservative MP 1924–29, 1931–45, 1945–64; junior office, Ministry of Supply 1940–42, Colonies 1942; Minister Resident, Algiers 1942–45; Air Minister 1945; Minister of Housing 1951–54; Defence Minister 1954–55; Foreign Secretary 1955; Chancellor of Exchequer 1955–57 during which time he withdrew his support for Eden's Suez campaign; Prime Minister and Party Leader 1957–63; after an undistinguished career during inter-war period, the ambitious Macmillan rose rapidly in post-war years delivering the party's target for new houses in 1953–54 and securing the leadership after Eden's resignation. Healed the wounds among the party post-Suez, and sought to restore the Anglo-American relationship, but failed to bring Britain into Europe. Economic successes earned him nickname 'Supermac' but scandal and political fragility marked his government's last years in office. Spent his long years of retirement writing a six-volume memoir. Created 1st Earl of Stockton, 1984.

Major John (1943–): Conservative MP 1979–2001; whip 1983–85; junior minister, Health 1985–87; chief secretary to Treasury 1987–89; foreign secretary 1989; Chancellor of Exchequer 1989–90; Party Leader and Prime Minister 1990–97; the rapid rise of the Brixton boy surprised many observers; the 'stop Heseltine' candidate in the 1990 leadership contest; his period in office was characterised by civil war among his own party. Against predictions he won in 1992 after his 'soapbox' campaign, but problems over Europe undermined his leadership and he led the Conservatives to their worst electoral defeat ever in 1997.

Malmesbury (James Howard Harris), 3rd Earl of (1807–89): Foreign Secretary 1852, 1858–59; Lord Privy Seal 1866–68, 1874–76; and Conservative leader in the Lords 1868. With a reputation as a womaniser, almost his entire career was spent in the House of Lords.

Manningham-Buller Reginald (1905–80): Conservative MP 1943–62 when created Baron Dilhorne; junior minister, Ministry of Works 1945; Solicitor-General 1951–54; Attorney-General 1954–62; Lord Chancellor 1962–64; undertook the informal 'soundings' of Cabinet figures in 1963 that led to the selection of Douglas-Home as Party Leader. Created 1st Viscount Dilhorne, 1964.

Margesson David (1890–1965): Conservative MP 1922–23, 1924–42; whip 1924–29; Chief Whip 1931–40; Secretary for War 1940–42; as Chief Whip he served four successive Prime Ministers. He established a reputation as a strict disciplinarian but also as a very personable individual. Created 1st Viscount Margesson, 1942.

Maude Angus (1912–93): Conservative MP 1950–58, 1963–83; Director, Conservative Political Centre 1951–55; opposition spokesman 1964–66; deputy chairman and chairman, Conservative Research Department 1975–79; shadow cabinet 1975–79; Paymaster-General 1979–81; member of Suez group, had whip withdrawn 1957–58; sacked as spokesman 1966 following article in *The Spectator*; voted against EEC entry 1971, leading critic of Heath's economic policies and leading member of New Right. Created Baron Maude, 1983.

Maudling Reginald (1912–79): Conservative MP 1950–79; Conservative Research Department 1945–50 where he worked on *Industrial Charter*; junior minister, civil aviation 1952, Treasury 1952–55; Minister of Supply 1955–57; Paymaster-General 1957–59; President of Board of Trade 1959–61; Colonial Secretary 1961–62; Chancellor of Exchequer 1962–64; shadow cabinet 1964–70; Home Secretary 1970–72 when he resigned. Unsuccessful candidate in 1963 and the 1965 Party Leadership contest, but consoled with position of deputy leader 1965–72. His career came to an ignominious end when his involvement in a dubious business deal led the House of Commons Select Committee on the Conduct of Members to criticise his actions.

Mawdsley James (1848–1902): Lancashire cotton spinner and Conservative trade unionist; member TUC Party Committee 1882–97; Conservative candidate Oldham 1899 in the double-member constituency running alongside Winston Churchill.

Maxse S.A. Marjorie (1891–1975): Deputy Principal Agent (Women's Organisation) 1921–30; Chief Organisation Officer Conservative Central Office 1930–39; Vice-chairman Conservative Party Organisation 1944–51.

Maxwell Fyfe David (1900–67): Conservative MP 1935–54; deputy chairman Post-war Problems Committee, 1941, chairman 1943; Solicitor-General 1942–45; Attorney-General 1945; Chief Prosecutor, Nuremberg War Crimes trials 1945–46; author 1948 'Maxwell Fyfe report' into party organisation, this report shaped the post-war Conservative party including ending the necessity of prospective candidates to bank-roll local constituency associations; chairman National Union 1950; Home Secretary 1951–54; Lord Chancellor, as 1st Viscount Kilmuir, 1954–62; despite declaring that loyalty was the Tories' secret weapon he was sacked by Macmillan in 'night of the long knives' in 1962.

Middleton Richard C.E. (1846–1905): Conservative agent West Kent 1883–84; Principal Agent Conservative Central Office 1885–1903. His nickname 'The Skipper' was in reference to the courtesy rank of captain he achieved on retirement from the Navy in 1882. Unlike his predecessors he was prepared to work under his leader. He had unprecedented access to 'the Chief' Salisbury, but also was on good terms with the aristocrats Douglas and McDonnell.

Milner (Alfred), 1st Viscount (1854–1925): Oxford don, barrister, financial civil servant 1887–97; High Commissioner South Africa 1897–1905 where gathered around him younger individuals, like Leo Amery, and formed the 'Kindergarten'; one of the founders of the Liberal Unionist Association; from 1905 a 'diehard' Unionist and leader of Lords' resistance to 1911 Parliament Act; war cabinet 1916–18; War Secretary 1918–19; Colonial Secretary 1919–21.

Monckton Walter (1891–1965): Conservative MP 1951–57; legal advisor to Royal Family during Abdication crisis; junior office 1939–42; UK delegate on Allied Reparations Commission, 1945; Minister of Labour and National Service 1951–55 where he was charged not to antagonise the trade union movement;

Minister of Defence 1955–56; Paymaster-General 1956–57. Created 1st Viscount Monckton of Brenchley, 1957.

Mosley Oswald 'Tom' (1896–1980): MP 1918–24 (Conservative to 1920, Independent 1920–24, Labour from 1924), 1926–31 (Labour to 1931 then New Party); Chancellor, Duchy of Lancaster 1929–30; leader, New Party 1931–32, of British Union of Fascists 1932–40, of Union Movement 1948–66; interned 1940–44; imitator of Mussolini and Hitler who abandoned the mainstream political parties for fascism.

Northcote (Stafford Henry), 1st Earl of Iddesleigh (1818–87): Conservative MP 1855–57 (Peelite); 1858–85 (Conservative); President Board of Trade 1866–67; India Secretary 1867–68; Chancellor of Exchequer 1874–80 committed to the orthodox economics of the Manchester School; Party Leader in House of Commons 1877–85, where he found himself under attack from the 'fourth party' and out-manoeuvred by Salisbury. He was not a good debater and was considered too apologetic as leader of the Commons; elevated to the House of Lords 1885; Foreign Secretary 1886–87 with a reputation for being liberal. For many years one of Disraeli's closest political allies, but failed to seize the inheritance offered by Disraeli.

Parkinson Cecil (1931–): Conservative MP 1970–92; whip 1974–76; opposition spokesman 1976–79; junior minister, Trade 1979–81; Paymaster-General 1981; Party Chairman 1981–83, 1997–98; Chancellor of the Duchy of Lancaster 1982–83; Minister for Trade and Industry 1983; Minister for Energy 1987–89; Secretary of State for Education 1989–90; Thatcher's golden boy obliged to resign after an affair with his secretary, Sara Keays, 1983; brought back by Hague to manage Central Office and provide a direct link back to the Thatcherite past. Created Baron Parkinson, 1992.

Patten Chris (1944–): Conservative MP 1979–92; junior minister, Northern Ireland 1983–85, Education 1985, Overseas Development 1986–89; Environment Secretary 1989–90; Chancellor of the Duchy of Lancaster and Party Chairman 1990–92; Governor of Hong Kong 1993–97; European Commissioner 1999– , although admitted to finding the job boring; a close friend of Major's it was ironic that just when he had helped mastermind victory in 1992 Patten should lose his own parliamentary seat – allegedly a result received gleefully by Thatcher. Produced Patten Report on the future of the Royal Ulster Constabulary.

Peel Robert (1788–1850): MP 1808–17, 1829–50; junior minister 1810–12; Chief Secretary for Ireland 1812–18 earning nickname 'Orange Peel'; Home Secretary 1822–27, 1828–30; Prime Minister 1834–35, 1841–46; Conservative Leader 1834–36, split party over Corn Laws 1846 (a foretaste of the events of 1992–97) and consigned the Conservatives to opposition for nearly three decades; subsequently the inspirer to the Peelite group and in death lionised as a wise and foresighted statesman.

Pitt William (the Younger) (1759–1806): Chancellor of Exchequer 1782–83; Prime Minister 1784–1801, 1804–6; considered by many Tories to be the party's founder, though Pitt always considered himself to be a Whig.

Portillo Michael (1953–): Conservative MP 1984–97, when his was one of the most memorable and high-profile defeats of the 1997 Tory debacle, 1999– after winning the 'safe' seat of Kensington and Chelsea vacated by the death of Alan Clark; junior minister, Health and Social Security 1987–88, Transport 1988–90; Minister for Local Government 1990–92; Chief Secretary to the Treasury 1992–94; Employment Minister 1994–95; Defence Minister 1995–97; during 1999 in an attempt to exorcise potential skeletons in the cupboard and ease his return to active politics Portillo admitted to homosexual experiences. Robust, right-wing Eurosceptic, dubbed one of 'the bastards' by Major, Portillo is seen as a potential leader of the Conservatives and has been seeking to widen his appeal since returning to Westminster. His return to parliament was quickly rewarded with the shadow Chancellorship.

Powell Enoch (1912–98): Conservative MP 1950–74, Ulster Unionist MP 1974–87; Professor of Greek, Sydney University 1938–39; Conservative Research Department 1945–50; junior minister, Housing 1955–57; Financial Secretary to Treasury 1957–58 when he resigned with the entire Treasury team; Minster of Health 1960–63; refused to serve under Home; shadow cabinet 1964–68 when sacked by Heath for the provocative nature of his Birmingham 'rivers of blood' speech. Always something of a maverick, Powell was an intensely intellectual politician. He added to his notoriety by urging voters to support Labour in 1970 and opposing EEC entry in 1971 before joining the Ulster Unionist Party. Many of the ideas behind Thatcherite economic policies can be traced back to Powell.

Prior James (1927–): Conservative MP 1959–87; vice-chairman, Conservative party 1965; Minster for Agriculture 1970–72; deputy chairman of party, Lord President of Council and Leader of House of Commons 1972–74; opposition spokesman 1974–79; Employment Secretary 1979–81; Northern Ireland Secretary 1981–84; one of the key 'wets' in the early Thatcher governments. Created Baron Prior, 1987.

Profumo John (1915–): Conservative MP 1940–45, 1950–63; junior minister, Civil Aviation 1952–53, Transport and Civil Aviation 1953–57, Colonies 1957–58, Foreign Office 1958–60; Defence Secretary 1960–63; forced to resign office and seat after he admitted lying to the House of Commons about the nature of his relationship with prostitute Christine Keeler.

Ripon (Frederick John Robinson, 1st Viscount Goderich), 1st Earl of (1782–1859): MP 1806–27; created Viscount Goderich 1827, Earl of Ripon 1833; President of the Board of Trade and Treasurer of the Navy 1818–23; Chancellor of Exchequer 1823–27; Secretary for War and Colonies 1827, 1830–33; Prime Minister 1827–28 upon the death of his friend Canning, but proved unable to control the factions within his cabinet. He resigned following the refusal of Huskisson and Herries to serve together; Lord Privy Seal 1833–34; President of Board of Trade 1841–43; President of Board of Control 1843–46.

Salisbury (Robert Gascoyne-Cecil), 3rd Marquess of (1830–1903): Conservative MP 1853–68; Secretary of State for India 1866–67 resigning in protest at 2nd Reform Act, 1874–78; Foreign Secretary 1878–80, 1885–86, 1887–92, 1895–1900; Prime Minister 1885–86, 1886–92, 1895–1902; Leader Conservative party 1885–1902. Having been a trenchant right-wing critic of Disraeli and Derby he became the dominant Conservative figure of latter part of nineteenth century who, despite his pessimism, oversaw the transformation of his party (partly through accident and partly through intent) in the age of mass democracy.

Salisbury (James Edward Hybert Gascoyne Cecil), 4th Marquess of (1861–1947): MP 1885–92, 1893–1903 as Viscount Cranborne; junior minister Foreign Office 1900–3; Lord Privy Seal 1903–5, 1924–29; President Board of Trade 1905; Lord President of Council 1922–24; Leader of Lords 1925–29; Leader Opposition Lords 1929–31 resigned; founder of 'Watching Committee' in April 1940 that played a role in fall of Chamberlain May 1940.

Salisbury (Robert – 'Bobbety' – Arthur James Gascoyne-Cecil), 5th Marquess of (1893–1972): Conservative MP 1929–41; junior minister, Foreign Office 1935–38 resigned in solidarity with Anthony Eden; Paymaster-general 1940; Dominions Secretary 1940–42, 1943–45; Lord Privy Seal 1942–43, 1951–52; Commonwealth Secretary 1952; Lord President 1952–57; Conservative leader House of Lords 1942–57; styled Viscount Cranborne 1903–47. Resigned from Macmillan's government in protest at the release of the Cypriot, Archbishop Makarios.

Sandys Duncan (1908–87): Conservative MP 1935–45, 1950–74; junior minister, War Office 1941–43, Ministry of Supply 1943–44; chairman of war cabinet committee on V weapons 1943–45; Minister of Works 1944–45; chairman of executive of European Movement 1947–50; Minister of Supply 1951–54; Minister of Housing 1954–57; Minister of Defence 1957–59; Commonwealth Secretary 1960–64; Colonial Secretary 1962–64; shadow cabinet 1964–66; leader of British delegation to Council of Europe 1970–72; son-in-law of Winston Churchill, Sandys stood loyally behind him during 1930s. He was one of most vociferous pro-Europeans post-1945. Introduced the 1957 Defence white paper with its reliance on nuclear deterrence in preference to conventional land forces. Created Baron Duncan-Sandys, 1974.

Selborne (William Waldegrave Palmer), 2nd Earl of (1859–1942): son-in-law of 3rd Marquess of Salisbury, as Lord Wolmer MP 1885–95 (Liberal and then Unionist); under-secretary, Colonies 1895–1900; First Lord of the Admiralty 1900–5; governor-general of Transvaal and South Africa 1905–10; president, Board of Agriculture 1915–16. His transition from Liberal to diehard Unionist, as he opposed the 1911 Parliament Act and Irish Home Rule, reflected the changes in the political climate at the dawn of the twentieth century.

Selwyn-Lloyd – *see* Lloyd

Smith F.E. – *see* Birkenhead, 1st Earl of

Smith William Henry (1825–91): Conservative MP 1868–91; First Lord of the Admiralty 1877–80; First Lord of Treasury and Leader of the House 1887–91; founder of W.H. Smith booksellers; opposed Lord Randolph Churchill's budgetary proposals for economics and succeeded him as Leader of the House. Appointment to the Admiralty provided the inspiration for W.S. Gilbert's satirical creation 'Sir Joseph Porter' in *HMS Pinafore*.

Smythe Hon. George A.F.P.S. (1818–57): MP 1841–52 ('Young England' and later Peelite); junior minister Foreign Office 1845–46; journalist *Morning Chronicle*.

Stanley Oliver (1896–1950): Conservative MP 1924–50; junior minister, Home Office 1931–33; Minister of Transport 1933–34; Minister of Labour 1934–35; President, Board of Education 1935–37; President, Board of Trade 1937–40; War Secretary 1940; Colonial Secretary 1942–45; member of the Derby political dynasty whose period as minister of war contributed to the fall of Chamberlain and who in his later years was seen as the third man in the party after Churchill and Eden.

Steel-Maitland Arthur (1876–1935): MP 1910–35; first Party Chairman 1911–17; junior minister 1915–19; opposed Lloyd George coalition 1922; Minister of Labour 1924–29; failed to fulfil early promise.

Swinton – *see* Cunliffe-Lister

Tebbit Norman (1931–): Conservative MP 1970–92; junior minister, Trade 1979–81, Industry 1981; Employment Secretary 1981–83 where he famously exhorted the unemployed to 'get on your bike'; Trade and Industry Secretary 1983–85; Chancellor of Duchy of Lancaster and chairman of party 1985–87; caught in the Brighton bomb blast which also seriously injured his wife. He was leading Thatcherite; oversaw Thatcher's third election victory, although clashed with Lord Young over strategy. He is a leading Eurosceptic. Created Baron Tebbit, 1992.

Thatcher Margaret Hilda (1925–): Conservative MP 1959–92; junior minister, Pensions 1961–64; opposition spokesman 1964–70; Education Secretary 1970–74; opposition spokesman 1974; Party Leader 1975–90; Prime Minister 1979–90; the 'Iron Lady' who was Party Leader for 15 years, in that time seeing off the Communist threat, cabinet wets and the Argentinians; gradual loss of natural allies and the 'poll tax' made her an electoral liability and led to her overthrow; many of her supporters, who were critical of Major, supported Hague in 1997 believing him to be a truer successor to her legacy. Created Baroness Thatcher, 1992.

Thorneycroft Peter (1909–94): Conservative MP 1938–66; junior minister, War Transport 1945; President, Board of Trade 1951–57; Chancellor of Exchequer 1957–58 resigning with entire Treasury team – resignations Macmillan dismissed as a 'little local difficulty'; Minister of Aviation 1960–62; Minister of Defence 1964; shadow cabinet 1963–66; Life Peer 1967; Party Chairman 1975–81.

Walker Peter (1932–): Conservative MP 1961–92; National Chairman, Young Conservatives 1958–60; Minister for Housing 1970; Environment Secretary 1970–72; Trade and Industry Secretary 1972–74; opposition spokesman 1974–75; Agriculture Minister 1979–83; Energy Secretary 1983–87; Welsh Secretary 1987–90. A 'Heathite' and 'wet' he ran Heath's two leadership campaigns. His leaking of the story during the 1975 leadership contest that Thatcher had hoarded food during the 1972 miners' strike backfired because it smacked of desperation in the Heath camp. Created Baron Walker, 1992.

Wellington (Arthur Wellesley), 1st Duke of (1769–1852): professional soldier with victories in the Napoleonic wars; Chief Secretary for Ireland 1807–9; Master General of the Ordnance 1819–27; member Liverpool Cabinet 1818–27; Prime Minister 1828–30, and acting Prime Minister November–December 1834; served in both of Peel's governments as Foreign Secretary 1834–35 and Minister without Portfolio and Leader of Lords 1841–46. As a politician Wellington lacked the skill of compromise and the acceptance of expediency. He was often at odds with his own cabinet viewing his role as one that fulfilled the duty of carrying on the King's government. An unwillingness to consider electoral reform destroyed his 1830 government.

Whitelaw William (1918–99): Conservative MP 1955–83; Whip 1959–62; junior minister, Labour Ministry 1962–64; Chief Whip 1964–70; Lord President of Council and Leader of House of Commons 1970–72; Northern Ireland Secretary 1972–73; Employment Secretary 1973–74; Party Chairman 1974–75; Deputy Leader of Party 1975–86; Deputy Prime Minister 1979–86; Home Secretary 1979–83; Lord President of the Council and Leader of House of Lords 1983–86 after unusually being granted an hereditary Viscountcy. A trusted lieutenant to Thatcher who affectionately referred to him as 'Her Willy'.

Willoughby de Broke (Richard Greville Verney), Baron (1869–1923): Conservative politician who came to prominence as a leading diehard in defence of the traditional powers of the House of Lords. Actively involved in the tariff reform campaign.

Wood – *see* Halifax, 3rd Viscount

Woolton (Frederick James Marquis), 1st Earl of (1883–1964): Minister of Food 1940–43; Minister of Reconstruction 1943–45; the man from Marks and Spencer whose experience of retailing led to his inclusion in the Churchill wartime coalition; joined party in 1945; Party Chairman 1946–55 where he reinvigorated the party organisation, secured funds and membership and formally merged the Liberal Nationals into the party; ill health after 1951.

Younger Sir George (1851–1929): Conservative MP 1906–22; Party Chairman 1916–23, who negotiated the 'coupon' deal of 1918 and who abandoned Lloyd George at the 1922 Carlton Club meeting; party treasurer 1923–29. A member of the Scottish brewing family. Created 1st Viscount Younger, 1923.

Part 6

GLOSSARY

6. GLOSSARY

Abbey House Conservative party headquarters 1946–58, Victoria Street, London SW1.

Abdication Crisis (1936): In 1936 King Edward VIII wanted to marry a twice-divorced American woman, Wallis Simpson. The Prime Minister, Stanley Baldwin, supported by the cabinet advised him that this would not be possible if he wished to remain King. On 11 December he renounced his throne and became Duke of Windsor, marrying Mrs Simpson in 1937. They lived in exile for the remainder of their lives.

Act of Union (1800): Established 'United Kingdom of Great Britain and Ireland'. Abolished Irish parliament, brought 100 Irish MPs to Westminster parliament; united the Churches of England and Ireland, but kept the financial systems distinct.

Advisory Committee on Policy: Chaired by R.A. Butler this committee was reconstituted in 1945 from the Post-war Problems Central Committee and then reformed under the 1949 Maxwell Fyfe reforms. Under this latter revision it was no longer a committee of the National Union and instead was responsible to the leader, advising upon policy recommendations.

Aliens Act (1905): Sought to restrict the entry of eastern European immigrants, particularly Jewish, into Britain. This followed widespread agitation by Conservative MPs, like Sir Howard Vincent (Sheffield), for entry restrictions and the Royal Commission on Alien Immigration that reported in August 1903. It was an issue that attracted working-class support.

Anglo-Irish Agreement (1985): This agreement signed by Thatcher and FitzGerald gave the Irish government a say in the affairs of Northern Ireland in return for recognition of the wishes of the majority population in Ulster. It was deeply resented by Ulster Unionist politicians and provoked a number of Conservative junior ministers to resign.

appalling frankness: Phrase used by Stanley Baldwin, November 1936, when responding to criticisms from Churchill. Contemporaries considered it a parliamentary triumph for Baldwin as he explained why he had felt unable to win an election on rearmament in 1933. Churchill later unjustly claimed that this was Baldwin putting party before country.

appeasement: A foreign policy that seeks concession to avoid war. Synonymous with the 1938 Munich agreement, since then it has been associated with British surrender in the face of Hitler's aggression. Historians debate whether it was a policy specific to the 1937–40 Chamberlain administration, or a phenomenon of British inter-war foreign policy, or whether in actuality it was a form of traditional British foreign policy dating from the mid-nineteenth century – the idea of aiming to maintain the balance of power in Europe by negotiation because it was recognised that Britain was too weak both financially and militarily to intervene.

Arcos raid: On 12 May 1927 police raided the offices of Arcos Ltd and the Soviet trade delegation in London. Undertaken with the permission of Joynson-Hicks (Home Secretary) the raid led to the suspension of diplomatic relations with Soviet Russia and hyped populist and establishment fears of a Soviet spying ring.

Arms for Iraq – *see* **Matrix Churchill case** and **Scott Inquiry**

Ashridge College: Hertfordshire site of Conservative Party College 1929–39.

back to basics: Conference slogan of John Major, October 1993. It sought to remind the country of the core values for which Conservatism stood. Intended to provide a new focus for the party after the disunity of the period since the 1992 general election (Maastricht, exit from ERM, the introduction of VAT on domestic fuel and record by-election defeats), the initiative backfired. Criticisms of single mothers made by other ministers, and then the exposure by the press of a series of extramarital affairs by a number of junior ministers and backbenchers punctured the morality of Major's message.

Barber boom: A period of economic prosperity 1972–73 fuelled by Chancellor Barber's 'dash for growth'. Although subsequently blamed for the inflation that followed, Barber claimed he had been reluctant to pursue such expansionist economic policies but that Heath had been determined upon this course of action.

bastards, the: Off the record phrase used by John Major in an interview with ITN's chief political correspondent, Michael Brunson, in July 1993 signalling the Prime Minister's frustration with right-wing Eurosceptic elements within his Cabinet. The conversation was picked up by a 'feed' cable from an earlier interview with the BBC and was piped into television studies in Millbank.

Beveridge Report (1942): Written by the liberal economist William Beveridge at the request of the Churchill coalition government it provided the framework for the post-war Labour government's Welfare State programme.

bimetallism: A concern during the late nineteenth century at Britain's apparent economic decline, which linked new economic 'demand-side' theories with government intervention in the financial markets.

Black Wednesday (16 September 1992): The day Britain was obliged to withdraw the pound from the European Exchange Rate Mechanism (ERM) after repeated, and substantial, interest rate increases failed to stop the collapse in the value of the pound on the money markets.

blood, toil, tears and sweat: Famous phrase uttered by Winston Churchill during his first parliamentary speech as Prime Minister in the dark days of May 1940 as Hitler's blitzkrieg swept through western Europe. It was repeated during the evening BBC radio broadcast on 13 May. The phraseology was illustrative of Churchill's ability to empathise with his listeners and of his combative war leadership.

borne down in a torrent of gin and beer: Quote from Gladstone in 1874 referring to the close association between the brewing industry and the Conservatives after Liberal attempts to reform the liquor licensing laws failed. Thus began a mutually beneficial relationship reinforced by the Conservative resistance to plans to nationalise brewing during the First World War and which ensured that the 'drinks' industry remained one of the party's core funders well into the twentieth century.

British Leyland: Britain's nationalised car industry that faced economic collapse in the 1970s.

British Nationalities Act (1981): The Thatcher government's legislative attempt to restrict the entry and citizenship of immigrants into Britain. It created three categories for citizenship: British, citizen of British dependent territories, and British overseas citizen. It revoked the automatic right to British citizenship for any child, including those born in the United Kingdom, unless at least one of the parents was a British citizen by birth. Children born overseas to parents of partial or naturalised British citizenship could be refused entry to UK.

British Union of Fascists (BUF): Led by former Conservative MP, Oswald Mosley, the 'Blackshirts' initially enjoyed support from a number of Conservative MPs. The violence of the June 1934 Olympia rally ended this support and that of press baron, Lord Rothermere. BUF membership declined but the organisation continued until many of its members, including Mosley, were interned in May 1940.

Butskellism: Term which refers to the perceived consensus between the Labour and Conservative parties in the years after 1945 on progressive social policies and the maintenance of a mixed economy with both private and public sectors. The word is a conflation of the names of R.A. Butler, Conservative Chancellor of Exchequer 1951–56 and Hugh Gaitskell, Labour Chancellor of Exchequer 1950–51 and later leader of the Labour party.

cash for questions: Reference applied to those Conservative MPs who were prepared to ask parliamentary questions in exchange for financial reward. Came to symbolise the 'sleaze' that tainted the Conservative party in the early 1990s.

Catherine Place: London home of Tristan Garel-Jones, and meeting place of a number of ministers on 20 November 1990, the night that Margaret Thatcher had failed to secure the necessary margin of support in the first round of the leadership contest against Heseltine. The impromptu supper gathering is represented as an anti-Thatcher cabal.

Catholic emancipation: Issue of removing disqualifications preventing Catholics from holding office, voting and serving in Parliament. Not finally secured until 1829.

Chinese slavery: This controversy arose over the Balfour government's decision to allow indentured Chinese labourers to be imported to work in South African mines. It alienated elements of the working class who felt that this would deprive them of their given right to seek gainful employment within the Empire, while others felt it demeaned workers' rights and feared British employers using the same tactic to circumvent strikes. Some have argued that this persuaded some working-class Conservatives to switch allegiance to the fledgling Labour party. Nonconformists were also offended by the suggestion of 'slavery' and the risk of homosexuality in the all-male compounds.

citizen's charter: Launched by John Major 22 July 1991 this was an attempt to make the public services more responsive to consumers' wishes. The individual charters for services, like education and the health service, gave pledges of guaranteed performance targets and greater information for consumers.

classless society: During Major's first speech as Leader to the party conference, October 1991, he set out the themes for his leadership. Drawing upon his experiences as a young man in Brixton he evoked the idea of the Conservative party providing opportunities for all, of creating a society without barriers to achievement.

clause 28: A section of the Local Government Act 1988 inserted by Conservative backbenchers that banned local authorities from promoting the acceptability of homosexuality. Attempts by the Labour government in 2000 to repeal the legislation have been thwarted by the opposition of the House of Lords.

closed shop: Compulsory trade union membership for all employees in a particular workplace. The closed shop was effectively ended by Conservative legislation during the 1980s.

Coldharbour Lane, Brixton, London: Childhood home of John Major 1955–59. It was a rented two-bedroom flat in a Victorian house. He featured it in his 1991 Blackpool party conference speech and in a party political broadcast of 1992 entitled *The Journey*. Directed by John Schlesinger the broadcast featured Major being driven around Brixton while talking about his life experiences.

collectivism: Term applied to policies that seek to utilise the powers of the state to promote social equality and common good, often at the expense of individual liberty. Advocates, such as the New Liberals, have argued that only through state intervention could individual freedom be guaranteed. Usually associated with welfare politics and the increase in state power it had proponents among the Conservative party such as the 'YMCA' group and was supported by Harold Macmillan's *Middle Way* (1938).

Common Agricultural Policy (CAP): An EEC-wide programme agreed in 1962 that dictated farming and other produce production targets of member states by allocating subsidies to encourage or discourage the production of certain goods. CAP has become synonymous with overproduction, wastefulness, inefficiencies and high prices.

Common Market: Popular name for the European Community or EC.

common sense revolution: Launched by William Hague in October 1999, and borrowing the vocabulary from the Canadian Conservative party and Labour's five electoral pledges in 1997, this was an attempt to give the British electorate the minimum guarantee of what could be expected of a Conservative government. The five themes were: the defence of sterling; reduced taxation; better educational opportunities; a tough stance on law and order; and a reduction in bureaucracy and red tape.

Commonwealth: A grouping of states that evolved from the former territories of the British Empire. Not all former territories of the British Empire are members, and there are members from outside the old Empire. The organisation works to improve economic collaboration and other forms of co-operation between member states.

community charge – *see* **poll tax**

conscription: Compulsory military service. First introduced in February 1916 it was abolished in 1920. In April 1939, a new National Service Act conscripted men aged 20 to 41, with the outbreak of the Second World War this was extended to the ages of 19 to 41 and again in December 1941 to ages 18 to 41 and single women of 20 to 30 years. With the return of peace women were once more exempt although the persistence of the Cold War obliged men to undertake an eighteen-month (later two-year) period of service. Conscription was abolished in 1960.

contracting in – *see* **political levy**

contracting out – *see* **political levy**

Corn Laws: Describes the 1815 Corn Law that prevented the import of foreign grain until the domestic price reached 80s. per quarter, and its 1828 successor which introduced a sliding scale of tariffs.

coupon: Derogatory nickname for the letters of support sent by Bonar Law and Lloyd George to Coalition candidates at the 1918 election.

Crichel Down affair: The refusal of the Ministry of Agriculture to allow the former owners of some Dorset farmland, compulsorily purchased in 1938, to buy it back after the war led to an inquiry by Sir Arthur Clark QC. He dismissed the Ministry's argument that the land could be more effectively farmed as a single unit and publicly criticised those civil servants involved for a faulty decision. The Agriculture Minister, Thomas Dugdale, assumed responsibility and resigned in July 1954.

cruiser crisis (1925): Provoked by the desire of Winston Churchill (Chancellor of Exchequer) to cut the naval budget to enable him to reduce income tax.

Ironically he employed arguments similar to those that he had so fiercely resisted when he had been First Lord of the Admiralty in 1913. William Bridgeman (First Lord of the Admiralty 1924–29) defended the navy against the Treasury's cost-cutting proposals, even threatening resignation. The Admiralty won the battle after the intervention of Baldwin (Prime Minister).

***Death on the Rock*:** Television documentary on the shooting on 6 March 1988 by soldiers from the Special Air Service (SAS) of three IRA members while allegedly preparing a bombing incident in Gibraltar. The programme alleged that the victims were not resisting when shot and challenged the assertion that they were planning an act of terrorism. The Conservative Home Secretary failed to prevent the programme's transmission. It encouraged Conservative antagonism towards independent television rather than solely, as in the past, the BBC.

denationalisation: A policy first seen under the Conservative government elected in 1951 whereby nationalised industries were returned to private ownership. Overtaken in the 1980s by the term privatisation.

deselection: Procedure whereby a local constituency party withdraws support for its MP or parliamentary candidate and undertakes measures to seek a new official party candidate. Conservative examples include George Gardiner (MP for Reigate) in 1997 for his anti-European views and attacks on Major, and Nigel Nicolson (MP for Bournemouth East and Christchurch) in 1958 because of his opposition to the death penalty and his Suez abstention.

Dizzyism: A play on Disraeli's nickname used by political opponents to imply the lack of principle displayed by the Conservative leader.

doctor's mandate: The 1931 manifesto appeal by the National Government for the power to take whatever measures were necessary, even tariffs, to resolve Britain's economic crisis. The mandate was deliberately vague in order not to alienate the support of free-trade Liberals.

Don Pacifico debate: In June 1850, Lord Palmerston (Whig Foreign Secretary) was forced to defend his actions to Parliament for authorising the British navy to support Don Pacifico's claim for damages against the Greeks after his home had been ransacked by a mob. The Peelites and Protectionists united to censure Palmerston.

Downing Street Declaration (1993): Agreement announced 15 December 1993 between John Major (British Prime Minister) and Albert Reynolds (Irish Prime Minister) from outside No. 10 Downing Street. It was an attempt to begin the peace process in Northern Ireland. The republican movement was offered the opportunity of joining multi-party talks within three months of a terrorist ceasefire. The IRA announced a ceasefire on 31 August 1994.

early day motion (EDM): Parliamentary procedure whereby an MP tables a motion for debate. Although it is unlikely to secure the parliamentary time to be debated, other MPs can add their signatures as a sign of support. It is a means of testing the strength of feeling on a given issue. Since 1945 the numbers of EDMs being tabled has risen dramatically.

Eden Plan (1952): This was a British plan to increase institutional ties between The Six and the Council of Europe. It proposed joint meetings and the use of shared facilities and was intended to show Britain's commitment to the Six. It failed.

European Community (EC) – *see* **European Union**

European Economic Community (EEC) – *see* **European Union**

European Exchange Rate Mechanism (ERM): Designed to establish a zone of currency stability and co-ordination across the European Community. Britain joined the ERM in 1990 but was forced to leave after Black Wednesday.

European Free Trade Association (EFTA): Alternative trading bloc to the Six created by Britain in 1959 after failure to agree on a Free Trade Area with the European Economic Community. Austria, Denmark, Norway, Portugal, Sweden and Switzerland joined Britain in EFTA under the Stockholm Convention. Britain left EFTA in 1973 on joining the European Common Market.

European Monetary System (EMS): Established in 1978, EMS was designed to formalise economic co-operation across the EEC with the longer-term objective of achieving economic convergence.

European Monetary Union (EMU): Adopted by 11 of the 15 European Union member states in January 1999. EMU was proposed as a three-stage process by Jacques Delors (President of the European Commission) in 1989 and was followed by the Maastricht treaty that established the timetable for EMU.

European Parliament: Under the Treaty of Rome each country's parliament was entitled to send nominated delegates to a European Parliament meeting monthly in Strasbourg. After Britain joined in 1973 the UK was entitled to send 36 members. 22 Conservatives were initially sent, while Labour boycotted the parliament. After the 1975 Referendum there were 16 Conservative delegates. From 1979 delegates were elected directly. Since 1999 MEPs have been elected by a system of regional list proportional representation.

European Union: The Common Market set up by the Treaty of Rome signed in 1957 by France, Germany, Italy, Belgium, the Netherlands and Luxembourg ('the Six'). Britain's applications to join in 1961 and 1967 were vetoed by General de Gaulle (French President). British entry was secured in 1973 alongside Ireland and Denmark ('the Nine'). The 1975 Referendum confirmed Britain's membership. The EEC became the European Community (EC) in 1980 and then, on 1 January 1994, the European Union (EU).

Falklands factor: Used to explain why Margaret Thatcher, after Britain's success in the Falklands War, was able to secure victory in the 1983 general election. Before the war she had been the most unpopular prime minister ever and was facing an electoral threat from the Liberal–SDP Alliance.

Falkland Islands (Malvinas): A small group of islands in the South Atlantic with a population of 2,000. Although under British control since 1833 the Argentinians have disputed sovereignty. In 1982 they seized the islands and neighbouring South Georgia. The Thatcher government dispatched a military task force, 2 April 1982, which recaptured the capital, Port Stanley, on 14 June.

free trade: The principle whereby imports should enter any country without being subjected to tariffs.

GCHQ – *see* **Government Communications Headquarters**

Geddes Axe: Committee of businessmen convened by Lloyd George's coalition government to recommend areas for cuts in public expenditure. This was a response to the series of by-election victories by anti-Waste candidates in 1921. When the 'Geddes Axe' fell it was to make cuts in the social services. This alienated Lloyd George from his supporters on the left and offended his moderate Conservative coalition partners who considered the cuts to be too arbitrary, while the remainder of the Conservative party felt it to be too little too late.

General Agreement on Tariff and Trade (GATT): Concluded in 1947 it is intended to liberalise trade based upon a reciprocal tariff reduction basis; developing into the Kennedy round in 1967, but involving disputes between the USA and the EU in the Uruguay negotiations in 1993.

gerrymandering: The influencing of electoral outcomes by redrawing boundaries or moving populations to give one section of the population, or a political party, unfair advantage. A method applied in Northern Ireland to give the Unionist community an even greater proportion of seats in the Stormont Parliament prior to 1972. More recently the former leaders of the Conservative-controlled Westminster City Council were accused of manipulating council houses sales in particular wards to retain political control.

Gestapo broadcast (1945): One of Winston Churchill's least successful wireless broadcasts. Made during the 1945 general election campaign he declared that the Labour party socialist programme was one that could not 'be established without a political police', that is to say by a 'Gestapo'. The speech had been drafted by Ralph Assheton (Party Chairman) and was crudely based on themes from F.A. Hayek's *Road to Serfdom.* Denounced by Labour for scaremongering Churchill's intended imagery backfired and was seen by the electorate as evidence that Churchill and the Conservatives were unprepared to lead Britain into reconstruction.

gold standard: International mechanism determining exchange rates according to gold reserves. Many considered that it had provided the basis for London's financial pre-eminence before 1914. Britain obliged by war to abandon it, and formally left in 1919. Winston Churchill, as Chancellor of Exchequer, oversaw the return in March 1925. The financial crisis of 1931 forced its abandonment in September.

Good Friday Agreement: Signed 10 April 1998 as a stage in Northern Ireland's search for peace. It was proposed to create an elected Assembly and introduce power-sharing devolved government while formalising the relationship between the North and the Republic of Ireland. It also included sections on the decommissioning of weapons and the early release of terrorist prisoners. The agreement secured 71 per cent endorsement by the Northern Irish electorate in a referendum in May 1998.

Government Communications Headquarters (GCHQ): Based in Cheltenham this is the location for collecting signals intelligence and co-ordinating a worldwide network of listening and electronic surveillance posts. The Conservative government banned GCHQ workers from trade union membership in January 1984. Those workers who refused to surrender their union membership were dismissed. The ban was lifted in 1997.

Grand Hotel, Brighton: Scene of IRA bomb attack on the Conservative Party Conference, 11 October 1984.

Great Tory democracy – *see* **Tory democracy**

Greater London Council (GLC): Established in 1963 the council was controlled by Labour for most of its existence. Under the leadership of Ken Livingstone from 1981 the GLC increasingly clashed with Thatcher's government. The Conservative government in 1986 abolished the GLC.

handbagging: A critical reference to the leadership style of Margaret Thatcher. Coined by backbencher Julian Critchley, who said 'she cannot see an institution without hitting it with her handbag'. The verb was 'born' in a 1982 *Economist* article that quoted Critchley. The handbag became synonymous with Thatcher. In 2000 an internet charity auction found itself attracting bids over £101,000 for a Thatcher handbag.

Hawarden kite (1885): This was the publicity surrounding Gladstone's conversion to Home Rule for Ireland. Leaked (whether intentionally or not) by his son Herbert to various newspaper editors (15 December 1885) and widely reported from 17 December. It enabled the Conservatives to break off their informal alliance with the Irish Nationalists.

High Church: Party within the Church of England upholding belief in sacraments and ritual, the authority of the church hierarchy, and the close relationship between church and state. Significant element within the Conservative party could be classified as such and included figures like 3rd Marquess of Salisbury.

hire purchase: A form of credit enabling someone to purchase an item by regular payments while having the use of it. Hire-purchase restrictions were employed by various post-war Conservative governments to control inflation.

Home Rule: Policy of granting partial self-government to Ireland, including the restoration of an Irish parliament. Irish Home Rule bills were introduced in 1886, 1893 and 1914.

Immigration Act (1962): The Macmillan government's response to the surge in non-white immigration from Asia, Africa and the Caribbean was to introduce legislation that restricted entry and citizenship for the 'Commonwealth' immigrant. Thereafter a voucher system for entry was imposed, giving priority to those with skills or guaranteed offers of work, and limiting the quotas for other types of immigrant worker.

***Industrial Charter, The* (1947):** Conservative party policy document providing the basis for much of the party's post-war domestic policy. It accepted that nationalisation could not be reversed and embraced the ideas of Keynes with commitments to demand-management policies and full employment. It was targeted as much at the party as at the floating voter.

Irish National Liberation Army (INLA): Irish terrorist group formed in 1975 by members of the Official IRA dissatisfied with its abandonment of violence. Responsible for the death of Conservative shadow Northern Ireland Secretary Airey Neave in a bombing at the House of Commons car park 3 March 1979. It declared a ceasefire in August 1999.

Irish Republican Army (IRA): Irish terrorist group and military wing of Sinn Fein. Responsible for numerous bomb and terrorist attacks in Northern Ireland and mainland Britain. Attempted to assassinate the Conservative leadership with a bomb attack on the Grand Hotel, Brighton 12 October 1984. The attack killed five people including a Conservative MP. Announced its first ceasefire 31 August 1994 but ended this with an attack on the London docklands February 1996. Subsequently returned to ceasefire.

Iron Curtain speech (1946): Made by Winston Churchill in March 1946 to an audience at the Westminster College, Fulton, Missouri in the presence of American President Harry Truman, predicting the division of Europe between capitalism and communism. Foresaw the rising of an 'iron curtain' from Stettin in the Baltic to Trieste in the Adriatic behind which lay all the capitals of the ancient states of Eastern and Central Europe.

Iron Lady: Nickname applied to Margaret Thatcher first coined by Soviet paper, *Red Star*, in January 1976 after she had made a speech at Kensington town hall sceptical of the likely success of détente and the forthcoming Helsinki conference to discuss nuclear arms restrictions. Thatcher poked fun at the label in a speech that same month to her Finchley constituents.

Keynesianism: Economic theory of full employment developed by John Maynard Keynes. It rejected the idea of a self-regulating economy arguing instead that government expenditure and state economic management should be used to maintain output and full employment. These ideas were influential until the rise of monetarism in the 1970s and the apparent inability of Keynesianism to cope with the combination of stagnation and inflation.

Khaki election (1900): Sought to exploit the patriotism behind the South African war and the Liberal party's weaknesses in the rather lacklustre House of

Commons elected in 1895. Some felt it was opportunist to seek an electoral mandate during wartime. The implications were not lost on future political leaders in 1918, 1945 and 1983. Joseph Chamberlain played upon the theme of hunting down the 'pro-Boer' Liberals and promoted the war feeling, but Central Office and many other Conservative candidates tried to play down the 'Khaki' nature in their campaigns.

kitchen table Conservatism: Launched in March 1999 by William Hague it was another attempt to re-launch Conservative fortunes in advance of the June 2000 European elections. The intention was to convey the message that the Conservatives formulated policy with the issues that matter most to ordinary people sitting around a family kitchen table: crime, public services, taxation, care for the elderly and genetically modified food. The theme was quickly dropped following the European elections as another re-launch, the Common Sense Revolution, in October with a more Eurosceptic tone was unveiled.

knockout blow: This was a scenario that gripped both ordinary people and decision-makers in 1930s Britain. It envisaged that upon the outbreak of a war Britain would be subjected to a massive aerial bombardment that would destroy vital communications, kill thousands of people and wreck the fabric of Britain leading to the rapid collapse of civilian morale and the defeat of Britain. Futuristic military novels perpetuated the myth as did the press empire of Lord Rothermere, faulty intelligence estimates of the bombing strength and aerial strategies of Germany and utterances from political leaders like Stanley Baldwin that 'the bomber will always get through'.

Labour's double whammy: Conservative slogan attacking Labour's tax plans and used on pre-election publicity material February 1992.

Liberal Toryism: Reforming Toryism associated with the later years of Lord Liverpool's administration (1812–28) and his leading ministers Canning, Peel and Huskisson.

life peer: Under the Life Peerages Act 1958, the sovereign can appoint men (or women) to the House of Lords with a title that lasts for a lifetime and cannot be inherited by their children. The Prime Minister and Opposition party leaders make recommendations for life peerages.

little local difficulty: Harold Macmillan's apparently casual dismissal of the domestic political crisis caused by the mass resignation of his Treasury team just prior to his departure for a Commonwealth tour, 7 January 1958, created an impression of unflappability. Over the previous weekend he had agonised about the press statement. Yet the phraseology was a successful political gamble re-uniting the Cabinet behind his leadership and providing a positive tone for his Commonwealth tour.

Locarno Treaty (1925): France, Germany and Belgium agreed to the drawing of Germany's western European frontier. Britain and Italy acted as guarantors. Germany was admitted to the League of Nations. In light of events in the late 1930s the failing of the treaty was to secure Germany's eastern European borders.

Looking Ahead**:** 1924 policy document drafted by Neville Chamberlain that provided the core of the party's 1924 election manifesto and much of the domestic legislation Baldwin's government administered 1924–29. It was the party's first ever comprehensive and practicable statement of policies and was wrongly attributed by contemporaries to be the work of Curzon.

Maastricht treaty (1991): Was signed following a summit of European leaders that set out agreements reached on the Treaty of European Union. John Major secured for Britain opt-out clauses on a single currency and the social chapter arguing these would adversely affect Britain. The treaty was ratified after considerable parliamentary opposition from Major's own Eurosceptic backbenchers and elements of the House of Lords who favoured a referendum on the issue.

Macquisten bill (1925): A private member's bill on trade union law. It carried widespread party support and proposed the abolition of the political levy system. Stanley Baldwin (Prime Minister) anxious not to harm industrial relations successfully opposed the bill.

market forces: This is an economic idea that believes that industry and service providers will become more efficient and productive if government intervention and bureaucracy is minimised leaving companies to compete against each other in competitive markets.

Matrix Churchill case: November 1992 prosecution of the directors of the machine tools company Matrix Churchill for illegal exports to Iraq. This 'arms for Iraq' trial collapsed after it emerged that ministers had signed 'gagging orders'. At the trial ex-minister Alan Clark, who had advised the company about preparing its export licences, admitted he had been economical with the truth about his role. Major forced to announce the creation of the Scott Inquiry into arms for Iraq.

May Report (1931): Issued in February 1931 by the Committee on National Expenditure it precipitated the fall of the Labour government and the formation of the National Government. The report had recommended that the Labour government make large cuts in public expenditure, particularly regarding unemployment benefit; however Ramsay MacDonald's Cabinet were unable to agree upon a course of action and the report heightened the fears of the City of London and the financial markets that Britain was in serious financial crisis.

Maynooth grant: This was Robert Peel's decision to provide financial assistance to the Roman Catholic seminary at Maynooth, Ireland. The increase in the institution's grant from £9,000 to £26,000 was partly to help meet the government's intentions of improving higher education for Catholics but also a deliberate attempt to detach moderate Catholic opinion from the repeal movement. The parliamentary bill provoked a large Conservative rebellion.

Member of Scottish Parliament (MSP): A representative who sits in the Scottish Parliament in Edinburgh created by the 1997 Scottish Act. The parliament has 129 members, 73 directly elected plus 56 'additional top-up members'. Voting for the first Scottish parliament since 1707 occurred in May 1999. Labour failed to secure an overall majority. The Conservatives failed to secure any directly elected members but did gain 18 top-up seats.

***Middle Way, The* (1938):** A book by Harold Macmillan that was the precursor for much of the Conservative post-1945 economic thinking. Macmillan advocated a centrist policy, government intervention and the adoption of Keynesian economic ideas.

Midlothian campaign: Famous electoral campaign undertaken by Gladstone beginning in November 1879. It transformed the practice of electioneering and increasingly obliged politicians to address their constituents directly.

monetarism: Means of influencing the economy's performance by a policy of controlling of the money supply. Rejecting Keynesian economics, monetarism emphasised money supply targets ensuring that economic indicators such as the Public Sector Borrowing Requirement became key in helping control inflation. These views gained influence during the 1970s, partly drawing upon the work of Milton Friedman, and propagated within the Conservative party by individuals like Keith Joseph. Thatcher's first administration from 1979 embraced monetarism imposing spending cuts on government expenditure, reducing government borrowing targets and emphasising market forces.

National Defence Contribution Tax (NDC): This was a proposal by Neville Chamberlain (Chancellor of Exchequer) in his April 1937 budget to introduce a new temporary tax to help fund Britain's rearmament programme. He proposed to tax business profits believing that this would forestall severe labour unrest in the event of serious price raises and prevent the possibility of excessive profiteering by defence contractors. The proposal was withdrawn the following month, by Chamberlain's successor, Sir John Simon, after sustained Conservative party opposition.

National Economic Development Council(s) (NEDCs): Formed in 1962 as a discussion forum between government, employers and the unions to examine methods of increasing the national growth rate to 4 per cent a year. Popularly known as 'Neddy'; 'Little Neddies' were set up in individual industries and services in 1964.

National Efficiency: Movement embracing at the turn of the nineteenth century Fabian socialists and collectivist Conservatives like Milner, Chamberlain and Balfour. It was a reaction to a perceived decline in Britain's standing, economically, militarily and diplomatically, a decline attributed to the failings of parliamentary government: it was too sectional and too amateurish. The South African war heightened these concerns and encouraged the advocacy of state intervention in social welfare reform. It was argued that a healthy population equalled a more efficient workforce and offered political stability.

National Government: Coalition formed in August 1931 after the collapse of MacDonald's Labour government. The coalition comprised elements from the Labour, Liberal and Conservative parties and would survive in hybrid form until 1945. Despite being foreseen as a temporary political solution to resolve the economic crisis it appealed for a 'doctor's mandate' at the 1931 general election and succeeded in securing one of the most emphatic electoral victories of the twentieth century.

***National Review*:** Influential Tory journal that, under the journalistic pen of Lord Cranborne (later Marquess of Salisbury), provided the moral conscience of the Tory party during the nineteenth century and frequently attacked the leadership and direction of Disraeli.

Neddy – *see* **National Economic Development Council(s)**

***Next Five Years*:** The Conservative's 1959 election manifesto. Intended to highlight the achievements of the Conservatives after two terms in office as well as presenting its vision for the next period in government, the manifesto evolved through a series of 'drafts'. Preparing for the election had begun as early as 1957. Macmillan asked colleagues to provide details for intended legislation; however original ideas were limited particularly in the economic sphere. Ultimately it was a compromise document generally defensive in tone.

Nigeria debate (1916): This was a debate in the House of Commons in November 1916 about the question of disposing of captured enemy (German) assets. It came at a time when Conservative backbenchers were frustrated with the Asquith coalition government's failure to prosecute the war with Germany and her allies more vigorously. These critics were grouped around Edward Carson. At the vote Bonar Law (Conservative leader) managed to convince a narrow majority of Conservatives to support the government. It made Bonar Law realise that his party expected a different sort of government and played a role in Asquith's decision to resign in December 1916.

night of the long knives: Nickname given to Harold Macmillan's cabinet reshuffle in July 1962 when he sacked one-third of his Cabinet including Selwyn Lloyd (Chancellor of Exchequer), Harold Watkinson (Secretary for Defence), David Eccles (Education Secretary), Christopher Hill (Housing Secretary) and Viscount Kilmuir (Lord Chancellor). It occurred in the wake of a Liberal electoral revival, notably at the Orpington by-election, but was viewed by many as an act of panic.

Nolan Committee: Created October 1994 in response to the *Guardian*'s allegations against Neil Hamilton and Tim Smith about asking parliamentary questions in exchange for cash. It presented its first report in May 1995 making recommendations covering the conduct of MPs, ministers and civil servants, quangos and NHS bodies. The Committee was highly unpopular with many backbench Conservatives.

North Atlantic Treaty Organisation (NATO): Created 4 April 1949 to provide for the collective defence and security of the western world against feared Soviet aggression. The original signatories were Belgium, Canada, Denmark, France, Iceland, Luxembourg, the Netherlands, Norway, Portugal, the United Kingdom and the USA. The membership has been expanded since inception and now includes former Communist countries like Poland, Hungary and the Czech Republic.

Norway debate: 7–8 May 1940 parliamentary debate to consider the British military reversals in Finland and Norway. It precipitated the fall of Chamberlain's National Government.

Old Queen Street: Site of Conservative Party headquarters 1941–46. Site of Conservative Research Department 1930–81.

OMOV – *see* **one member one vote**

one member one vote (OMOV): Introduced in the February 1998 revision of the Conservative leadership rules enabling all party members to vote in the final ballot round. The Labour party had introduced OMOV to its leadership elections rules in 1993.

Optimist Clubs: Name given to Conservative women's clubs established among young women working in factories during 1930s. These clubs deliberately steered away from overt political activity, but sought to provide a personal and social forum for young women.

opting out: Introduced in the 1988 Education Reform Act it gave a school the right to leave local education authority control if a majority of parents and governors voted to do so. The school was then directly funded by central government and the governing body made responsible for spending and performance for a period of five years.

orange card: Refers to the support given by British politicians to Ulster Protestants in their attempts to preserve the 1800 Act of Union and frustrate home rule. Particularly associated with Conservative opposition to Home Rule for Ireland in the period 1880–1914.

Palace Chambers: Headquarters of Conservative Party 1922–41.

Parliament Acts (1911 and 1947): These acts weakened the ability of the House of Lords to defeat Government legislation already approved by the House of Commons. Introduced by Liberal and Labour governments respectively they were intended to limit the ability of the Conservative party to 'wreck' legislation by using their majority in the Lords. The 1911 Act meant legislation could no longer be defeated, instead being delayed for a two-year period. The 1947 Act reduced this delaying period to one year.

Patten Report: The report of the Patten Commission (chaired by former Conservative party chairman and former Hong Kong Governor Chris Patten) on the future of policing in Northern Ireland. Published in September 1999 it recommended sweeping changes to the Royal Ulster Constabulary. The report has proved unpopular with many of Patten's former Conservative colleagues.

pay pause: Euphemism used by Selwyn Lloyd (Chancellor of Exchequer) to describe the freezing of public sector wages introduced in July 1961.

peace for our time: The words of Neville Chamberlain spoken from No. 10, September 1938, indicating his apparent satisfaction at the avoidance of war with the Munich agreement. Legend suggests he immediately expressed regret at having using such positive language, but in doing so he was aping his predecessor, Benjamin Disraeli, who returned from the 1880 Congress of Berlin declaring 'peace with honour'.

Pentonville Five: Five miners jailed under terms of 1971 Industrial Relations Act, but released in November 1973 after the intervention of the official solicitor.

Plan G (1956): Proposal formulated by Macmillan (Chancellor of Exchequer) and Thorneycroft (President of Board of Trade) in July 1956 which envisaged creating a free trade area between European countries. It failed to achieve fruition and was overtaken by events, particularly the signing of the 1957 Treaty of Rome.

political levy: Money raised by trade unions from their members to be devoted to political campaigning and, in the case of those affiliated unions, to the Labour party. Conservatives have resented this arrangement and have sought to introduce legislation that requires members to specify their wish to 'contract in' to the pay the levy, for example 1927 Trade Disputes Act. Conservative legislation in the 1980s forced trade unions to hold ballots on the retention of political funds.

poll tax: Euphemism for the Community Charge. Introduced by Thatcher's third administration in 1987 it was intended to replace the unpopular domestic rates with a broader-based system of financing local government that targeted the individual adult. Enthusiastic grass-roots support at the 1987 party conference led to its rapid implementation with little cushioning of the higher costs faced by many. The resulting unpopularity played a large party in Thatcher's downfall. The Community Charge was replaced with the Council Tax in 1992.

Primrose League: Founded in 1883 by the Fourth Party as part of an attempt to democratise the party by broadening its base of support and reforming its organisation. Expounded the virtues of monarchy, empire, religion and national unity. Played an important role in electioneering politics. Social function in that it provided the catalyst for women to combine politics and public life. Name was chosen because the Primrose was the favourite flower of former party leader Disraeli.

privatisation: Deliberate policy of Conservative governments since 1979 to reduce the role of the state and extend the influence of market forces. This manifested itself in the sale of shares in publicly owned or partly owned corporations, e.g. 1984 sale of British Telecom, 1986 sale of British Gas, and in legislating to enable private firms to tender for work previously undertaken by public bodies such as refuse collection.

Profumo affair: Political scandal involving John Profumo (Conservative War Minister). He denied to Parliament, and Harold Macmillan (Prime Minister), that he had conducted an affair with the prostitute, Christine Keeler, who was known to be sleeping with the Soviet naval attaché. The revelation that he was lying forced his resignation on 4 June 1963. The timing of the scandal from the government's perspective was unfortunate occurring in a pre-election year at a time when the polls showed electorate dissatisfaction and coinciding with the growing popularity of political satire.

protection: System that subjected imports to duties ('tariffs') on entry into Britain. The issue had divided the Edwardian Conservative party and proved controversial throughout the inter-war years. In the 1923 general election the Conservatives, led by Baldwin, campaigned for protection and lost. As a result protectionism was renounced. However, the Empire Crusaders, led by Beaverbrook and Rothermere, waged a campaign for its reintroduction. A move Baldwin resisted until 1930 when a pro-tariff policy was reverted to as free-trade sympathies evaporated with the doubling of unemployment. In 1932 the Import Duties Act imposed tariffs on most non-food imports.

quango: Quasi-autonomous non-governmental organisation: a government-appointed body that has the power to spend public money but is not directly answerable to Parliament. Although the Conservatives were elected to government in 1979 committed to reduce their number, even more were created during their period in office.

rate-capping: Introduced in Scotland in 1982 and two years later in England and Wales it was a device used by Thatcher's Conservative administrations to limit the revenue which local authorities (which were at the time largely Labour controlled) could raise from the rates. In 1985–86, 18 councils were rate-capped for exceeding spending targets.

Referendum Pledge (1910): Pledge by Balfour in November that the next Conservative government would submit the issue of tariff reform to a referendum. This pledge alleviated the fear of some Conservatives that the party would be hit by a popular backlash against 'food taxes'. But it failed to help the party win the December general election.

retail price maintenance (RPM): This was a system that allowed manufacturers to stipulate the price at which retailers sold their goods. Its abolition was championed by Edward Heath (Secretary for Trade, Industry and Regional Development) in 1964 and pushed through despite the hostility of backbenchers, party activists and Tory shopkeepers who foresaw the destruction of their livelihoods as supermarkets undercut their prices. Some historians have labelled the episode as Douglas-Home's poll tax.

***Right Road for Britain, The* (1949):** Conservative's first full-length policy document since 1945, incorporating much of the Conservative Research Department's work. It was typical of the intellectual strain of Conservatism prevalent during the 1950s.

***Road to Serfdom, The* (1944):** Written by the London School of Economics don F.A. Hayek, the book became the bible of post-war libertarianism. Hayek argued that Britain was rapidly moving towards totalitarian socialism because of people's adherence to the middle way between competition and central government intervention. From the 1970s his arguments were crucial to those Conservatives who wished to abandon Keynesianism and feared the ratchet effect of collectivism.

safety first: The 1929 general election slogan for the Conservatives. Intended as an appeal to the conservative nature of the electorate, especially the newly enfranchised female vote, it characterised the uninspirational nature of Baldwin's campaign.

Samuelite Liberals: Faction of Liberal Party that followed the lead of Viscount Samuel and resigned from the National Government in September 1932 in protest at the adoption of tariffs agreed at the Ottawa conference.

Schuman Plan (1950): Proposed 8 May 1950 by the French foreign minister, Robert Schuman it sought to tie the emergent West Germany economically to France by limited institutional controls over coal and steel, the backbone of European economies. The opportunity to join the 'Plan' was widened to other Western European governments, but the British remained wary and the Labour government eventually rejected it.

Scott Inquiry: Established by John Major in 1992 under the chairmanship of Lord Chief Justice Scott to investigate the role of ministers in the issuing of armaments export licences to Iraq. This emerged during the Matrix Churchill trial that collapsed in November 1992. The report published in February 1996 caused acute embarrassment for Major's government, but it narrowly survived a parliamentary vote, 319–318.

secondary picketing: Picketing by strikers of places not directly involved in their dispute. This form of industrial action was outlawed under the Conservative Government by its 1980s trade union legislation.

section 28 – *see* **clause 28**

Selsdon Park conference: Meeting of the shadow Cabinet over weekend 30 January–1 February 1970 at a hotel in Croydon to 'brainstorm' and focus attention on policy ideas that would form the basis of the Conservatives' next election campaign. The meeting attracted widespread publicity and provoked Labour's quip from Harold Wilson about the emergence of 'Selsdon man': that the Conservatives were acolytes to an ancient breed of economics that worshipped laissez-faire and market economics.

set the people free: Conservative campaign slogan for the 1950 general election. Intended to emphasise Conservative freedom from controls and rationing, consumer choice and opportunity. While it helped the Conservatives regain votes in the suburban and commuter areas, Labour still secured a majority of six seats.

shadow cabinet: Alternative government-in-waiting formed by the parliamentary opposition party. A spokesman is appointed to 'shadow' government ministers, for example Michael Portillo was appointed Shadow Chancellor of Exchequer in 2000 to 'shadow' Gordon Brown Labour's Chancellor of Exchequer. The first Conservative shadow cabinet was formed following the 1906 general election defeat.

sleaze: Generic label applied to the various political scandals (e.g. David Mellor's extramarital affair, Stephen Milligan's accidental death playing a sex game, and 'cash for questions') that plagued the Major administration 1992–97. The exposure of sex scandals, political corruption and moral ambiguities played a considerable role in the 1997 rejection of the Conservatives at the polls. Mr Major's political response was to create the Nolan Committee into Public Standards.

Smith Square: Conservative Party headquarters since 1958.

social chapter: Section of the Treaty of European Union rejected by the Thatcher and Major governments. Concerned with workers' rights and health and safety issues, these Conservative governments considered that they would increase the bureaucratic burden on industry, push up costs and reduce British industrial competitiveness.

social imperialism: Exemplified by the 1867 Abyssinian War whereby the use of British arms to win easy victories abroad was intended to impress domestic voters rather than cower native populations.

St Stephen's Chambers: Site of Conservative Party headquarters 1900–18.

St Stephen's Club: Established in 1870 in Bridge Street, Westminster it was the club for Central Office and National Union lesser functionaries.

Sunningdale Agreement (1973): Agreement on a Protestant–Catholic power-sharing assembly and the creation of a Council of Ireland reached at the Civil Service College at Sunningdale, Surrey following a conference on Northern Ireland 6–9 December 1973.

Supermac: Nickname for Harold Macmillan coined by the cartoonist Vicky in 1958. Intended as a critique of the Prime Minister it rebounded becoming used with affectionate admiration making the intended victim something of a folk hero.

swing: Terminology used to describe the movement in votes from one party to another at an election compared with the previous contest. The phrase has been popularised by the television presenter Peter Snow's 'swingometer'. Various mathematical formulas exist to calculate swing.

Swinton College: Yorkshire home of Lord Swinton. Donated to Conservative Party and became the Conservative Party College 1948–71.

Taff Vale: Legal judgment reached by the House of Lords in July 1901 that ruled that a trade union was liable for the acts of its agents. This ruling effectively prevented trade unions from undertaking industrial action. The case brought by the Taff Vale Railway Company was against the Amalgamated Society of Railway Servants who had picketed Cardiff Station. The Liberal government's 1906 Trade Disputes Act overturned the ruling.

tariff reform: A movement which sought to re-apply duties on foreign imports, particularly grain. The issue divided the Conservative party for most of the Edwardian period.

Thatcherism: -ism coined by the Marxist academic, Stuart Hall, in 1976, to identify the political philosophy of recently selected leader, Margaret Thatcher. She is the only Prime Minister whose name has given rise to an 'ism'.

The Nine – *see* **European Union**

The Six: Nickname applied to the six European Countries (France, Germany, Italy, Belgium, the Netherlands and Luxembourg) who signed the Treaty of Rome in 1957 and formed the European Economic Community – *see also* **European Union**.

think twice campaign: Was run by Scottish Conservatives opposed to Labour's devolution plans prior to the September 1997 referendum. The campaign title was meant to make Scottish voters question the viability of a Scottish Parliament and of Scotland exercising tax-raising powers. Ultimately they failed to convince voters who overwhelmingly supported the 'devolution' camp.

three circles: Churchill's interpretation of the international world order after 1945. He saw three blocks: the Commonwealth and Empire, America 'the English-speaking world', and western Europe. Since these three circles overlapped with Britain as the common denominator that left Britain in a unique position for leadership, enabling her to maintain a leading world role.

Tory: Label derived from the name for Irish cattle thieves, it was first applied politically to a group of former Cavaliers during the reign of Charles II. A Tory typically came to signify a landed gentleman who was opposed to change. Despite the adoption of the name Conservative the label Tory continues to be applied often as a term of abuse by political opponents, however some Conservatives still refer to themselves as Tories to imply an association with tradition and gradual reform.

Tory democracy: Description of the policies advocated by Disraeli and Lord Randolph Churchill, combining maintenance of established institutions with cautious social reform in an attempt to win working-class support for the Conservative party.

Treaty of Rome (1957): Saw the creation of the European Economic Community and has provided the framework for the moves towards European economic and political integration – *see* **The Six**, **European Union**.

two nations: Phrase from Disraeli's 1845 novel *Sybil*. He was seeking to describe the polarisation of early Victorian society into rich and poor. This idea has profoundly impacted upon Conservative philosophy based upon a mythical notion that Disraeli was committed to 'One Nation Toryism' with its intention of improving the conditions of the working classes and preventing the emergence of a divided society. Subsequent leaders, like Baldwin, Macmillan and Heath, were seen to be operating within this tradition.

Unionist: The 'union' referred to was that between Britain and Ireland. The name was generally applied to Conservatives and Liberal Unionists. With the end of the Union in 1921 the term 'Conservative' returned to general usage, but many continued to call themselves 'Unionist' or 'Conservative and Unionist'.

valentine letters: Public exchange of correspondence between Balfour and Joseph Chamberlain, February 1906, in which Balfour accepted the case for imperial preference and that this was an aim of the Conservative party. In return Chamberlain accepted this definition of party policy and gave a promise of loyalty.

value added tax (VAT): Introduced in 1973 by the Conservatives it levied an additional rate of taxation on products and goods. The decision to introduce the tax was motivated by Heath's desire to make Britain's application for membership of the EEC more acceptable to the existing members. The decision to apply VAT to fuel in March 1993 provoked outrage from Conservative backbenchers and old age pensioners.

Vassall case (1962): Spying scandal when it emerged that a minor Admiralty official, John Vassall, was a homosexual and a Russian spy. Macmillan insisted upon the resignation of a junior minister, Galbraith, but he was later exonerated of any wrongdoing.

villa Toryism: Reference to suburbia and the idea that it was the social staple and demographic foundation of the Conservative party in the age of Salisbury.

Westland Helicopters dispute: Cabinet dispute over the sale of British company Westland Helicopters in January 1986. Thatcher preferred a bid by the American firm, Sikorski, while Michael Heseltine (Defence Secretary) favoured a European consortium takeover. When he failed to win the argument Heseltine dramatically walked out of the cabinet and resigned. The affair claimed the ministerial scalp of Leon Brittan, Trade and Industry Secretary, when it emerged that he was responsible for leaking material on the dispute to the press. The whole drama raised issues about Britain's European role, Thatcher's conduct of cabinet government and her relations with senior ministers. Ultimately these were to lead to her downfall in 1990.

Westminster City Council scandal: Investigation into activities of Conservative-controlled Westminster City Council for its policy on the sale of council houses. Dame Shirley Porter, former leader of the Council, was accused of vote rigging to retain Conservative control of the Council and the findings of the district auditor led to Porter and two other Conservative councillors being given large surcharges. The case has gone before the High Court on appeal. *See also* **gerrymandering**.

wets: Label applied to those Conservatives after 1979 who were not Thatcherites, particularly in their economic thinking. Thatcher used her first administration to weaken their authority, and to marginalise those whom she considered to be 'not one of us'. They were particularly critical of Howe's 1981 budget but failed to make a stand.

Whigs: Political grouping from eighteenth century who were disposed to change and associated with the interests of trade. Remnants of the Whigs joined the Liberal Party in the nineteenth century.

winds of change: Harold Macmillan's acknowledgement in February 1960, while addressing the Joint Assembly of the South African Parliament, that the issues of anti-colonialism and nationalism were political facts among the nations of the British Empire. It was seen as a signal of intent by the British to hasten the speed of decolonisation.

winter of discontent (1978–79): A series of public and private sector strikes during the winter of 1978–79 as the Labour government sought to limit pay increases. The disruption, and scenes of violence on picket lines, was exploited by the Conservative party and contributed to their electoral success in 1979. The repetition of the phrase continued to undermine Labour in successive general elections.

Woolton–Treviot agreement (1947): formally merged the Liberal National Party with the Conservative Party.

Zinoviev letter (1924): A letter supposedly written by Zinoviev, president of the Communist International (Comintern) to British Communists shortly before the 1924 general election calling for them to agitate and prepare for a revolutionary seizure of power. Knowledge of the letter came into the possession of the Conservative party, via Joseph Ball and Donald im Thurn, before it was leaked to the *Daily Mail.* Once in the public domain it was used to damage the Labour party in a campaign orchestrated by Central Office. A *Sunday Times* investigation in 1967 questioned the letter's authenticity suggesting that it had been forged in Poland by Russian émigrés in order to prevent the British government from giving aid to Soviet Russia. Documents released by the Public Record Office in 1998 confirmed it was a forgery.

Part 7

BIBLIOGRAPHY

7. BIBLIOGRAPHY

Topics

- History
- Ideology and beliefs
- Organisation and membership
- The leadership
- Biographies of other Conservatives
- Electoral support
- Policies and policy-making

Topic themes: Conservatives and . . .

- Women
- Immigration
- Trade unions
- Europe
- Economic policy
- Social policy
- Ireland
- The Union
- Foreign and imperial policy
- Defence policy

Specific eras

- Repeal of the Corn Laws
- Age of Disraeli
- Salisbury's ascendancy
- Crisis of Edwardian Conservatism
- Age of Baldwin
- Chamberlain and appeasement
- Conservative hegemony 1951–64
- Heath years
- Thatcherism

Published documentary sources, diaries and memoirs

List of abbreviations

BIHR	*Bulletin of the Institute of Historical Research*
BJPS	*British Journal of Political Science*
CBH	*Contemporary British History*
CR	*Contemporary Record*
EconHR	*Economic History Review*

EHR	*English Historical Review*
H	*History*
HJ	*The Historical Journal*
IHS	*Irish Historical Studies*
IPS	*Irish Political Studies*
JBS	*Journal of British Studies*
JCH	*Journal of Contemporary History*
JICH	*Journal of Imperial and Commonwealth History*
JP	*Journal of Politics*
PA	*Parliamentary Affairs*
PH	*Parliamentary History*
PP	*Past and Present*
PPrej	*Patterns of Prejudice*
PQ	*Political Quarterly*
RP	*Review of Politics*
TCBH	*Twentieth Century British History*
TRHS	*Transactions of Royal Historical Society*
VS	*Victorian Studies*

Introductory note

This bibliography has been arranged by themes and also chronologically and is intended to represent a fair selection of the themes and issues that concern the Conservative party since 1830. The reading is deliberately greater than would be required for an average essay, but does reflect the wealth of bibliographical material now available for most of these subjects and allows a degree of specialisation on particular aspects of a topic. Similarly, the article literature mentioned, while not an exhaustive list, is intended as a guide to some of the most important material from which a selection can be made according to preference.

TOPICS

History

All historians of the Conservative party owe an enormous debt to the *Longman History of the Conservative Party* that comprises six volumes and tells the story of the party from 1830 to 1975:

R. Stewart, *The Foundation of the Conservative Party 1830–1867* (1978)
R. Shannon, *The Age of Disraeli, 1868–1881: the Rise of Tory Democracy* (1992)

R. Shannon, *The Age of Salisbury, 1881–1902: Unionism and Empire* (1996)
J.A. Ramsden, *The Age of Balfour and Baldwin 1902–1940* (1978)
J.A. Ramsden, *The Age of Churchill and Eden, 1940–1957* (1995)
J.A. Ramsden, *The Winds of Change: Macmillan to Heath 1957–1975* (1996)

Professor Ramsden has subsequently condensed his thoughts into an accessible one-volume history, *An Appetite for Power: A History of the Conservative Party since 1830* (1998); Lord Blake's *The Conservative Party from Peel to Major* (1999), despite first appearing in 1970, has been revised and re-issued several times and is still a useful narrative starting point, although the approach is strictly high political. Also of use is Bruce Coleman, *Conservatives and Conservatism in the Nineteenth Century* (1988).

No longer can historians get away with the claim that the history of the party has been neglected. Evidence of the breadth of work on the Conservative party can be seen from the thematic essays in A. Seldon and S. Ball (eds), *Conservative Century: The Conservative Party since 1900* (1994). Apart from essays on most aspects of the party, Stuart Ball's essay 'The Conservative party since 1900: a bibliography' is a must for anyone wishing to branch out further than this select reading list. For further reading also consult the relevant volume of the *Longman History of the Conservative Party.*

For suitable political facts and figures see D. Butler and G. Butler, *Twentieth Century British Political Facts 1900–2000* (2000). There is nothing comparable for the nineteenth century, although C. Cook and B. Keith, *British Historical Facts 1830–1900* (1975) is the best available.

Ideology and beliefs

A useful starting point is Robert Eccleshall, 'Conservatism' in R. Eccleshall *et al.* (eds), *Political Ideologies* (1984), as are the opening two chapters of Philip Norton and Arthur Aughey, *Conservatives and Conservatism* (1981). For a sceptical but accessible evaluation and selection of extracts from various Conservative thinkers see Robert Eccleshall, *English Conservatism since the Restoration* (1990); also aimed at the general student is Frank O'Gorman (ed.), *British Conservatism: Conservative Thought from Burke to Thatcher* (1986). For a more sympathetic anthology see Kenneth Baker (ed.), *The Faber Book of Conservatism* (1993). R.B. McDowell, *British Conservatism 1832–1914* (1959) remains valuable for the development of ideas during the Victorian age. Maurice Cowling (ed.), *Conservative Essays* (1978) comprises a series of essays from Conservative journalists, academics and politicians. Also Robert Nisbet, *Conservatism: Dream and Reality* (1986) admirably summarises Conservatism in an international context in less than 120 pages! A sceptical interpretation is offered by Andrew Gamble, *Conservative Nation* (1974), which covers the period 1945–74.

On specific themes see Ian Packer, 'The Conservatives and the ideology of landownership 1910–1914' and M. Francis, 'Set the people free? Conservatives and the State 1920–1960', both in Martin Francis and Ina Zweiniger-Bargielowska (eds), *The Conservatives and British Society 1880–1990* (1996).

For examples of Conservative politicians willing to explain their ideology see the classic Quintin Hogg, *The Case for Conservatism* (1947) and more recently David Willetts, *Modern Conservatism* (1992).

Organisation and membership

The standard starting point is R. McKenzie, *British Political Parties* (2nd edn, 1963), which examines all aspects of the party machine and offers a historical perspective. All volumes of the *Longman History of the Conservative Party* have sections on organisational development.

Professional

For the origins of the party organisation see Edgar Feuchtwanger, *Disraeli, Democracy and the Tory Party* (1968), also his article 'J.E. Gorst and the central organisation of the Conservative Party 1870–1882' in *BIHR* (1959). Also vital to understanding the political system during the mid-Victorian era is H.J. Hanham, *Elections and Party Management: Politics in the time of Gladstone and Disraeli* (2nd edn, 1978) and Cornelius O'Leary, *The Elimination of Corrupt Practices from British Elections 1868–1911* (1962); for twentieth-century developments Stuart Ball, 'The national and regional party structure' in Ball and Seldon, *Conservative Century* (1994). For the constituency agent, see R. Frasure and A. Kornberg, 'Constituency agents and British politics' *BJPS* 5 (1975). The role of the party conference is given a rehabilitation by Richard Kelly, *Conservative Party Conference: The Hidden System* (1989). The delicate matter of party funding is considered by Michael Pinto-Duschinsky, *British Political Finance 1830–1980* (1981) and the various articles of Justin Fisher offer a contemporary analysis, including 'Political donations to the Conservative party' *PA* 47, 1 (1994). The role of the Conservative Research Department is evaluated in John Ramsden, *The Making of Conservative Party Policy* (1980) and Arnold Beichman, 'Hugger-Mugger in Old Queen Street: the origins of the Conservative Research Department', *JCH* 13, 4 (1978). For the party in Scotland see D.W. Urwin, 'Scottish Conservatism: a party organisation in transition', *Political Studies* 14 (1966), J.T. Ward, *The First Century: A History of Scottish Tory Organisation* (1982), James Kellas, 'The party in Scotland' in Ball and Seldon (eds), *Conservative Century* (1994), S. Kendrick and D. McCrone, 'Politics in a cold climate: The Conservative decline in Scotland', *Political Studies* 37 (1989).

Voluntary

For the role of Conservative Associations see Stuart Ball, 'Local Conservatism and the evolution of the party organisation' in Ball and Seldon (eds), *Conservative Century* (1994). Party membership was subject to scrutiny in a 1992 survey by Paul Whitely, Patrick Seyd and Jeremy Richardson, *True Blues: The Politics of Conservative Party Membership* (1994). They concluded that apart from being in rapid decline it was also an ageing membership. See also Patrick Seyd and Paul Whitely, 'Conservative grassroots: an overview' in S. Ludlam and

M. Smith (eds), *Contemporary British Conservatism* (1996). Anecdotal impressions of the condition of party members in the early 1990s can be gathered from Rupert Morris, *Tories: From Village Hall to Westminster* (1991). The party's youth movement is considered in Zig Layton-Henry, 'The Young Conservatives 1945–1970', *JCH* 8 (1973) and in a rather idiosyncratic manner by John Holroyd-Doveton, *Young Conservatives* (1996).

Parliamentary

For the composition and ideology of the parliamentary party, see J. Cornford, 'The parliamentary foundations of Hotel Cecil' in R. Robson (ed.), *Ideas and Institutions of Victorian Britain* (1967), W.L. Guttsman, *The British Political Elite* (1963), J.F.S. Ross, *Elections and Electors: Studies in Democratic Representation* (1955) and D. Baker, A. Gamble and S. Ludlam, 'More "classless" and less "Thatcherite"? Conservative MPs after the 1992 election', *PA* 45 (1992). Philip Norton, 'The parliamentary party and party committees' and Bryon Criddle, 'Members of Parliament' in Ball and Seldon, *Conservative Century* (1994) both consider the activities of the parliamentary party in the twentieth century.

For the 1922 Committee, see Philip Goodhart and Ursula Branston, *The 1922: The Story of the Conservative Backbenchers' Parliamentary Committee* (1973) and Stuart Ball, 'The 1922 Committee: the formative years 1922–1945', *PH* 9 (1990) which argues that during this period it was little more than a lecture club, but that the Second World War changed its role. For the activities of the whips' office, see Viscount Chilston, *Chief Whip: The Political Life and Times of Aretas Akers-Douglas* (1961) for an insider's view of the late Victorian and Edwardian period; for a more contemporary perspective, see Gyles Brandreth, *Breaking the Code: Westminster Diaries 1990–1997* (1999), offering the views of a junior whip during the last years of the Major government. The post-war issue of discipline is considered by R. Jackson, *Rebels and Whips: Dissension and Cohesion in British Political Parties since 1945* (1968) and the two studies by Phillip Norton, *Dissension in the House of Commons: Intra-Party Dissent in the House of Commons Division Lobbies 1945–74* (1975) and *Dissension in the House of Commons 1974–79* (1980).

The leadership

Overviews

Lord Blake's survey of Conservative leaders, from Peel to Major, is a useful starting point (see above); also of some use is Donald Southgate (ed.), *The Conservative Leadership 1832–1932* (1974) which curiously stopped the story in 1932. Robert Shepherd, *The Power Brokers: The Tory Party and Its Leaders* (1991), although concerned mainly with the fall of Thatcher, is full of insider insight and covers the issue of leadership selection and removal over the twentieth century. Peter Hennessy, *The Prime Minister: The Office and Its Holders since 1945* (2000) provides an engaging and readable portrait of the various Prime Ministers since 1945 combining his journalistic flair with academic scrutiny.

For individual leaders

Peel

Norman Gash, *Peel* (1976) or his *Sir Robert Peel* (1972) remain the standard lives. See also D. Reed, *Peel and the Victorians* (1987) and E.J. Evans, *Sir Robert Peel: Statesmanship, Power and the Party* (1991). Also worth consulting is Norman Gash, 'Peel and the party system', *TRHS* (1951).

Derby

Robert Stewart, *The Politics of Protection: Lord Derby and the Protectionist Party 1841–1852* (1971). Also essential is W.D. Jones, *Lord Derby and Victorian Conservatism* (1959). Much can be gleaned on Derby's leadership from John Vincent (ed.), *Disraeli, Derby and the Conservative Party: Journals and Diaries of Edward Henry, Lord Stanley 1849–1869* (1978).

Disraeli

The authority is Robert Blake, *Disraeli* (1966), but it is a massive work. For more recent scholarly assessments see Paul Smith, *Disraeli: A Brief Life* (1996), while Edgar Feuchtwanger has produced a succinct volume for Arnold's Reputations series that takes account of the most recent research: E. Feuchtwanger, *Disraeli* (2000).

Northcote

Still awaiting a modern biographer.

Salisbury

Peter Marsh, *Discipline of Popular Government: Lord Salisbury's Domestic Statecraft 1881–1902* (1978) for many years was the standard point of reference; however, recently two large biographies have appeared: Andrew Roberts, *Salisbury: Victorian Titan* (1999) which runs to over 900 pages and the slimmer but impeccably researched David Steele, *Lord Salisbury: A Political Biography* (1999). For the evolution of Salisbury's political ideology see M. Pinto-Duschinsky, *The Political Thought of Lord Salisbury 1854–1868* (1967).

Balfour

Although dated much of use can still be gleaned from Blanche Dugdale, *Arthur James Balfour* (2 vols, 1936). More recent studies include Ruddock MacKay, *Balfour: Intellectual Statesman* (1983) and Max Egremeont, *Balfour* (1980), but there is a feeling that none of these is quite satisfactory. It will be worth looking out for R.J.Q. Adams's forthcoming study that will be published by John Murray.

Bonar Law

For many decades the standard reference point was Robert Blake, *The Unknown Prime Minister: Bonar Law* (1955) but a fresh rehabilitation has been recently offered by R.J.Q. Adams, *Bonar Law* (1999).

Austen Chamberlain

David Dutton, *Austen Chamberlain: A Gentleman in Politics* (1985).

Baldwin

The standard point of reference is the massive volume by J. Barnes and K. Middlemas, *Baldwin* (1969); Roy Jenkins, *Baldwin* (1987) is shorter and more elegant to read. Historical research has since then moved in new directions offering fresh perspectives on the dominant political figure of the inter-war period such as Philip Williamson, *Stanley Baldwin* (1999) which examines Baldwin in the context of political leadership and offers perspective on his moral and intellectual influences.

Neville Chamberlain

Keith Fielding's *A Life of Neville Chamberlain* (1946) is a sympathetic study and remains the best single-volume study to date. An officially sanctioned two-volume study has only seen the completion of Part I: David Dilks, *Neville Chamberlain* (1984) which takes the story as far as 1929, but it appears unlikely the sister volume will be published. Look out for David Dutton's forthcoming volume in Arnold's Reputations series that will evaluate the evolution of Chamberlain's reputation from the 1920s to date. A number of historians are waiting in the wings to write a single-volume study. To get an idea of the 'inner man' see Robert Self (ed.), *The Neville Chamberlain Diary and Letters: vol. 1: 1915–20, vol. 2 1921–27* (2000, 2001); a third volume is forthcoming.

Churchill

There is no shortage of studies of Churchill. It seems that every aspect of his life has been considered. The official biography runs to 8 massive volumes and 11 companion volumes of documents: Randolph Churchill (vols 1–2), Martin Gilbert (vols 3–8), *Winston S. Churchill* (1966–90). Robert Rhodes James, *Churchill: A Study in Failure* (1970), as its title suggests sees the limitations in his career, but only takes the story as far as 1939. John Charmley, *Churchill: The End of Glory* (1993) provoked a storm of publicity with its publication and seeks to challenge the myths surrounding Churchill. Robert Blake and Roger William Louis (eds), *Churchill* (1993) is a series of thematic essays by leading experts and is very accessible. John Ramsden, 'Winston Churchill and the leadership of the Conservative Party', *CR* 9, 1 (1995) is useful. Paul Addison, *Churchill on the Home Front 1900–1955* (1992), as the title suggests, considers Churchill's domestic career. Also of interest is John Ramsden, 'How Winston Churchill became "The greatest living Englishman"', *CBH* 12, 3 (1998). See also Dennis Kavanagh, *Crisis, Charisma and British Political Leadership* (1974). Short single-volume review studies of Churchill include Keith Robbins, *Churchill* (1992) which takes a standard chronological approach and Ian S. Wood, *Churchill* (2000) which takes a thematic approach.

Eden

The prosecution case is presented by David Carlton, *Anthony Eden: A Biography* (1981); the defence by Robert Rhodes James, *Anthony Eden* (1986). A thematic study of Eden is offered by David Dutton, *Anthony Eden: A Life and Reputation* (1997) which gives greater analysis of Eden's domestic policies than previous studies.

Macmillan

His authorised biography appeared in two volumes, Alistair Horne, *Harold Macmillan* (1986–1988). The best, and most concise, single-volume study is John Turner, *Macmillan* (1994). Specific aspects of Macmillan's career from appeasement to Ireland to war are considered in a collection of essays: Richard Aldous and Sabine Lee (eds), *Harold Macmillan: A Political Portrait* (1999).

Home

The shortness of Home's premiership has meant he has been ill-served by the biographer; however D.R. Thorpe, *Alec Douglas-Home* (1996) has begun the revisionary process.

Heath

David Campbell, *Edward Heath: A Biography* (1993) is the standard point of departure.

Thatcher

Hugo Young, *One of Us* (final edition, 1991) has provided the standard point of reference, although it is not an exercise in hagiography. See also John Campbell, *Margaret Thatcher: Volume One: The Grocer's Daughter* (2000). It will shortly be joined by a second volume.

Major

The authority is Anthony Seldon, *Major: A Political Life* (1997) based upon extensive interviews with those close to the Prime Minister. Much of use can be gleaned from Sarah Hogg and Jonathan Hill, *Too Close to Call: Power and Politics, John Major at No. 10* (1995), which offers an insider's view of working at the heart of the Major administration. See also P. Jones and J. Hudson, 'The quality of political leadership: a case study of John Major', *BJPS* 26, 2 (1996).

Hague

The verdict of history is still awaited!

Leadership selection

Vernon Bogdanor, 'The selection of the party leader' in Ball and Seldon, *Conservative Century* (1994) offers an overview of the selection process; while Leonard Stark, *Choosing A Leader* (1996) considers the Conservative process alongside the other British political parties. On specific leadership contests see Mark Wickham-Jones, 'Right turn: a revisionist account of the 1975 Conservative Party leadership election', *TCBH* 8, 1 (1997); Philip Norton, 'Choosing the leader: the 1989 Conservative contest', *CR* 4 (1990–91); R.K. Alderman and N. Carter, 'A very Tory coup: the ousting of Mrs Thatcher', *PA* 44 (1991); Keith Alderman, 'The Conservative party leadership election of 1995', *PA* 49, 2 (1996) and 'The Conservative party leadership election of 1997', *PA* 51, 1 (1998).

Biographies of other Conservatives

Age of Peel

J.T. Ward, *Sir James Graham* (1967); Richard Shannon, *Gladstone 1809–1865* (1982); Muriel Chamberlain, *Lord Aberdeen: A Political Biography* (1983); Elizabeth Longford, *Wellington: Pillar of State* (1972).

Age of Disraeli

Viscount Chilston, *W.H. Smith* (1965).

Age of Salisbury

Viscount Chilston, *Chief Whip: The Political Life and Times of Aretas Akers-Douglas, 1st Viscount Chilston* (1961); Roy Forster, *Lord Randolph Churchill* (1981); Peter Marsh, *Joseph Chamberlain* (1994); Richard Jay, *Joseph Chamberlain* (1981).

Edwardian era

John Campbell, *F.E. Smith: 1st Earl of Birkenhead* (1983); Richard Cosgrave, 'Lord Halsbury' in J.A. Thompson and Arthur Mejia (eds), *Edwardian Conservatism: Five Studies in Adaptation* (1988); Larry Witherell, *Rebel on the Right: Henry Page Croft and the Crisis of British Conservatism* (1997).

Inter-war years

A.J.P. Taylor, *Beaverbrook* (1972); John Charmley, *Duff Cooper: The Authorised Biography* (1986); Randolph S. Churchill, *Lord Derby: King of Lancashire* (1959); Andrew Roberts, *Holy Fox: A Biography of Lord Halifax* (1991); J.A. Cross, *Sir Samuel Hoare* (1977); John Charmley, *Lord Lloyd and the Decline of the British Empire* (1987).

1940–65

Mark Garnett, *Alport: A Study in Loyalty* (1999); Anthony Howard, *Rab: A Life of R.A. Butler* (1986); D.R. Thorpe, *Selwyn Lloyd* (1989); Robert Shepherd, *Iain Macleod* (1994); Robert Rhodes James, *Bob Boothby: A Portrait* (1991); Simon Heffer, *Enoch Powell: Like a Roman* (1998).

Heath years

Andrew Denham and Mark Garnett, *Keith Joseph* (2001).

Thatcher and Major years

Patrick Cosgrave, *Carrington: A Life and a Policy* (1985); Michael Crick, *Michael Heseltine: A Biography* (1997); Mark Stuart, *Douglas Hurd: The Public Servant* (1998); Bruce Anderson, *Whitelaw: On the Right Track* (1988).

Electoral support

The electoral statistics bibles are the multi-volume compilations of the late F.W.S. Craig, *British Parliamentary Election Results* and *British Electoral Facts.* This last volume has now been up-dated and revised by Rallings and Thrasher, *British Electoral Facts 1832–1999* (2000).

For the debates about who supports the Conservatives, see: Jon Lawrence, 'Class and gender in the making of urban Toryism 1880–1914', *EHR* 108 (1993); Derek Jarvis, 'The shaping of Conservative electoral hegemony' in J. Lawrence and M. Taylor (eds), *Party, State and Society: Electoral Behaviour in Modern Britain* (1997); Robert Waller, 'Conservative electoral support and social class' in S. Ball and A. Seldon (eds), *Conservative Century* (1994); Martin Pugh, 'Popular Conservatism in Britain: continuity and change 1880–1987', *JBS* 27 (1988); Neil R. McCrillis, *The British Conservative Party in the Age of Universal Suffrage* (1998); and Charles Pattie and Ron Johnston, 'The Conservative party and the electorate' in S. Ludlam and M. Smith (eds), *Contemporary British Conservatism* (1996). For the Primrose League, see Martin Pugh, *The Tories and the People 1880–1935* (1985). For the arguments about working-class support for Conservatism, see the seminal R. McKenzie and J. Silver, *Angels in Marble* (1968) also Eric Nordlinger, *The Working Class Tories* (1967) and P. Joyce, *Work, Society and Politics* (1980).

Policies and policy-making

The party's election manifestos are always a useful source. Iain Dale (ed.), *Conservative Party General Election Manifestos 1900–1997* (2000) reprints the lot with a useful introduction from Alistair Cooke, formerly of Conservative Central Office.

For examination of the process of policy-making in the party the classic study is R.T. MacKenzie, *British Political Parties* (1955, 2nd edn 1963). Historians have begun to revise MacKenzie's interpretation of the Conservative party as an oligarchy with policy handed down from upon high. See the essays by Ball, Kelly and Cockett in Ball and Seldon (eds), *Conservative Century* (1994). See also R. Kelly (ed.), *Changing Party Policy in Britain* (1999). Articles worth consulting are Ivor Bulmer-Thomas, 'How Conservative policy is formed', *Political Quarterly* 24 (1953) and Michael Wolff, 'Policy-making within the Conservative party' in J.P. Mackintosh (ed.), *People and Parliament* (1978). See also the ICBH witness seminar 'Conservative party policy making 1964–1970' in *CR* 3, 3–4 (1990). See also Richard Cockett, *Thinking the Unthinkable: Think-tanks and the Economic Counter-Revolution 1931–1983* (1994).

TOPIC THEMES

Women

The essays by David Jarvis and Ina Zweiniger-Bargielowska in M. Francis and Ina Zweiniger-Bargielowska (eds), *The Conservatives and British Society 1880–1990* (1996) discuss the party's appeal to the female vote. G.M. Maguire, *Conservative Women: A History of Women and the Conservative Party 1874–1997* (1998) is patchy in its coverage, though it has some things of interest. Joni Lovenduski *et al.*, 'The Party and women' in Ball and Seldon, *Conservative Century* (1994) explores the party's treatment of the 'woman question'.

Immigration

N.J. Crowson, 'The British Conservative party and the Jews during the late 1930s', *PPrej* (1995) considers the types of Conservative anti-semitism and the impact this had upon the conduct of foreign policy towards Hitler and Mussolini; Zig Layton-Henry, *The Politics of Immigration* (1992) is an engaging and balanced analysis of the post-war issues. For an introduction to governmental policy see Ian Spencer, *British Immigration Policy since 1939* (1997) and Randall Hansen, *Citizenship and Immigration in Post-war Britain* (2000) who argues that immigration policy was not racist in intention, but was racist in effect. For specific governmental episodes see D.W. Dean, 'Conservative governments and the restriction of Commonwealth immigration in the 1950s' *HJ* (1992) and David Welsh, 'The principle of the thing: the Conservative government and the control of Commonwealth immigration 1957–1959', *CBH* 12, 2 (1998) as well as S. Brooke, 'The Conservative party, immigration and national identity 1948–1968' in M. Francis and Ina Zweiniger-Bargielowska (eds), *The Conservatives and British Society 1880–1990* (1996) and Zig Layton-Henry, 'Immigration and the Heath government' in Ball and Seldon, *The Heath Government* (1996). Worth consulting is P. Rich, 'Conservative ideology and race in modern British politics' in Zig Layton-Henry and P. Rich (eds), *Race, Government and Politics in Britain* (1986).

Trade unions

Andrew Taylor, 'The Party and the trade unions' in Ball and Seldon (eds), *Conservative Century* (1994) provides a historical overview of the twentieth century. Peter Dorey, *The Conservative Party and the Trade Unions* (1995) should be consulted. The 1927 Trades Disputes Act is considered by M.C. Shefftz, 'The trade disputes and Trade Union Act of 1927', *RP* 29 (1967). For the post-war story see Robert Taylor, *The Trade Union Question in British Politics since 1945* (1993). Consult also Andrew Taylor, 'Conservatives and trade unions since 1945', *CR* 4 (1990–91). See also Justin Smith, *The Attlee and Churchill Administrations and Industrial Unrest 1945–55* (1990). For the Heath years: Robert Taylor, 'The Heath government and industrial relations: myth and reality' in Ball and

Seldon (eds), *The Heath Government 1970–1974* (1996); for the early years of Thatcher's leadership: R. Behrens, '"Blinkers for the cart horse": the Conservative party and the trade unions 1974–78' and Andrew Rowe, 'Conservatives and trades unionists' in Zig Layton-Henry (ed.), *Conservative Party Politics* (1980), while two articles by Peter Dorey, 'One step at a time: the Conservative government's approach to the reform of industrial relations since 1979', *PQ* 64 (1993) and 'Thatcherism's impact on the trade unions', *CR* 4 (1990–91) provide good overviews as does Christopher Johnson, *The Economy under Mrs Thatcher 1979–1990* (1991). For the Major years see Ben Rosamond, 'Whatever happened to the "enemy within"? Contemporary Conservatism and trade unionism' in Smith and Ludlam (eds), *Contemporary Conservatism* (1996).

Europe

An overview is offered by N.J. Crowson, 'The Conservative party and Europe' in R. Broad and V. Preston (eds), *Moored to the Continent: Britain and Europe since 1945* (2001). General studies worth consulting include Hugo Young, *This Blessed Plot* (1998) and Stephen George, *An Awkward Partner: Britain in the European Community* (1990, 2nd edn 1994); For specific episodes, see Sue Onslow, *Backbench Debate within the Conservative Party and its influence on British Foreign Policy 1948–1957* (1997), Wolfram Kaiser, *Using Europe, Abusing the Europeans: Britain and European Integration 1945–63* (1996) and Ronald Butt, 'The Common Market and Conservative party politics 1961–62', *PQ* 36 (1965) which offers a contemporary analysis of the party's response to Britain's first EEC application, while David Dutton, 'Anticipating Maastricht: the Conservative party and Britain's first application to join the European Community', *CR* 7 (1993) provides a historical analysis. For the Heath government see John W. Young, 'The Heath government and British entry into the European Community' in Ball and Seldon (eds), *The Heath Government 1970–1974* (1996); for the problems during the 1990s, see David Baker *et al.*, 'The parliamentary siege of Maastricht 1993', *PA* (1994) and 'Backbench Conservative attitudes to European integration', *PQ* (1995) and Matthew Sowemimo, 'The Conservative party and European integration 1988–1995', *Party Politics* 2, 1 (1995).

Economic policy

For a Marxist but nevertheless perceptive analysis, see Nigel Harris, *Competition and the Corporate Society: British Conservatives, the State and Industry 1945–1964* (1972). A different interpretation is offered by Keith Middlemas over three volumes, *Power, Competition and the State: Britain in Search of Balance 1940–1961* (1986), *Threats to the Post-war Settlement: Britain 1961–1974* (1990) and *The End of the Post-war Era: Britain since 1974* (1991); also his chapter 'The party, industry and the city' in Ball and Seldon (eds), *Conservative Century*. The period of Conservative hegemony is considered by N. Tiratsoo and J. Tomlinson, *The Conservatives and Industrial Efficiency 1951–1964* (1998), Jim Tomlinson, 'Liberty with order: Conservative economic policy 1951–64' in M. Francis and

I. Zweiniger-Bargielowska (eds), *The Conservatives and British Society 1880–1990* (1996), while in the same volume taxation policy is considered by Martin Daunton, 'A kind of tax prison: rethinking Conservative taxation policy 1960–1970'. The Heath years are considered in the chapters by Alex Cairncross and Robert Taylor in Ball and Seldon (eds), *The Heath Government 1970–1974* (1996) as well as Martin Holmes, *Political Pressure and Economic Pressure: British Government 1970–1974* (1982). For policy since 1979, see Helen Thompson, 'Economic policy under Thatcher and Major' in Smith and Ludlam (eds), *Contemporary Conservatism* (1996) and Christopher Johnson, *The Economy under Mrs Thatcher 1979–1990* (1991).

Social policy

An overview of nineteenth-century policy is offered by D. Englander, *Poverty and Poor Law reform in Nineteenth Century Britain 1834–1914* (1998). More specifically, see W.O. Aydelotte, 'The Conservative and Radical interpretations of early Victorian social legislation', *VS* (1967) and J. Hart, 'Nineteenth century social reform: a Tory interpretation of history', *PP* (1965). The seminal study of Disraeli and social reform is Paul Smith, *Disraelian Conservatism and Social Reform* (1967) but consider also P.R. Ghosh, 'Style and substance in Disraelian social reform *c.* 1860–80' in P.J. Waller (ed.), *Politics and Social Change in Modern Britain* (1987); for the Edwardian party, see David Dutton, 'The Unionist party and social policy', *HJ* 24 (1981) and E.H.H. Green, 'The Conservative party, the state and social policy 1880–1914' in M. Francis and I. Zweiniger-Bargielowska (eds), *The Conservatives and British Society 1880–1990* (1996); the impact of the Beveridge report is considered by Rodney Lowe, 'The Second World War, consensus and the foundations of the welfare state', *TCBH* 1, 2 (1990); the post-1945 era is surveyed by Howard Glennerster, *British Social Policy since 1945* (2nd edn 2000). Consider Paul Addison, 'Churchill and social reform' in R. Blake and Roger William Louis (eds), *Churchill* (1993). See also Timothy Raison, *Tories and the Welfare State* (1990) and Harriet Jones, 'New tricks for an old dog? The Conservatives and social policy 1951–55' in A. Gorst *et al., CBH 1931–1961* (1991) and Paul Bridgen, 'The one nation idea and state welfare: The Conservatives and pensions in the 1950s', *CBH* 14, 3 (2000); while the chapters by Jones and Lowe in M. Francis and I. Zweiniger-Bargielowska (eds), *The Conservatives and British Society 1880–1990* (1996) consider the period 1945–64. For more recent developments see Rodney Lowe, 'The social policy of the Heath government' in Ball and Seldon, *The Heath Government 1970–74* (1996) and Chris Pierson, 'Social Policy under Thatcher and Major' in Smith and Ludlam (eds), *Contemporary Conservatism* (1996).

Ireland

A good starting point is D.G. Boyce, *The Irish Question and British Politics 1868–1988* (1988); for specific eras, see Allen Warren, 'Disraeli, the Conservatives and the Governments of Ireland', Part 1 1837–1868 and Part 2 1868–1881, *PH*

18, 1–2 (1999); Ronan Fanning, 'The Unionist Party and Ireland 1906–1910', *IHS* 15 (1966–67); the attitude of the party to Home Rule is examined in L.P. Curtis, *Coercion and Conciliation in Ireland 1880–1892: A Study in Conservative Unionism* (1963), Paul Bew, *Conflict and Conciliation in Ireland 1890–1910* (1986) and W.C. Lubenow, *Parliamentary Politics and the Home Rule Crisis* (1988). L.J. McCaffrey, 'Home Rule and the general election of 1874', *IHS* (1954–55) considers the electoral impact of the Irish question. Worth consulting is L.P. Curtis, 'Government policy and the Irish Party crisis 1890–92', *IHS* (1962–63). The third Home Rule bill is considered by A.T.Q. Stewart, *The Ulster Crisis: Resistance to Home Rule 1912–1914* (1967) and re-evaluated by Jeremy Smith, 'Bluff, bluster and brinkmanship: Andrew Bonar Law and the 3rd Home Rule Bill', *HJ* 36 (1993). For the moves towards concession and the 1921 Anglo-Irish treaty see D.G. Boyce, 'British Conservative opinion, the Ulster question and the partition of Ireland 1912–21', *IHS* (1970–71), John Stubbs, 'The Unionists and Ireland 1914–18', *HJ* 33 (1990) and John Fair, 'The Anglo-Irish Treaty of 1921: Unionist aspects of the peace', *JBS* 12 (1972). For Irish policy during the Macmillan years see R.A. Aldous, 'Perfect peace? Macmillan and Ireland' in R.A. Aldous and S. Lee (eds), *Harold Macmillan: A Political Portrait* (1999). For the Heath years, see Philip Norton, 'Conservative politics and the abolition of Stormont' in Peter Catterall and Sean McDougall (eds), *The Northern Ireland Question in British Politics* (1996) and Paul Arthur, 'The Heath government and Northern Ireland' in Ball and Seldon (eds), *The Heath Government 1970–1974* (1996). On British policy to Northern Ireland see M.J. Cunningham, *British Government Policy in Northern Ireland 1969–1989* (1991) as well as his article 'Conservative dissidents and the Irish question: the "pro-integrationists" lobby 1973–1994', *IPS* 10 (1995).

The Union

J. Mitchell, *Conservatives and the Union* (1990); C. MacDonald, *Unionist Scotland 1800–1997* (1998). The issue of devolution is considered by M. Burch and I. Holliday, 'The Conservative party and constitutional reform: The case for devolution', *PA* 45 (1992) and Vernon Bogdanor, 'Devolution' in Zig Layton-Henry (ed.), *Conservative Party Politics* (1980). Consult also Jeremy Smith, 'Conservative ideology and representations of the Union with Ireland 1885–1914', Felix Aubel, 'The Conservatives in Wales 1880–1935' and Richard Finlay, 'Scottish Conservatism and Unionism since 1918', all in M. Francis and Ina Zweiniger-Bargielowska (eds), *The Conservatives and British Society 1880–1990* (1996); the dwindling fortunes of the party in Scotland are considered by D. Seawright and J. Curtice, 'The decline of the Scottish Conservative and Unionist Party 1950–1992: religion, ideology or economics?', *CR* 9, 2 (1995).

Foreign and imperial policy

A useful introduction to nineteenth-century foreign policy is provided by M. Chamberlain, *Pax Britannica? British Foreign Policy 1789–1914* (1989);

similarly for colonial policy B. Porter, *The Lion's Share: A Short History of British Imperialism 1850–1970* (3rd edn 1996). See C.C. Eldridge, *Disraeli and the Rise of New Imperialism* (1996) for the Disraelian era. Andrew Thompson, *Imperial Britain: The Empire in British Politics* c. *1880–1932* (2000) considers how imperialism impacted upon the British political culture. See also D. Judd, *Balfour and the British Empire* (1968). For the Boer War see A.N. Porter, *The Origins of the South African War: Joseph Chamberlain and the Diplomacy of Imperialism* (1980). For inter-war considerations, see Carl Bridge, 'Conservatism and Indian Reform 1929–1939', *JICH* 4 (1974–75); John Darwin, 'Imperialism in decline? Tendencies in British Imperial Policy between the wars', *HJ* 23, 3 (1980) and N.J. Crowson, *Facing Fascism: the Conservative Party and the European Dictators 1935–1940* (1997). For governmental policy see J.W. Young (ed.), *The Foreign Policy of Churchill's Peacetime Administration 1951–55* (1988); an important study is Sue Onslow, *Backbench Debate within the Conservative Party and its Influence on British Foreign Policy 1948–1957* (1997). For the impact of Suez, see Max Beloff, 'The crisis and its consequences for the British Conservative party' in R. Louis and R. Owen (eds), *Suez, 1956* (1989) and Leon Epstein, *British Politics in the Suez Crisis* (1964). For the problems associated with the retreat from Empire, see Philip Murphy, *Party Politics and Decolonisation: The Conservative Party and British Colonial Policy in Tropical Africa 1951–1964* (1995).

Defence policy

For an overview consult Michael Dockrill, *British Defence since 1945* (1988). For the Edwardian era, see A.J.A. Morris, *The Scaremongers: The Advocacy of War and Rearmament 1896–1914* (1984) and R.J.Q. Adams and Philip Poirier, *The Conscription Controversy in Britain 1900–1918*. Conservative support for conscription in the 1930s is considered in N.J. Crowson, 'The Conservative party and the question of national service, 1937–39: compulsion versus voluntarism', *CR* 9, 3 (1995); while the debate about whether to retain compulsory military service after 1945 is also examined in N.J. Crowson, 'Citizen defence: the Conservative Party and its attitude to national service 1937–1957' in R. Weight and A. Beach (eds), *The Right to Belong: Citizenship and National Identity in Britain 1930–1960* (1998). An important contemporary analysis is William Snyder, *The Politics of British Defence Policy 1945–61* (1964) whose conclusions were validated by the release of official documents – see Simon Ball, 'Harold Macmillan and the politics of defence: the market for strategic ideas during the Sandys era revisited', *TCBH* 6, 1 (1995).

SPECIFIC ERAS

Repeal of the Corn Laws

A useful overview of the politics of the period is provided by Robert Stewart, *Party and Politics 1830–1852* (1989), while Asa Briggs, *The Age of Improvement*

1783–1867 (1959), ch. 6, has a good brief introduction to the politics of the 1840s. Useful is G. Kitson Clark, 'The repeal of the Corn Laws and the politics of the forties', *EconHR* (1951). The suggested biographies of Peel are relevant as is the Stewart volume of the Longman history of the party. The Anti-Corn Law league is considered in N. McCord, *The Anti-Corn Law League* (1959), while Robert Stewart, *The Politics of Protection: Lord Derby and the Protectionist Party 1841–1852* (1971) considered this strand of Tory reaction as does R. Faber, *Young England* (1987). The party political dimension is also considered by N. Gash, 'Peel and the party system', *TRHS* (1951) and A. Aydelotte, 'The House of Commons in the 1840s', *H* (1954). The political consequences for the Peelites are considered by J.B. Conacher, *The Peelites and Party System 1846–1852* (1972) and W.D. Jones and A.B. Erickson, *The Peelites* (1973). For the protectionist Conservative party after 1846 see W.D. Jones, *Lord Derby and Victorian Conservatism* (1956) and Angus Hawkins, *Parliament, Party and the Art of Politics in Britain 1855–59* (1987).

Age of Disraeli

A helpful introduction is Paul Adelman, *Gladstone, Disraeli and Later Victorian Politics* (3rd edn 1997). For Disraeli's climb to the top of the greasy pole see Robert Blake, 'The rise of Disraeli' in Hugh Trevor-Roper (ed.), *Essays in British History* (1965). For Disraeli and the party see Bruce Coleman, *Conservatism and the Conservative Party in Nineteenth Century Britain* (1988) and T.A. Jenkin, *Disraeli and Victorian Conservatism* (1996). For the second Reform Act, see F.B. Smith, *The Making of the Second Reform Act* (1966) and its consequences, E.J. Feuchtwanger, 'The Conservative party under the impact of the second Reform Act', *VS* (1959), while G. Himmelfarb, 'The politics of democracy: the English Reform Act of 1867', *JBS* (1966) reviews the debate on the Act. P.R. Gosh, 'Disraelian Conservatism: a financial approach', *EHR* 99 (1984) considers a neglected aspect. Worth consulting is Allen Warren, 'Disraeli, the Conservatives and the National Church 1837–1881' in J.P. Parry and S. Taylor (eds), *Parliament and the Church 1529–1961* (special edition of *PH*). For social policy see Paul Smith (above). Important articles also include C.J. Lewis, 'Theory and expediency in the policy of Disraeli', *VS* (1960–61); James Cornford, 'The transformation of conservatism in the late nineteenth century', *VS* (1963–64); J.P. Dunbabin, 'Parliamentary elections in Great Britain 1868–1900: a psephological note', *EHR* (1966). For foreign policy, see M. Swartz, *The Politics of British Foreign Policy in the Era of Disraeli and Gladstone* (1985).

Salisbury's ascendancy

A useful starting point is Martin Pugh, *The Making of Modern British Politics* (2nd edn 1993) while his volume *The Tories and the People 1880–1925* (1985) and Henry Pelling, *Popular Politics and Society in Later Victorian Britain* (1968) explain the popular appeal of the Conservatives. Peter Marsh, *The Discipline of Popular Government: Lord Salisbury's Domestic Statecraft 1881–1902* (1978) is essential as is J. Cornford, 'The parliamentary foundations of the Hotel Cecil' in R. Robson (ed.), *Ideas and Institutions of Victorian Britain* (1967). Lord Randolph Churchill's influence on the Tory party is discussed in R. Foster, *Lord Randolph Churchill* (1982) and Roland Quinault, 'Randolph Churchill and Tory Democracy', *HJ* (1979), while Joseph Chamberlain's eventual alliance with the party can be charted in Richard Jay, *Joseph Chamberlain* (1981) and Peter Marsh, *Joseph Chamberlain: Entrepreneur in Politics* (1994). The role of the Liberal Unionists and Chamberlain is discussed in P. Fraser, 'The Liberal Unionist alliance: Chamberlain, Hartington and the Conservatives 1886–1904', *EHR* (1962). See also Leigh Michael Powell, 'Sir Michael Hicks Beach and Conservative politics 1880–1888', *PH* 19, 3 (2000).

Crisis of Edwardian Conservatism

A useful survey of the period is David Dutton, *His Majesty's Loyal Opposition: The Unionist Party in Opposition 1905–1915* (1992). The best analysis of the Edwardian crisis is E.H. Green, *The Crisis of Conservatism* (1996); also worth consulting is G.R. Searle, *The Quest for National Efficiency: A Study in British Politics and Political Thought 1899–1914* (1971) and Alan Sykes, *Tariff Reform in British Politics* (1979); for the party see J.A. Ramsden, *The Age of Balfour and Baldwin* (1978). M. Fforde, *Conservatism and Collectivism 1886–1914* (1990) artificially seeks to superimpose a 1980s debate onto the Edwardian era; Franz Coetzee, *For Party or Country* (1990) considers the multitude of leagues and their significance for popular Conservatism; R. Williams, *Defending the Empire: The Conservative Party and British Defence Policy 1899–1915* (1991) examines the myriad quasi-Conservative military leagues and illustrates their impotence at imposing policy upon Balfour. Larry Witherell, *Rebel on the Right: Henry Page Croft and the Crisis of British Conservatism* (1997) explores how the tariff issues impacted upon one wannabe Conservative politician. The Party's strategy at the ballot boxes can be assessed from A.K. Russell, *Liberal Landslide: The General Election of 1906* (1973) and Neal Blewett, *The Peers, the Parties and the People: The General Elections of 1910* (1972).

Age of Baldwin

Siân Nicholas, 'The construction of national identity: Stanley Baldwin, "Englishness" and the mass media in inter-war Britain' in M. Francis and Ina Zweiniger-Bargielowska (eds), *The Conservatives and British Society 1880–1990* (1996) examines Baldwin's success with the radio and newsreels, which made him the first premier to be recognisable both by sight and sound to the majority of the electorate. For the crisis years of Baldwin's leadership see Stuart Ball, *Baldwin and the Conservative Party* (1988) and Gillian Peele, 'St George's and the Empire Crusade' in Chris Cook and John Ramsden (eds), *By-Elections in British Politics* (2nd edn 1997). For the economic crisis that precipitated the National Government, see Philip Williamson, *National Crisis and National Government* (1992). For the Conservatives' role in the formation of the National

Government, compare John Fair, 'The Conservative basis for the formation of the National Government of 1931', *JBS* 19 (1980) with Stuart Ball, 'The Conservative Party and the formation of the National Government: August 1931', *HJ* 29 (1986). For Baldwin's electoral tactics, see Robert Self's important article, 'Conservative reunion and the general election of 1923: a reassessment', *TCBH* 3 (1992); see also Chris Cook, *The Age of Alignment: Electoral Politics in Britain 1922–1929* (1975), Philip Williamson, '"Safety First": Baldwin, the Conservative party and the 1929 general election', *HJ* 25 (1982) as well as Andrew Thorpe, *The British General Election of 1931* (1991) and Tom Stannage, *Baldwin Thwarts the Opposition: The British General Election of 1935* (1980).

Chamberlain and appeasement

John Charmley, *Chamberlain and the Lost Peace* (1989) is a staunch revisionist defence of Chamberlain, although critics have suggested Charmley allowed too much hindsight in arguing that the two outcomes Chamberlain feared from war, Bolshevik domination of Europe and the end of the British Empire, was the result in 1945. R.A.C. Parker, *Chamberlain and Appeasement* (1994) is the best survey that accepts that Chamberlain was genuine in seeking peace, but that from late 1938 he missed an opportunity to revise policy. See also R.A.C. Parker, *Churchill and Appeasement* (2000). For a defence of Halifax at the Foreign Office, see Andrew Roberts, *The Holy Fox: A Biography of Lord Halifax* (1991). For the issue of media manipulation, see Richard Cockett, *Twilight of Truth: Chamberlain, Appeasement and the Manipulation of the Press* (1989). For the response of the wider Conservative party, see N.J. Crowson, *Facing Fascism: The Conservative Party and the European Dictators 1935–1940* (1997). For the anti-appeasers see Neville Thompson, *The Anti-Appeasers* (1971) which rebutted the idea that the critics of appeasement were a strong and coherent force, and N.J. Crowson, 'Parliamentary dissent over foreign policy during the premiership of Neville Chamberlain', *PH* (1995). For the critics during the phoney war look out for Larry Witherell, 'Lord Salisbury's Watching Committee and the fall of Neville Chamberlain May 1940', *EHR* (forthcoming). For the fall of the Chamberlain government, compare Nick Smart, 'Four days in May: The Norway debate and the downfall of Neville Chamberlain', *PH* 17, 2 (1998) with Jorgen Rasmussen, 'Party discipline in wartime: the downfall of Neville Chamberlain', *JP* 32 (1970).

Conservative hegemony 1951–64

For the 1945 election defeat and after, see M.D. Kandiah, 'The Conservative party and the 1945 general election', *CR* 9, 1 (1995). For particular administrations, see Anthony Seldon, *Churchill's Indian Summer: The Conservative Government 1951–55* (1981); Henry Pelling, *Churchill's Peacetime Ministry* (1997); Richard Lamb, *The Failure of the Eden Government* (1987) and Richard Lamb, *The Macmillan Years: The Emerging Truth* (1995). The debate about the success, or not, of the 1951–64 administrations was opened by Michael

Pinto-Duschinsky, 'Bread and Circuses? The Conservatives in Office 1951–1964' in Bogdanor and Skidelsky (eds), *The Age of Affluence 1951–1964* (1970) and has been returned to frequently by historians including John Barnes and Anthony Seldon, '1951–1964: thirteen wasted years?', *CR* 2, 5 (1989); see also ICBH witness seminar '1961–64: Did the Conservatives lose direction?', *CR* 2, 5 (1989). An important article is John Ramsden, 'A party for owners or a party for earners? How far did the Conservative party really change after 1945?', *TRHS* 5th series, 37 (1987) as is John Turner, '"A land fit for Tories to live in": the political ecology of the British Conservative Party 1944–1994', *Contemporary European History* 4, 2 (1995). For the economy, see Peter Oppenheimer, 'Muddling through: the economy 1951–64' in V. Bogdanor and R. Skidelsky (eds), *The Age of Affluence 1951–1964* (1970). For the internal politics, see Keith Alderman, 'Harold Macmillan's night of the long knives', *CR* 6, 2 (1992). For the theme of consensus, see Harriet Jones and Michael Kandiah (eds), *The Myth of Consensus: New Views on British History 1945–1964* (1996).

Heath years

S. Ball and A. Seldon (eds), *The Heath Government 1970–1974* is a collection of essays, many using the archives of the Conservative party, that reappraise particular themes of Heath's premiership. A Thatcherite critique is offered by Martin Holmes, *The Failure of the Heath Government* (2nd edn 1997); see also his article 'Heath's government reassessed', *CR* 3, 2 (1989). For the ill-fated Industrial Relations Act, see M. Moran, *The Politics of the Industrial Relations Act of 1971* (1977). For Heath on himself, see Edward Heath, *Course of My Life* (1998). For an insider's account, see Douglas Hurd, *An End to Promises: Sketch of a Government 1970–1974* (1978) and the ICBH witness seminar 'The Heath Government', *CR* 9, 1 (1995). For the problems of managing the parliamentary party, see Philip Norton, *Conservative Dissidents: Dissent within the Parliamentary Conservative Party 1970–1974* (1978).

Thatcherism

For an introduction start with Anthony Seldon and Daniel Collings, *Britain Under Thatcher* (2000). See also Eric Evans, *Thatcher and Thatcherism* (1997), who challenges the idea that Thatcherism had any originality and ideological coherence and suggests that ultimately it failed to achieve its objectives. Other useful books include Dennis Kavanagh, *Thatcherism and British Politics* (1987) and D. Kavanagh and A. Seldon (eds), *The Thatcher Effect* (1989), which is a collection of thematic essays. For Thatcher's leadership in relation to others, see Peter Clarke, 'Margaret Thatcher's leadership in historical perspective', *PA* 45 (1992) and Mark Garnett and Lord Gilmour, 'Thatcherism and the Conservative tradition' in M. Francis *et al.*, *Conservatives and Society* (1996). The historical origins of Thatcherism and her ideas on political economy can be traced in E.H.H. Green, 'Thatcherism: an historical perspective', *Royal Historical Society Transactions* 6th series, 9 (1999). Other articles worth reading are

Brian Harrison, 'Historians and the intellectuals' and B. Porter '"Though not a historian myself": Margaret Thatcher and the historians', which both appeared in *TCBH* 5, 2 (1994) alongside a review of the Thatcher memoirs. See also Stephen Evans, 'The Earl of Stockton's critique of Thatcherism', *PA* 51, 1 (1998).

PUBLISHED DOCUMENTARY SOURCES, DIARIES AND MEMOIRS

For any reader wishing to undertake research on the Conservative party two articles introduce possible sources. Sarah Street (Archivist of the Conservative Party Archive 1987–1993), 'The Conservative Party Archive', *TCBH* 3 (1992) provides an introduction to the archive held at the Bodleian Library, Oxford. Stuart Ball, 'National politics and local history: the regional and local archives of the Conservative party 1867–1945', *Archives* (1996) explains about the types of constituency party records available and some of the problems associated with their use.

Age of Peel

Primary sources

Peel's *Tamworth Manifesto* can be found reprinted in H.J. Hanham (ed.), *The Victorian Constitution: Documents and Commentary* (1969). A selection of documentary extracts will be found in Paul Adelman, *Peel and the Conservative Party 1830–1950* (1989).

Age of Disraeli

Primary sources

A selection of documentary extracts can be found in Paul Adelman, *Gladstone, Disraeli and Later Victorian Politics* (3rd edn 1983).

Two useful edited diaries are John Vincent (ed.), *Disraeli, Derby and the Conservative Party: Journals and Diaries of Edward Henry, Lord Stanley, 1849–69* (1978) and Nancy Johnson (ed.), *The Diary of Gathorne Hardy, later Lord Cranbrook, 1866–1892* (1981).

Age of Salisbury

Primary sources

Some relevant documentary extracts can be found in Adelman cited above.

In addition to the Gathorne Hardy journal cited above, see A.B. Cooke and A.P.W. Malcomson (eds), *The Ashbourne Papers 1869–1912* (1974) and Robin Harcourt-Williams (ed.), *The Salisbury–Balfour Correspondence 1869–92* (1988).

Edwardian era

Primary sources

There exists a wealth of published primary material for this period. See John Ramsden (ed.), *Real Old Tory Politics: The Political Diaries of Sir Robert Sanders, Lord Bayford 1910–1930* (1984); John Vincent (ed.), *The Crawford Papers: The Journals of David Lindsay, 10th Earl of Balcarres 1892–1940* (1984); George Boyce (ed.), *The Crisis of British Unionism: Lord Selborne's Domestic Political Papers 1885–1922* (1987); Philip Williamson (ed.), *The Modernisation of Conservative Politics, the Diaries and Letters of William Bridgeman, 1904–1935* (1988).

Inter-war years

Primary sources

A selection of documentary extracts will be found in Stuart Ball, *The Conservative Party and British Politics 1902–1951* (1986).

In addition to the Sanders, Crawford, Selborne and Bridgeman papers cited above see Robert Self (ed.), *The Austen Chamberlain Diary and Letters 1916–1937* (1995); Robert Self (ed.), *The Neville Chamberlain Diary and Letters* (3 vols, 2000, 2001, forthcoming); Keith Middlemas (ed.), *Thomas Jones' Whitehall Diary 1916–1930* (3 vols, 1971), Thomas Jones, *A Diary with Letters 1931–1950* (1954); John Barnes and David Nicolson (eds), *The Leo Amery Diaries* (2 vols, 1980, 1988), Robert Rhodes James (ed.), *Chips: The Diaries of Sir Henry Channon* (1967); N.J. Crowson (ed.), *Fleet Street, Press Barons and Party Politics: The Journals of Collin Brooks 1932–1940* (1999); Stuart Ball (ed.), *Parliament and Politics in the Age of Baldwin and MacDonald: The Cuthbert Headlam Diaries 1924–35* (1990) and *Parliament and Politics in the Age of Churchill and Attlee: The Cuthbert Headlam Diaries 1935–1951* (2000); Robert Rhodes James (ed.), *Memoirs of a Conservative: J.C.C. Davidson's Memoirs and Papers 1910–1937* (1967).

Memoirs

Alfred Duff Cooper, *Old Men Forget* (1954) Viscount Templewood [Samuel Hoare], *Nine Troubled Years* (1954); Earl of Winterton, *Orders of the Day* (1953).

Age of Churchill, Eden and Macmillan

Primary sources

For the post-1945 party see Stuart Ball, *The Conservative Party since 1945* (1998) that has a wide range of pithy and original extracts covering all aspects of the party. A short selection of documentary extracts will be found in Andrew Boxer, *The Conservative Governments 1951–1964* (1996).

In addition to the second volume of the Headlam diaries and the Channon diaries cited above, see Richard Cockett (ed.), *My Dear Max: The Letters of Brendan Bracken to Lord Beaverbrook 1925–58* (1990); John Colville, *The Fringes of Power: Downing Street Diaries 1939–1955* (1985); Nigel Nicolson (ed.), *Diaries and Letters of Harold Nicolson* (3 vols, 1966–68); Ben Pimlott (ed.), *Hugh Dalton Diaries* (2 vols, 1986); Harold Evans, *Downing Street Diary 1957–63* (1963).

Memoirs

Lord Butler, *The Art of the Possible* (1971); Lord Hailsham, *A Sparrow's Flight* (1990); Earl of Kilmuir, *Political Adventure* (1964); Harold Macmillan, *Memoirs* (6 vols, 1966–73); Reginald Maudling, *Memoirs* (1978); James Stuart, *Within the Fringe* (1967); Earl of Woolton, *Memoirs of the Rt Hon. Earl of Woolton* (1959)

Heath years

Primary sources

Ion Trewin (ed.), *Alan Clark Diaries: Into Politics* (2000).

Memoirs

Douglas Hurd, *An End to Promises: Sketches of a Government 1970–74* (1978); Peter Walker, *Staying Power* (1991); Edward Heath, *Course of My Life* (1988).

Thatcher and Major years

Primary sources

A short selection of documents can be found in Anthony Seldon and Daniel Collings, *Britain Under Thatcher* (2000). See also Alan Clark, *Diaries* (1993); Gyles Brandreth, *Breaking the Code: Westminster Diaries 1990–1997* (1999).

Memoirs

Kenneth Baker, *The Turbulent Years* (1993); Norman Fowler, *Ministers Decide* (1991); Michael Heseltine, *Life in the Jungle* (2000); Geoffrey Howe, *Conflict of Loyalty* (1994); Norman Lamont, *In Office* (1999); Nigel Lawson, *The View From Number 11* (1992); John Major, *Memoirs* (1999); Cecil Parkinson, *Right At The Centre* (1992); Jim Prior, *A Balance of Power* (1986); Norman Tebbit, *Upwardly Mobile* (1988); Margaret Thatcher, *The Downing Street Years* (1993); Peter Walker, *Staying Power* (1991).

INDEX